T0284748

SHARING A HOUSE
with the
NEVER-ENDING
MAN

SHARING A HOUSE
with the
NEVER-ENDING MAN

~~~~~~~~~~~~~~~~~~~~~~

15 YEARS AT STUDIO GHIBLI

Steve Alpert

Stone Bridge Press • *Berkeley, California*

Published by
Stone Bridge Press
P. O. Box 8208, Berkeley, CA 94707
tel 510-524-8732 • sbp@stonebridge.com • www.stonebridge.com

Front cover design by Linda Ronan, incorporating an image from *Kaze Tachinu (The Wind Rises)*. Depicted is the character Castorp, modeled on the author (who does not smoke). Image © 2013 Studio Ghibli - NDHDMTK.

All photographs provided by the author. Film images provided by Studio Ghibli; respective copyright notices provided on each.

Printed in the United States of America.

10 9 8 7 6 5 4 3 2 1   2023 2022 2021 2020

p-ISBN 978-1-61172-057-0 (paperback)
p-ISBN 978-1-61172-060-0 (casebound)
e-ISBN 978-1-61172-941-2 (e-book)

CONTENTS

INTRODUCTION

~~~~~~~~~

Studio Ghibli

Studio Ghibli was for more than three decades Japan's best known and most successful creator of hand-drawn feature-length animated motion pictures. Its huge success has been both artistic and commercial. Since its founding in 1984 Ghibli has produced more than twenty feature films, including *Spirited Away*, winner of an Academy Award for Best Animated Feature and a Golden Bear for Best Picture at the Berlin International Film Festival—and the most commercially successful Japanese film ever made. Other Ghibli films, including *Princess Mononoke, My Neighbor Totoro, Kiki's Delivery Service,* and *Grave of the Fireflies,* have smashed box office records, won numerous awards, and influenced generations of filmmakers and moviegoers young and old.

Studio Ghibli was founded by the directors Hayao Miyazaki and Isao Takahata, the producer Suzuki Toshio, and Yasuyoshi Tokuma, who was the head of Ghibli's former parent company, the Tokuma Shoten Publishing Company. *Nausicaä of the Valley of the Wind*, the studio's first film, is a tale of a dystopian future in which the world's ecosystems have been decimated. It was the first Japanese feature-length animated film to draw over a million people to the movie theaters, proving that a commercially viable studio could be created to make *only* feature-length theatrical animation.

Studio Ghibli's films have influenced and inspired both

animated and live-action filmmakers worldwide. Reflections and versions of images originally created by Hayao Miyazaki can be found in the films of well-known independent and Hollywood motion picture directors, including some major box office hits. Hayao Miyazaki has been called the Walt Disney and the Steven Spielberg of Japanese film. His influence on other filmmakers has been enormous.

Studio Ghibli is located in the leafy residential suburb of Koganei in the western part of Tokyo. Visitors are surprised by its size (small). The studio has made twenty-two feature-length animated films since its inception, and director Hayao Miyazaki is currently working on the studio's twenty-third.

1. *Nausicaä of the Valley of the Wind* (1984)
2. *Castle in the Sky* (1986)
3. *My Neighbor Totoro* (1988)
4. *Grave of the Fireflies* (1988)
5. *Kiki's Delivery Service* (1989)
6. *Only Yesterday* (1991)
7. *Porco Rosso* (1992)
8. *The Ocean Waves* (1993)
9. *Pom Poko* (1994)
10. *Whisper of the Heart* (1995)
11. *Princess Mononoke* (1997)
12. *My Neighbors the Yamadas* (1999)
13. *Spirited Away* (2001)
14. *The Cat Returns* (2002)
15. *Howl's Moving Castle* (2004)
16. *Tales from Earthsea* (2006)
17. *Ponyo* (2008)
18. *The Secret World of Arrietty* (2010)
19. *From Up on Poppy Hill* (2011)
20. *The Wind Rises* (2013)
21. *The Tale of Princess Kaguya* (2013)
22. *When Marnie Was There* (2014)
23. *How Do You Live?* (2020)

For about fifteen years beginning in 1996 I was a senior executive at Studio Ghibli and a member of the studio's board of directors. I was the only *gaijin* (foreigner) in a very traditional Japanese company. When I graduated from business school in 1981, a business computer was something that was very large and that you kept in a basement. Only qualified technicians could operate them. They were fed cardboard punch cards that the user gave the tech guys in the late afternoon and then waited until the next day for the results. Computer technology has advanced somewhat since then. The Japanese way of doing business, on the other hand, for the most part has not. It still retains elements popular in the 1800s or earlier.

In most American business schools professors taught (and may well still teach) that Japan is a country populated by people who are arguably the world's most ideal employees. They were said to possess a world-beating tolerance for hard work and long hours. Their dedication to their jobs and their companies meant that even ordinary assembly-line workers analyzed their own work processes and offered suggestions for improving them and making them even more efficient.

American business school students were urged to emulate the innovative business practices of Japanese companies. Ideas such as the lifetime-employment system and the just-in-time manufacturing process were raised as examples of business practices that gave Japanese companies a competitive edge and made them successful.

For a long time Japan was the world's number-two economy, although recently it has been surpassed by China. Japan had maintained its position despite its small size, relatively small population, and lack of natural resources. So when I first joined a Japanese company, I looked forward to seeing all the things I'd been hearing about in actual practice. What a shock it was to discover that almost none of it was true.

Finally, a brief word about the title of this book. *The Never-Ending Man: Hayao Miyazaki* is a 2016 Japanese television documentary film directed by Kaku Arakawa. The name "The Never-Ending Man" refers to Hayao Miyazaki and was coined to describe him by his long-time producer Toshio Suzuki. The title in Japanese, *Owaranai Hito*, is a bit more nuanced. It might be better translated as "The Man Who's Never Finished," a subtle reference to Miyazaki's feeling that his films are never finished and that, but for the demands of the business of cinema and meeting screening deadlines, he might never finish a film. It also carries the meaning of a man who is never finished making films.

I wanted to use this title for my book because when I saw the documentary it seemed *exactly* what it felt like for me to work at Studio Ghibli. The camera in the documentary could have been me, right down to the early morning conversations over coffee in the kitchen in Miyazaki's atelier, where my office at Ghibli was for most of the time I worked there.

1

Salaryman

Fools Rush In

I had been working in Tokyo for ten years, most recently at the Walt Disney Company, when Toshio Suzuki, the head of Studio Ghibli and the producer of nearly all of its films, hired me to start up the international division of Studio Ghibli and its parent company, Tokuma Shoten. With few exceptions, Ghibli's films hadn't been released outside of Japan. Suzuki thought it was time Ghibli's films got the international audience they deserved.

But Studio Ghibli had its own nonconventional way of doing things. This was both the reason for its success in Japan and its inability to get its films screened outside of Japan. Suzuki needed a *gaijin* for his new international division. But he needed more than a *gaijin* with the appropriate business talents and experience. He needed a *gaijin* who could appreciate the subtleties of the way Ghibli/Tokuma functioned. I was a graduate student in Japanese literature before I switched to an MBA program, so I fit the bill. Theoretically.

Suzuki was concerned that even a Japanese-speaking *gaijin* might not be able to function in the pure and thoroughly Japanese environment that was Ghibli/Tokuma. He went to great lengths to insure that my transition to the new company would be smooth. To begin with he established my new division as a completely independent company within the Tokuma Group. The new company was called Tokuma International. Hayao Miyazaki designed our business cards. The logo was an image of Yasuyoshi Tokuma, the chairman of the Tokuma Group, sprouting wings and flying, presumably, out of Japan.

Suzuki at that time seemed to me to be both the busiest person and the person with the most free time on his hands of anyone I had ever met. This, as I would later learn, is what it's like to be in the movie business.

Suzuki was based at Studio Ghibli in Higashi Koganei on the western outskirts of Tokyo. He ran the operational side of the studio while also keeping the production of the film on schedule and creatively on track. He provided support and a shoulder to lean on for the film's director, Hayao Miyazaki, and he was the person to whom Miyazaki would turn in order to bounce ideas off of. Every time Miyazaki conceived a possible ending for his film, he would seek out Suzuki to get his reaction. If Suzuki approved right away, Miyazaki would discard the idea and begin again.

In addition to his duties at Ghibli, Suzuki was also the number-two man at Tokuma Shoten, a company that had businesses in publishing, movies, music, and computer games. His boss and mentor, Yasuyoshi Tokuma, chairman and sole owner of the parent company, was in his early seventies and had a penchant for causing trouble and creating situations. It was often Suzuki's job to unravel the problems his boss had caused. This generally involved many time-consuming meetings and private, in-person visits.

Suzuki lived in central Tokyo and would start his day with a one-hour-plus drive out to Ghibli in suburban Koganei. He would work there for several hours, then drive back into central Tokyo to attend a meeting or meetings in Shinbashi, where Tokuma Shoten was located. Most meetings in Tokyo were followed by a side meeting, or meetings, in a coffee shop or restaurant. Then Suzuki would drive back again to Ghibli to see how

Mononoke Hime (Princess Mononoke) was coming along. On some days he would drive back again to Shinbashi for another meeting and then back again to Ghibli. Suzuki often held meetings out at Koganei or back in Tokyo that began at 10 pm and lasted for hours. He usually left the studio at 1 am or 2 am for his drive back home to Tokyo. He rarely slept more than four hours a night.

Suzuki is not a particularly large man, but he radiates a palpable energy, intelligence, and wit. Like Hayao Miyazaki, who is older than Suzuki by about a decade, Suzuki is instantly recognizable by anyone almost anywhere in Japan. His narrow face with John Lennon–style round glasses and a perpetual five-day beard and his extremely casual style of dress make him look like a person no one would ever mistake for a Japanese salaryman or believe was a director of a major company.

Despite living a good deal of his life in a car or in meeting rooms, Suzuki always had time to see every major Japanese and Hollywood film then playing. He had an unusually thorough and detailed knowledge of the roads, paths, and hidden alleyways of the Koganei-Mitaka area. None of these roads were ones Suzuki would have crossed in his back-and-forth travels between Ghibli and Shinbashi, and they often led to the most interesting hidden parks and special restaurants in the area. For someone so eternally busy, Suzuki managed to spend long periods of time alone and just thinking. He also spent long hours locked in windowless rooms attending to the excruciatingly time-consuming process of filmmaking. And somehow he still found time to mentor the people who worked for him.

The Tokuma Group of companies then consisted of Studio Ghibli (animation), Daiei Pictures (live-action films), Tokuma Publishing (the main company and a large publisher of a range of books from graphic novels to literature, nonfiction, magazines, and even poetry), Tokuma Japan Communications (music), Tokuma Intermedia (computer games and computer game magazines), Toko Tokuma (joint venture movie projects in China and independent films using Chinese directors), and

Tokuma International (my company, engaged in sales of Tokuma's entertainment products outside of Japan).

When I joined Tokuma International, all media companies in Japan were just beginning to experience the serious challenges to their traditional business models posed by computer-based entertainment products and a decline in the demand for things printed on paper, formerly known as books, magazines, and newspapers. Over at Ghibli, the studio's primary creator, Hayao Miyazaki, was simultaneously working himself nearly to death on his new film, *Princess Mononoke*, and facing a monumental writer's block in his struggle to come up with an ending for the film. Miyazaki would always work by writing the endings to his screenplays while the beginning and middle parts of it were already in production. When the production of the film would catch up to the unwritten parts of the screenplay, a general panic would set in. Ghibli produced approximately one film every two years, and to miss a release date could conceivably mean financial ruin for the studio.

With the business problems at Tokuma, the production problems at Ghibli, and the teething problems with the brand new Tokuma/Disney relationship in which Disney had contracted to distribute Ghibli's films worldwide, Suzuki was driving back and forth between Shinbashi and Koganei quite a lot. He therefore spent a good part of his day in his car.

Toshio Suzuki was then and continues to be what is known as an early adopter. If a certain new technology is available, he will be one of the very first to start using it. Owing to his position in the entertainment business, major Japanese electronics manufacturers would often seek him out to try their prototypes of new devices. Spending so much time in his car, Suzuki was always looking for ways to turn his car into a mobile office, so that he would never lose working time driving from place to place.

Years before hands-free mobile phones became readily available in cars, Suzuki had one in his. Years before GPS systems became readily available in cars, Suzuki had one in his. He had an audio CD system in the trunk of his car that automatically rotated and played either a preselected menu of music or randomly selected music for him to listen to. The system was attached to four very fine speakers that replaced the ones that had come with the car. All of this gadgetry allowed Suzuki to conduct business during his hours on the road and to listen to his favorite music when he wasn't on the phone.

Thanks to his hands-free phone system, Suzuki was among the very first humans capable of gesturing wildly and yelling at someone while driving (legally) as he commuted to work. Thanks to his mobile GPS and sophisticated music players, he could plot his escape from Tokyo's famous traffic jams while steeped in the sounds of 1950s and 1960s pop music ("Big Girls Don't Cry," "She Loves You," and "House of the Rising Sun"). Many of his gadgets were specially made for him and were designed to be installed in various places in his car, including on the dashboard on the passenger side.

I would often ride with Suzuki between Tokuma Shoten and Studio Ghibli. Once as we were cruising through relatively light Tokyo traffic, it occurred to me that his car was equipped with air bags.

"Suzuki-san, does this car have a passenger side air bag?" I asked.

"Yes, of course," he said.

"So if we get into an accident, the air bag will deploy and the GPS thing and the phone thing and the CD player controller thing will all be driven into my body at warp speed and with lethal force, killing me instantly?"

"Well . . . yes, now that you mention it, I suppose it would."

The systems in his car were down for a few weeks after that. No one would agree to ride shotgun until his technology friends had figured out how to place everything so as not to kill the front-seat passenger in the event of an accident.

No matter how busy Suzuki was, he always had time to do what was needed to make sure that my transition from a large

American entertainment company (Disney) to Tokuma Shoten went as smoothly as possible. Most of his efforts in this respect involved keeping me isolated from contact with the company's other divisions.

The mission statement for the new company and my job description was to sell the rights outside of Japan to anything owned or produced by any of the Tokuma companies and to handle any business of the Tokuma companies that involved dealings outside of Japan. This included managing the Disney relationship for the Ghibli films they would distribute, but it also included the Daiei films (*Shall We Dance?*) in markets where they had not been sold and the music, video games, and the Chinese-produced or -directed films.

One reason for setting up a separate company for the international business was to avoid the work rules of the rest of the Tokuma Group. Japanese companies then still worked a six-day week. Overtime, if required, was not compensated, even for hourly workers. Vacations and holidays, though earned, were rarely taken. And duties such as cleaning the office and serving tea or coffee were mandatory for all female employees (only). Suzuki understood that *gaijin* lacked the proper work ethic to submit to the normal working conditions in a Japanese company and would also resist applying the work rules to the new company's Japanese staff as well. In order to function harmoniously in a Japanese company, the new company had to be separate and to have its own work rules.

Many years ago when I was still a student in Japan, I was out drinking with a Japanese friend in a backstreet section of Osaka's Dotonbori entertainment district. It was late, maybe 2 am, and we were stumbling around looking for a taxi, having had a lot to drink in the bars and clubs called "snacks" that my friend often frequented. We came to a very narrow street, so narrow you could have stretched out a leg and reached the other side in a single step. The street had a pedestrian traffic light. The light was red. The streets were completely and totally deserted except for the two of us. Having lived for years in New York I instinctively moved to cross. My friend reached out his arm and prevented me.

"Red light," he said.

"Oh come on," I said. "It's completely deserted. No cars are coming. No one else is around. Why would we let a dumb, inanimate machine tell us if it's safe to cross?"

"Arupaato-san, of course I know it is safe to cross. But I have the inner strength to stand here and wait for the green signal. That is the problem with you *gaijin*. You are weak. You lack the discipline to stand here and wait for the green light."

It was an argument that was hard to refute, from the Japanese perspective anyway. We *gaijin* don't work on Saturdays. We might do overtime once in a while, but not as a regular thing, and we expect to get paid extra for it. We don't share desks at work and expect to have a whole desk all to ourselves. We complain if the offices we work in are more crowded than the legal limits imposed by the municipal fire department. We don't think smoking should be allowed in the office. We don't think women with the same job description as men should automatically be required to make tea (coffee), wear uniforms when men doing the same job don't, or neaten up everyone's desk at the end of the day. We sometimes allow the people who work for us to tell us that we're wrong and we even get angry when they fail to advise us that the truck they see roaring down the road, which we haven't noticed, is about to flatten us. Not only don't *gaijin* do the many basic things that every Japanese company worker understands, is expected to do, and expects others to do, but we're not even aware of most of them.

Hence the solution of physically walling off the office that was Tokuma International from the rest of the Tokuma companies housed in the same building. Not only were the walls meant to protect the *gaijin* within from clashing with the normal Japanese people working nearby, but they were also meant to protect the Japanese workers from exposure to the *gaijin* next door and its *gaijin*-friendly Japanese staff. Tokuma International was the only no-smoking part of the company. No one worked on Saturday. The secretary didn't wear a standard issue office lady (OL) uniform or clean desks (OK, she did make coffee). Each person had their own desk. And we had a reasonable amount of space to work in.

For those unfamiliar with the look and feel of a typical Japanese corporate business office, they typically look very much like the chaotic homicide squad rooms in American TV crime dramas, only more crowded and less well organized, and with no private offices for the lieutenants. The meeting rooms look exactly like the interrogation rooms where the suspects are grilled and bullied into confessing to crimes. Only the company's president on the executive floor would have his own office. Even presidents of smaller subsidiary companies might share a desk with one or more assistants, though they would have larger desks than everyone else.

Even the offices of major Japanese corporations look as if Godzilla came rampaging through and management decided the cost of cleaning up or repair wasn't justified. The employees are Japanese. They'll make do. Each floor of a Japanese office building is generally designed to be used as a single, large open space. In even the most famous corporations, the staff share desks. Four or six employees to a desk, seated on both sides of it, facing each other with a computer or stacks of files serving as a semi-porous middle barrier. A single printer, copier, and fax machine is shared by an entire floor. Sometimes by two floors, and people might have to make a trip upstairs or down to pick up a printed or faxed document.

Tokuma Shoten's offices sat in an impressively stylish architect-designed building. But the offices themselves were designed for Japanese employees. The Tokuma International office on the other hand, was designed for *gaijin*. Inside its newly erected walls, each of the four original Tokuma International employees had his/her own reasonably sized desk and computer. We had a printer, copier and fax machine for four people. We had a sofa and two armchairs for casual meetings and a table and four desk chairs for meetings where papers and documents had to be spread out. We had bookcases full of relevant but seldom-used legal and industry tomes plus massive Japanese-English and English-Japanese dictionaries. We had a display cabinet containing one of every consumer product or book Studio Ghibli had ever produced.

Our tenth-floor office also had large corner windows with views that extended all the way out to Tokyo Bay. From my desk I could see all of Japan's various modes of transportation at a single glance. There was the *shinkansen* Bullet Train just slowing on its final glide toward Tokyo Station. The various color-coded JR local and long-distance lines came and went every few minutes. The newly built and driverless Yurikamome train zipped along on rubber wheels toward the Odaiba entertainment area and the Big Site convention center. The aging but still graceful Monorail, a leftover from the 1964 Olympics, leaned precariously leftward as it rounded a curve on its way to Haneda Airport.

There were the gracefully arching branches of the Shuto, the overhead highways. These were clogged with traffic that barely moved all day. Once or twice a day I could spot a ferry just easing into its berth at the Takeshiba piers after completing its twenty-four-hour trip from one of the far-away Izu-Ogasawara Islands, incongruously an official part of metropolitan Tokyo. There was the newly built Rainbow Bridge standing astride the harbor and linking it to the island of Odaiba. The bridge was silvery white in the morning sunshine or bathed in colored lights against a hazy pink and purple sky at dusk.

All day, passenger jet aircraft banked low over Tokyo Bay on their final approach to Haneda Airport. Immediately below, bustling Shinbashi's wide main streets were packed with cars and busses mired in the heavy traffic. The warren of narrow pedestrian-only alleys in the *mizu shobai* (bar) district were mostly empty in the morning and crammed with wandering pedestrians once the evening rush began. At the beginning and end of the lunch hour, which everyone took at exactly the same time, the sidewalks were full of people.

Just behind our building, ground had been broken for the soon-to-be new modern high-rise district of Shiodome. But the initial digging had unearthed a forgotten mansion, a *daimyo yashiki*, and now all construction was on hiatus while anthropologists used toothbrushes to excavate Edo-era teacups and teapots from the muddy soil. The original Shinbashi train station, Japan's very first, had also been discovered nearby and was similarly being excavated and restored.

It was a spectacular view out my office window. And I have to admit, I spent time enjoying it. Only Mr. Tokuma's own office two floors up had so special and so expansive a view of Tokyo. His was, of course, much bigger and much better.

To populate our special office, Suzuki, always conscious of the interpersonal dynamics of the workplace, had hand-picked Tokuma International's initial operating staff. To begin with, there was one male from the Tokuma publishing side of the business with experience in computer games and accounting. And there was one female from Daiei Pictures with experience in overseas film sales and a good knowledge of Tokuma politics.

To avoid the potential for sexual complications at work, Suzuki made sure that the male staff member was younger and *majime* (boring), and that the female staff member was the *senpai* (senior) in terms of industry knowledge and experience. This, he believed, combined with his having specifically chosen two people who he was sure would not find each other attractive, would preclude any workplace complications from an office romance. As it turned out, these two original employees ended up marrying each other about a year later and left the company.

Since nearly all of Tokuma International's business was with people from outside of Japan, a secretary who could speak English was needed, or at least one who could receive phone calls convincingly in English. None was available from inside the Tokuma Group (a sign of a truly Japanese company), so we proceeded to hire one from the outside. This gave me the opportunity for firsthand experience of how Japanese companies hire their employees, a process that differs somewhat from how Western companies do it.

Suzuki let me know that he had contacted an employment agency and had scheduled appointments with three prospective candidates. The first candidate, a young woman in her early twenties, was shown into a conference room accompanied by a representative from the agency, and we were joined by three managers from Tokuma Shoten. To my surprise, there would be a single interview at which all parties would be present. In America we tend to do it one-on-one.

The questions asked also differed from what would typically be asked in an employment interview in the US. What were the young woman's religious beliefs? Did she have a boyfriend? If not, why not? If she had a boyfriend before but not now, was it she who left him or did he dump her? How much money did she have in her bank account? Was she planning on having children any time soon? Generally these types of questions are considered bad form in an American employment interview or are possibly actually illegal.

The hardest part of the interview for the first candidate came when she was suddenly told to start talking in English to the *gaijin*. The girl looked around the table at five unsmiling faces and at one face trying hard to look friendly. She hesitated briefly, and then she burst into tears. The situation did seem unfair to her, though when hiring a secretary for a company that mainly does business with non-Japanese people, you probably do not want to hire someone who breaks down and cries when asked to speak English with a foreigner.

This first candidate was not hired. I asked Suzuki if we could do the subsequent interviews with fewer people present. I thought that if we were going to make the candidates talk about their sex lives, their religion, and how much money they had in the bank, it might be better with a smaller group. Suzuki seemed puzzled by the request but agreed.

The next candidate arrived with a representative from her agency and her mother. This time the Tokuma side was represented by Suzuki and myself and one other person. The questions were as before (the mother looked uncomfortable), but the English part of the interview was between only the girl and myself. We ended up hiring her. However, as it turned out she did have an unfortunate tendency to burst into tears from time to time, and eventually we had to replace her. She ended up marrying someone in the office next door.

Our beginning staff of four people spent the first few weeks in the office just setting things up. I immediately discovered that there are two major things about working in a Japanese company that set it apart from working in an American company: frequent and pointless internal meetings and *aisatsu*.

We don't really have *aisatsu* in the USA. It can be roughly translated, depending on the context, as greetings. In this case, in-person greetings. For about the first week in the new company, every single Japanese person I had ever known, or had even ever met, stopped by unannounced to congratulate me on my new position and to sit and chat for five to ten minutes about nothing in particular. People I had never met dropped by unannounced to congratulate me on joining my new company. The office was filled with pots of lovely white orchids: gifts from people who had wanted to drop by but couldn't make it. Some were even from the heads of major Japanese corporations. Although I was impressed, I could never understand how, with this many people always just dropping by and having nothing in particular to talk about, anyone could ever get any work done. At least for the first few weeks of a new company's existence.

Once the external ceremonial *aisatsu* had begun to die down, I was visited by various people from within the Tokuma companies. The first was Mori-san from Toko Tokuma, the company that worked with partners in China to produce Chinese films by Chinese directors. Mori-san was a serious-looking man with a large scar running down the side of his face, gleaming yellow eyes, and tobacco-stained brownish teeth. He was rumored to have worked for the Japanese CIA in Taiwan during the War. Mori-san sat with me in my office and mustered what for him passed as a pleasant voice and told me he had just dropped by to warn me to stay out of his China business.

The head of Daiei Pictures, the live-action movie production group, dropped by with a few of his senior managers to let me know that yes, they had been told that I was in charge of selling their films abroad, but no, Daiei didn't need any help from me. They had their own people who had managed perfectly well before my arrival and they would continue to do so without me.

The head of the Tokuma legal department dropped by to let me know that he was in charge of all contracts and that I was not to even think about negotiating a contract without consulting him first. The head of book publishing came by to say that he'd heard I would be helping him with book deals outside of Japan, but that since I didn't have any publishing experience, I should just leave all that to him. And the head of the interactive games business came by to thank me for not bothering to use my Disney contacts to try to expand his distribution business outside of Japan. The head of the music division delivered this same message by not even bothering to come over to see me.

Unlike the *aisatsu* visits from people outside the company, the *aisatsu* visits from the people within the company at least seemed to serve some kind of obvious purpose. The same could not be said for the frequent internal meetings I was required to attend. I understood that the real discussion of any issue in a Japanese enterprise takes place before any meeting is called. If there is an issue that needs to be resolved or a plan someone is seeking to have approved, the relevant parties meet informally, usually one-on-one or in very small groups, and often at a bar or restaurant somewhere. In a less formal setting, fueled by alcohol or not, company employees float ideas and get a sense of who might be in favor or who might oppose a thing, and crucially, what the real reasons for being for or against might be. The process of visiting and obtaining the approval of all required persons in advance is called *nemawashi* (securing the roots). In this way the arguments for or against any proposal or new idea and the decision makers' positions on the proposal have all been fixed long before any formal meeting takes place.

Once the *nemawashi* has occurred, a meeting is called to pretend to discuss the matter in question, and the attendees vote on the outcome in accordance with the positions they have previously (and privately) confirmed they would take. By the time the meeting has been called, everyone attending already knows what's been decided. In the meetings I attended, I always hoped that there would be at least one guy who never got the memo or who was out of town or something, and would come to the meeting, be astonished at what was being proposed, and argue about the decision. Of course that never happened. It always surprised me how much time and energy went into the fake and pointless discussion of something that had already been decided, and that I was always the only one in the room who seemed to mind.

When setting up our new company, Tokuma International, we had hours and hours of "discussion" meetings to determine the new company's official policies and work rules. Japanese law requires any incorporated company to have official policies on a number of things, including rules governing employment, though surprisingly no one seems to pay much attention to them once they're finalized and written down. Suzuki and I had worked them out in advance, and Suzuki had done the *nemawashi* with some of the other division heads and explained the rules to Mr. Tokuma and gotten his approval.

Nonetheless, a series of meetings were held to discuss the policies and rules. The meetings were attended by no fewer than a dozen people, including Mr. Tokuma himself. We slogged through the minutiae of potential human resources issues and rules and regulations. We once spent the better part of an hour deciding whether an employee making his/her first business trip should be allowed to purchase a suitcase at the company's expense, which was the rule in the other Tokuma

Group companies, and if so, exactly what kind of suitcase it could be and how much such a suitcase would cost.

We also briefly touched on larger issues like maternity leave, long-term sickness leave, grounds for dismissal, employee evaluations, and performance review frequency, though none of these topics held the attention of the participants the way the suitcase issue had. All of this seemed like overkill for a company that had only three employees and was never expected to have as many as a dozen—especially since the rules that Suzuki and I had decided on and Mr. Tokuma had approved were already being printed up for submission to the government agency that monitors such things. And it wasn't as if the other people in the meetings didn't know this.

Another feature of Japanese meetings that has always puzzled me is that once a person begins to talk, no matter what he/she has to say, the floor is his/hers for as long as he/she thinks he/she needs to say it. Even when the person is saying something completely and wildly off topic, overlong, or embarrassingly inaccurate, no one ever intercedes, politely or otherwise, to end or limit the speech. The person just keeps going on until he/she is done.

Japanese people are used to *happyo*, a term that roughly translates as "presentation." Long speeches mark many of Japan's social occasions. Weddings and farewell parties require an endless series of long speeches. From an early age Japanese people are often pointed to at random, in school say, or at social gatherings, and asked to stand up and talk. And they almost always do, whether or not they actually have anything to say. At a Japanese business meeting, every single person in the room must talk, whether or not they have anything to say. There is never a sense of trying to come to a conclusion or challenging or discussing the opinions being talked about. Just a series of each person in the room articulating a position that may or may not have direct or even indirect relevance to whatever is being discussed.

On the other hand, even a meeting where everything is

decided or has been decided behind the scenes can serve other functions. Where people sit matters. Who sits closest to the president matters. Who is asked to speak in what order reveals things about the company's power structure, which does shift from time to time. Who is invited to the meeting in the first place matters. The meetings may not bring forward the actual business of the company through critical discussion and evaluation of options. But they do let the people in it know a good deal about what is actually going on inside the company. The important information that you took away from a meeting often had very little to do with the topic that was being discussed.

Tokuma-*shacho*

The chairman of the Tokuma Group was Yasuyoshi Tokuma, also variously known as Tokuma Kokai or Tokuma-*shacho*. Whatever stereotypical images there are of Japanese businessmen, Tokuma-*shacho* conformed to none of them. A consensus building, risk-averse team player, indistinguishable from his peers in a blue suit he was not. He was a quirky, self-confident, opinionated, strong-willed, blustering individual capable of swimming gleefully against the tide of public opinion and conventional wisdom. He consciously sought to appear bigger than life. He was exuberant and joyful but also capable of rage and thunder. He was a tall, good-looking man who projected an aura of authority. He was your grandfather on steroids (if your grandfather was Japanese). He spewed out transparent untruths so convincingly and entertainingly that no one believed them for a moment yet acted as if they did. He was capable of infinitely subtle Machiavellian intrigue that succeeded because it came wrapped in motives that seemed so comically obvious he was often underestimated. What you thought was really going on was often just diversion.

It took me quite a while to realize that Tokuma-*shacho*'s self-aggrandizing, obviously exaggerated fabrications were meant to be dismissed as folly, because while you were congratulating yourself on seeing through the pretense, you were missing the real story. Tokuma-*shacho* could transform himself from a blustering, self-absorbed egoist into a wise elder statesman sharing his wisdom with you, secretly and off the record, in the space of a few sentences. His advice, when he gave it, could seem profound and usually made good practical sense. His mottos, which he repeated frequently, were "never let anyone else write the screenplay of your life" and "never let a lack of money stop you, because the banks have plenty of it just for the asking." Knowing how to borrow large sums of money was his greatest talent.

When I joined Tokuma Shoten, Tokuma-*shacho* was in his seventies. He was strongly built and handsome in the manner of an aging or retired movie star. He had a deep, gravelly voice that he broadcast stirringly to an audience of hundreds without a microphone. In private, the voice could drop to a sandpapery stage whisper, if he wasn't yelling at you for something. He had the demeanor of an old-time politician or *yakuza* don. It was difficult to imagine him sitting down to give advice to famous Japanese politicians, or to heads of major modern corporations like SONY or Nintendo or to Japan's first-tier major banks, as he often claimed. Yet there were newspaper articles, complete with photos, to prove that at least some of his stories were actually true. You were always sure that he was making up most or at least some of what he said, embellishing the details and adding here and there to make a good story, but there was always just enough verifiable truth in it to make you stop and wonder. No one ever believed his stories, and yet no one completely disbelieved them either.

Mr. Tokuma was a fixer. He was a man who could get things done behind the scenes. If Politician A needed to speak to Politician B or Captain of Industry C, but couldn't be seen in public doing so, he could speak to Mr. Tokuma and Mr. Tokuma would pass along the message. He was famously a friend of the Prime Minister Uno Sosuke. In 1989 when the *Mainichi Shinbun* broke with tradition and reported that then Prime Minister Uno had been keeping a geisha, Uno rode out the media firestorm hidden away in Mr. Tokuma's twelfth-floor office suite for the better part of a week. Uno was later forced to resign after only three months in office. It was unclear whether the cause had been the public outrage over the moral issue of a prime minister having a kept woman, or the Uno regime's being blamed for the prior administration's imposition of an unpopular nationwide consumption tax, or that Uno had kept the geisha on such a pitiful allowance she had sought out a newspaper reporter to complain about it. In any event, it had been Mr. Tokuma who kept Uno out of sight while his political party tried to contain the damage.

Once when returning from lunch and entering one of the two elevators in the lobby of the Tokuma Shoten Building, I noticed that people were avoiding the elevator I had just entered. People in public in Japan sometimes avoid sitting next to *gaijin* on trains or standing next to them in elevators (we are unpredictable, apparently), but this rarely happened in the Tokuma office building. Then I noticed that the other person in the elevator with me was clearly a *yakuza*. He was as wide as he was tall, muscular, wearing a dark suit with a narrow tie, had on sunglasses, and had facial scars, a crew cut, and an unambiguous attitude. He was carrying a large paper shopping bag in each hand. I casually glanced down to see what was in them. Though they were covered on top with loosely positioned Hello Kitty hand towels, I could clearly see that underneath the towels the bags were full of cash: bundles of ¥10,000 notes bound with rubber bands. No one else got on the elevator and the doors closed. I pushed the button for 10 and my companion asked me to push 12, the executive floor containing only Mr. Tokuma's office and his private meeting rooms.

The twelfth floor of the Tokuma Shoten Building was a kind of world unto itself. It contained the Tokuma boardroom, a very beautifully appointed president's office with an adjoining smaller conference room, and a few secret rooms in the back, including a storeroom full of gifts that the *shacho* had received or that the *shacho* would eventually give to others. There was expensive-looking original art everywhere. The gatekeeper to the president's office was Tokuma-shacho's personal secretary, a very elegant woman named Oshiro-san.

If you were summoned into the *shacho*'s presence you would get a call from Oshiro-san. If you needed to see Tokuma-*shacho* for some reason, you phoned Oshiro-san and she would either fit you in as appropriate or politely inform you that your request had been rejected. If you were a visitor from the outside or if you came up to the twelfth floor in the company of a visitor from the outside, at the end of the audience you would receive either a package of something called *dokudamicha*, a kind of supposedly healthful green tea, or a small present *and* a package of *dokudamicha*. Somewhere on the twelfth floor there was a storeroom containing a mountain of packages of *dokudamicha*.

Any summons to the twelfth floor was guaranteed to be interesting. If there was something Tokuma-*shacho* wanted you to do for him, Oshiro-san would call you up. It was never come up at 3 pm or be here on Tuesday at noon. Advance notice was rare. When Oshiro-san called, the *shacho* wanted you right away. You dropped whatever it was you were doing and you went.

Being ushered into Tokuma-*shacho*'s office always felt special. He had an enormous, beautiful mahogany desk that seemed to be overflowing with presents or framed documents he had just received and unwrapped. Two of the walls were all glass with sweeping views all the way out into Tokyo Harbor. It was a philosopher's view of the city, similar to my own view from my office, but much grander. From up here the Bullet Trains rushing to and from Tokyo Station, the ferries docking or departing for Tokyo's outer islands, and the planes banking low for their descent into Haneda Airport seemed somehow more significant. As if the person with this view of Tokyo had the kind of real power to change what you were seeing down below.

If you stood by the window in Mr. Tokuma's office, you

could see down into the Hama Rikyu Imperial Gardens where the emperor of Japan had once hunted ducks by day and held moon-viewing parties at night. With no taller buildings nearby, you had a sense that you were up on top of the world. Even the emperor of Japan and the real estate that he owned was down below you.

Whether first-time visitor or company employee, once you got the required dose of the art on the walls and the view out the windows, you were ushered to a suite of sofas and chairs arranged around a large glass-topped coffee table. This is where you were invited to sit and wait for the *shacho* to join you while observing him in action. He was usually on the phone when you came in. The single armchair looking outward was reserved for Tokuma-*shacho*, and on the table in front of it was his personal teacup, a very beautiful and very rare Edo-era blue and white Imari porcelain with a mountain and waterfall landscape baked into it. The two chairs facing the desk were usually reserved for in-house visitors. The sofa with its back to the desk was usually stacked high with books or more items that Tokuma-*shacho* had received as gifts but was cleared off to be used by outside visitors.

No meeting with the *shacho* ever began until Oshiro-san had brought in a tray with freshly brewed coffee and fancy French cookies or little cakes, followed by Japanese tea. Once the *shacho* settled into his chair, which was bigger than the others, he never seemed to be in a hurry. He asked how you were doing, what you were up to. There was personal conversation while you ate the cookies and sipped tea and/or coffee. And eventually he would get around to whatever it was that he wanted you to do for him. One such theme, for example, was his wanting to meet personally with Disney's then chairman Michael Eisner. How could this be arranged and when? Several times he asked me up to his office for advice on how he could arrange to meet with Bill Clinton (Harvey Weinstein had suggested that he could arrange it).

Sometimes the meeting with Mr. Tokuma would be about

an offer he had received from someone not Japanese, and he wanted a response drafted in English. Michael Ovitz once invited him to meet Christie Hefner to see if Tokuma Shoten would be interested in publishing *Playboy* in Japan (he wasn't). Steven Segal wanted him to invest in one of his films (he didn't). Every three or four months he received an invitation to executive produce a film somewhere in Europe that included a financial summary, and he asked me to look it over.

Sometimes Mr. Tokuma would ask me and Moriyoshi-san, who worked with me, to come up to his office, and there would be no point to the meeting or request at all. Oshiro-san would come in with individual cups of Häagen-Dazs (always vanilla) or little plastic containers of crème brulée. We would eat. There would be no talking at all sometimes; just eating. We would finish eating, he would thank us, and we would leave. That would be it. Moriyoshi-san and I would leave, look at each other but not voice the question "what was that about?" at least until we got back downstairs.

The actual business of Tokuma Shoten was entertainment and publishing. Mr. Tokuma had started his company by recognizing talent and promoting it. Writers and other artists loved to be represented by Tokuma because he firmly believed that the creative part was up to them, and he seldom interfered in any way with what they did. Once he selected someone he had decided to work with, he left the creative side of things entirely in their hands. It helped that he was always less interested in their actual work than he was in what use he could make of the relationship. He published books. He hired writers and other staff and let them create magazines. His companies funded the films of Akira Kurosawa when no one else would. He invested in Chinese filmmakers whose government threatened to ban their films. And he started Studio Ghibli by finding the money to finance the then relatively unknown Japanese directors Isao Takahata and Hayao Miyazaki.

Studio Ghibli was founded in order to keep the team that had produced *Kaze no Tani no Nausicaä* (*Nausicaä of the Valley of the Wind*) together so they could go on to make more films. A great deal of mythology surrounds the creation of Studio Ghibli. Toshio Suzuki has said that the name for the studio was chosen because Ghibli is a term WWI Italian fighter pilots used for the hot wind that blows out of the Sahara Desert. Suzuki maintained that Ghibli's purpose was to blow a hot new wind into the world of Japanese film animation. Hayao Miyazaki, when asked why the name Ghibli, said the name was chosen when Suzuki told him they were getting their own studio and it needed a name. Miyazaki says he was looking at a book of WWI aircraft when Suzuki came in, and randomly pointed to a plane on the page he had open at the time. Both or neither may be true. Either way, it was Yasuyoshi Tokuma who came up with the money to make it happen.

Public Speaking

To manage his companies, or perhaps more accurately, to hear the reports on what was happening in his companies and create a narrative to describe it to the outside world, Tokuma-*shacho* held three monthly meetings on a regular schedule. There was a department heads meeting, a board of directors meeting, and an all–Tokuma Group employees meeting. The latter was a monthly address to the assembled employees of the companies that made up the Tokuma Group. There was also a semiannual stockholders meeting. Each meeting began with a speech by Tokuma-*shacho*. The speech took a slightly different form depending on Mr. Tokuma's mood and what was going on at the time. It was somewhere between a comedian's stand-up monologue and a politician's formal address.

Each of the meetings had its own purpose and its own audience even though there was a good deal of overlap in the contents. At the department heads meeting attended by thirty or so department heads or subheads seated around the huge board room table on the top floor of the Tokuma Shoten Building, each department head was required to stand and relate the highlights of his/her department's activities that month and say what kind of things were expected to happen in the coming months. All seats were assigned. You had to be on time. The meeting started at 10 am and if you were not in your seat by 9:55 am you were late.

The current status of each person in the company was revealed by his/her proximity to Tokuma-*shacho* seated at the head of the table. Toshio Suzuki was always seated to his right. No one managed to hold the seat to his left for more than a meeting or two. Because Mr. Tokuma loved intrigue, most of the other positions at the table often changed, and rivals of equal status sat equidistant from the boss, facing each other at the table. I always sat next to Suzuki, partly because the idea of having a *gaijin* at the table in the first place was meant as a kind of status for the company and partly because the *gaijin* needed frequent whispered commentary to understand what was going on.

Tokuma-*shacho* always opened the meeting and for the first half hour regaled the assembled group with a reading of selections from his current month's diary. The diary, the parts of it he read anyway, contained secrets and glimpses behind the scenes of Japan's centers of commercial and political power. He used the diary as a kind of jumping-off point for his monologues. He would tell stories about famous people. Sometimes he would interrupt himself with his thoughts on politics and society or just to tell a joke. He was one of the most riveting public speakers I have ever heard. And he expected no less of each person in the room when it was his/her turn to speak.

When you spoke at one of these meetings, you had to speak up in a loud, confident, and manly voice (even if you were a woman). Often not much happened in a particular department from month to month. Listening to a speaker trying to embellish his/her business activities and make it sound as though progress were being made could be either painful or sleep-inducing (sleeping in a Japanese business meeting is OK if done correctly; the proper position is arms folded across chest, chin resting on top of chest, and facial expression ambiguous enough to be interpreted as listening with eyes closed). Often the topic being reported was some business-related failure that everyone in the room understood Tokuma-*shacho* himself had caused but would not admit to. The publishing division's numbers were down because a highly touted new book by Sidney Sheldon had failed to do any business. Tokuma-*shacho* had taken pride in negotiating the outrageously generous contract with the author by himself, against the advice of his head of publishing. Because no one could actually blame Mr. Tokuma aloud at a meeting, the head of publishing had to take responsibility for vastly overpaying Sidney Sheldon.

No remedies or actionable plans were ever offered at the meetings, and there were rarely comments or questions. The department head or subdepartment head said his/her piece, heads nodded, and the next person was called on. There were to be no surprises and no introduction of brand-new information. But at first I didn't know that.

At the very first department heads meeting I attended, all I had to do was to stand up and introduce myself. That went fairly well. At the second meeting, though, I got a little carried away and got into trouble. Some of the international business had been handled by Tokuma Shoten executives. There was a group of them who took on whatever project came up that didn't fit into another category or that no one else wanted to deal with. The people in charge of the various foreign projects were more than happy to turn them over to me. One of the more senior generalists, a man named Ohtsuka-san, had been assigned to be my in-house Tokuma liaison (probably because Tokuma-*shacho* didn't trust Suzuki-san to be my only mentor). Ohtsuka-san had been in charge of Korea. There was a Korean company that Tokuma did various kinds of business with, and Ohtsuka-san wanted me to meet its chairman and take over the business relationship.

Ohtsuka-san had arranged for the first face-to-face meeting with the chairman of the Korean company to take place over dinner. The dinner was scheduled at 4 in the afternoon in a fairly expensive sushi restaurant in nearby Higashi Ginza. I thought it was odd that a dinner would be scheduled so early and wondered if the sushi restaurant would even be open then. I went to the appointed place at the appointed time and was introduced to the head of the Korean company, Chairman Wook of Daigen Communications (we always referred to him as the Kaicho). After ordering beer, Ohtsuka-san downed his as soon as it arrived and then, to my astonishment, stood up, gave a curt bow, and just left.

For the next three and a half hours over sushi and beer, Wook-*kaicho* explained to me everything I didn't know about the film business in Korea. Most of what I didn't know had to do with the historical relationship between Korea and Japan. It was illegal to screen Japanese films in Korea, partly because of the lingering animosity felt by many Koreans toward Japan after WWII, but also due to economic protectionism. Korea wanted its own film industry to flourish, and Japanese films, popular with Korean young people, were a threat.

The ban on Japanese films was gradually being loosened, but only for Japanese live-action films. The ban on animated films was less likely to be lifted, because of the many indigenous fledgling Korean animation studios and the fact that animated films were watched by children. After a good deal of expensive lobbying by companies like Daigen that wanted to import Japanese animation, the only exception the Korean lawmakers would concede was for films that had won major international awards. Theatrical distribution would be allowed for those films but not TV broadcast or video sales.

Wook-*kaicho* explained that there were Korean businessmen and a few Korean politicians who were actively campaigning to reverse this unnecessary remnant from another era, and that things were changing and certainly would change in the near future. Soon, he said, all Japanese live-action films would be allowed in and the ban on airing them on TV would be lifted. The ban on animated films and TV shows would remain in place for a while, but it was only a matter of time before that too would be lifted.

I asked the Kaicho how he knew the Korean government would lift the ban. He leaned in closely and spoke in a low voice. "We know the people who make these decisions," he said. "We have ways to influence them."

"You mean bribes?" I asked.

He leaned back, picked up his glass, and had another sip of beer.

"I know for a fact that the ban will be lifted by the end of this year," he said.

"What is it you want me to do?" I asked.

The Kaicho's problem was that he had been a very early supporter of Ghibli films. He had entered into a ten-year license contract to distribute the films in Korea. The end of his contract was fast approaching. The contract stipulated that if the ban on Japanese animated films was still in place when the contract expired, Daigen would lose the large minimum guarantee it had paid up front to Tokuma for the Korean rights to the films. Ten years had nearly passed. The ban had not been lifted. The Kaicho wanted me to extend the license for another ten years for free. "I know politicians. I'm spending money. I promise you the ban will be lifted by the end of the year. I guarantee it," he said.

At the next department heads meeting when it was my turn to speak I announced that the longstanding Korean ban on animated films was about to be lifted. My statement was met with a tsunami of uproarious laughter. Waves and waves of it washed over me. Tokuma-*shacho* turned to me and in an almost kindly, grandfatherly voice said, "Ah, you've been talking to Wook-*kaicho*. You see Arubahto-san (Mr. Tokuma could never pronounce my name correctly), Wook-*kaicho* has been coming to Tokyo twice a year for the last ten years telling us exactly the same thing. We believed him at first too. The ban won't be lifted any time soon, no matter what he tells you."

And of course, it was not.

In addition to standing up to speak at the department heads meeting, every month each department head was required to make a short speech in front of a large group representing the roughly thirteen hundred employees of the Tokuma Group. The meeting took place in the Tokuma Shoten Building's in-house theater, Tokuma Hall. Each department head in turn mounted the big stage and addressed the three hundred assembled employees. The prospect of speaking in Japanese on stage in front of a large auditorium full of people terrified me, and it happened once a month.

I knew I would always be the third speaker. After Tokuma-*shacho* himself and just after Suzuki-san. Tokuma-*shacho* was a consummate performer. His speech would always be in equal measure topical, thought-provoking, humorous, and altogether relevant. It was delivered in the booming, stentorian tones of an accomplished stage actor, but also dropped to a coarse and earthy intimacy as required. He could be grandfatherly and wise or thundering and angry, or very, very funny. Of course, almost everything he said was completely made up and most of it untrue, and his audience stayed riveted to his every word. He was a really good public speaker.

Then Mr. Tokuma's protégé Toshio Suzuki would stand up and speak. Usually Suzuki was even better than Tokuma-*shacho*. Suzuki's speeches had the same qualities, and what he lacked in gravelly tone and the mellowness of age he made up for in the sharpness of his wit and the fact that his content wasn't made up. What he said was clear, concise, and unobvious. He often said out loud what others were only thinking. He had a good strong speaking voice. He was also a really good public speaker.

These are the two guys I followed when it was my turn to speak.

The only way I could deliver a speech in Japanese was to practice it beforehand. I would write out what I wanted to say and then I would translate it into Japanese. Then I would show my Japanese translation to someone and make sure there were no obvious translation errors. And then, on the day I had to deliver this speech, I would spend the entire morning and early afternoon in the bayside park inside Hama Rikyu that was a five-minute walk from the Tokuma Shoten Building. I chose a secluded part of the park and spent hours there memorizing my speech and practicing its delivery out loud. I suppose if it had ever rained on the day of the speech I would have had to cancel it and go into hiding.

With nothing in my head but my speech, I would return to Tokuma Hall and take my front row seat next to the Tokuma Japan Communications starlet of the month. Tokuma Japan Communications was the music division of the Tokuma Group. They represented many talented and even occasionally very successful musicians, and also some who sold CDs based on how good they looked on the CD's cover. New, young, female artists were introduced to the company at the monthly meetings.

For some reason, usually sitting next to me as I awaited my turn to take the stage was the newest of Tokuma Japan Communication's starlets. Typically she was a girl of about sixteen with an adult woman's body that was more or less contained in an attention-getting mini-skirt and abbreviated top. Before the speeches began, her name was announced and she stood up, teetered on her vertiginous platform heels, and turned to nod, jiggle, and wave to the audience. Upon seeing her move at close range, parts of my speech would suddenly disappear from my memory. For some reason, these young women always made me think of evolution, biology, and natural selection. Even a gigantic dinosaur could function with a brain the size of a peanut.

Tokuma's and Suzuki's speeches having wowed the audience, my name would be announced. I cast one final glance at the lovely starlet, now back in her seat again crossing her legs to get comfortable. Then I strode confidently forward to take the stage. Speaking in a foreign language, no matter how skilled you might be, can be like trying to eat or drink immediately after a visit to the dentist. You've had your gums injected with Novocain and you may or may not be going through the food and drink intake motions properly, but you just don't feel a thing. You think you're doing it right, but you can't really tell. If you've just said something completely and devastatingly wrong, you will only know it when your audience reacts. US President Bill Clinton had a translator on a state trip to Poland who translated a presidential greeting for the Polish press saying that the president had a deeply felt need to have sexual relations with Poland. Probably it was a grammatically correct translation. Only the colloquial usage was off.

Although I was emphatically not a good enough speaker to follow Tokuma or Suzuki, I was very lucky in what I had to say when I got up on the stage. We were in the midst of the seemingly endless process of making the English-dubbed version of Hayao Miyazaki's record-breaking film *Princess Mononoke* with Miramax, then a subsidiary of the Walt Disney Company. Every week Harvey Weinstein, the chairman of Miramax, was claiming that he was about to hire someone new and amazing for the film's English-language cast. All I had to do was report it. The other department heads were doing updates from their increasingly struggling businesses. There wasn't much good news to report, and Mr. Tokuma didn't like to hear bad news at the big meeting, so mentioning crowd-pleasing topics like business disasters and potential financial collapse was out. While everyone else was struggling with their topics, I was delivering Entertainment Tonight, name-dropping the names of America's most famous movie stars courtesy of Harvey Weinstein's expansive vision of the possible (but the very unlikely).

Up I would go onto the big stage with hundreds of pairs of eyes trained on me, the audience's ears alert from having been enlightened and entertained by the dynamic duo of Mr. Tokuma and his old-world (samurai era) blustering brilliance and Mr. Suzuki and his hip, insightful, and funny message that the company was about to harness new technologies and ride them to success. I took the microphone and tried my best to sound good in Japanese. I did my best to deliver my speech in manly, confident Japanese.

It is a fairly well-kept secret in Japan—something that the Japanese will not tell you until you've been there for twenty-five years (if then)—that most foreign males speak like women. The vast majority of Japanese-language teachers are women, and they never really dwell on the fact that men and women speak the Japanese language very differently, and that for a man to speak like a woman immediately reduces his effectiveness as a public speaker to near zero.

The Japanese in general are still fairly open about how they consider blacks and gay people to be inferior (though less open about how they think the same of Chinese and Koreans and a group of Japanese former outcasts known euphemistically as *burakumin*, "village people"). As a man, when you speak like a woman, the first impression you give is that you are effeminate or gay or both (or Chinese, depending on how you look). When I first learned this, it was pretty much already too late to correct. I also felt even more self-conscious about public speaking than before. And thanks to our chairman, Tokuma Shoten had a particularly manly-man culture of behavior. But then, how hard is it after all to stand up on a stage and reel off the names of America's most paparazzi-plagued movie stars?

I would begin my talk by doing a little business updating, giving some information about the overseas sales of the company's animated and live-action films. Miramax had also bought Daiei's hit film *Shall We Dance?* and had big plans for the US release. After putting up some numbers, which always sounded more impressive expressed in dollars or euros because most people couldn't do the math in their heads, I would launch into the report on the casting of the US version of *Princess Mononoke*. The cast list changed weekly and Harvey Weinstein rarely distinguished between wished for and confirmed. Leonardo DiCaprio agreed to play Ashitaka. Robin Williams is going to perform Jigo Bo. Juliet Binoche will be Lady Eboshi. Cameron Diaz will be San. Meryl Streep is going to do Moro. The audience was impressed and didn't even seem to notice or mind that actors who had committed one month before would then be out in the next. I was on the verge of discovering one of Tokuma-*shacho*'s own secrets: for some audiences, if you're entertaining enough, it doesn't really matter that what you are saying isn't factually accurate or strictly true. A whiff of truthiness will suffice.

Also, if you are a *gaijin* giving a speech in Japanese you start out with a huge advantage. You get a lot of points just for the fact that you can speak and are speaking a more or less recognizable version of the Japanese language. Yes, if you are a *gaijin* and male you are probably using mostly the female forms of speech that you learned from your female Japanese teacher. Many of the words you choose are wrong, like in the film *Sophie's Choice* when Meryl Streep's character misidentifies a seersucker suit as a cocksucker suit or like President Clinton's Polish translator getting the wrong word for "delighted."

As a *gaijin* you're lovable and amusing and maybe less threatening by being imperfect. The audience forgives you for your cultural and linguistic mistakes because at least you're trying. Like a little kid, you're not expected to understand the complexities that make up the Japanese psyche or the subtleties of the language that give it a voice. Whatever you do know about it just makes you seem precocious. So, as a public speaker you succeed even when you're not really good at it.

It may not be fair, but fair after all, is not really an Asian concept.

2

A Different Kind of Princess

Princess Mononoke

The Studio Ghibli film *Mononoke Hime* (*Princess Mononoke*) directed by Hayao Miyazaki was released in theaters in Japan in July of 1997. Set in Japan's Muromachi period, the story follows Prince Ashitaka, who is caught in a struggle between the gods of a forest and the humans who consume its resources. The film was a critical and commercial blockbuster, became the highest-grossing film in Japan of 1997, and held Japan's box office record for Japanese-made films until 2001 when Miyazaki's *Spirited Away* broke that record. On each and every weekend in the months of July and August, people stood in long lines outside movie theaters all across Japan to see *Princess Mononoke*. For the first two months of its release every showing was completely sold out.

Princess Mononoke played in movie theaters in Japan for more than one year. Ticket sales reached 19 billion yen ($160 million). This was a new Japanese box office record, nearly double the biggest box office success for a Japanese film. The previous Japanese-film record-holder, *Nankyoku Monogatari,* had grossed about $89 million. Steven Spielberg's *E.T.*, the previous all-time record holder, had earned $133 million in Japan and had held the record since 1983. For fifteen years, no other film had even come close to *E.T.*'s record. Even big Hollywood block-buster movies in Japan rarely earned more than $60 million. *Princess Mononoke*, a non-Hollywood film, and a hand-drawn animated film, had nearly tripled that.

This unprecedented box office success was a cultural phenomenon so big that even foreign news agencies and big international newspapers and TV networks took notice. *Princess Mononoke* did not conform to anyone's idea of what a Japanese hit movie would be. And once the foreign press began to notice, the Japanese took an even greater interest.

When I joined Tokuma Shoten, the parent company of Studio Ghibli, *Princess Mononoke* was still being furiously drawn in pencil. The finished drawings were painstakingly hand-painted onto transparent single sheets of cellulous acetate called cels. The cels were individually photographed to be joined together to make a film. It was October 1996 and production of the new film at Studio Ghibli was only about halfway through. Although the film was in full production, its director, Hayao Miyazaki, had not finished writing the final fifth of the film. He hadn't yet decided how it would end.

My boss when I joined Tokuma/Ghibli, Toshio Suzuki, insisted that it wouldn't be possible for me to do my job unless I learned the full, start-to-finish process of making an animated film. He believed that the only way to really learn about animated filmmaking was by direct experience.

When I made my first visit to Studio Ghibli, what struck me most was how small the studio was. The main building, then the studio's only building, was designed by Hayao Miyazaki. Miyazaki famously enjoyed designing buildings for his films. When Ghibli was established he got his first chance to design one that would actually be built.

Ghibli's main building was designed to be both compact and flexible. Every part of the building had to be able to be used for multiple purposes. The downstairs "bar" where the staff ate their *bento* lunchbox meals also served as a kitchen, a meeting room where the whole company could gather, a place to hold meetings for outsiders, and a screening room where the day's rushes could be viewed. The compactness and self-contained utility of its design reminded me of a submarine: a submarine with large windows letting in light and a beautiful garden on its roof.

The area where the animators worked had retractable overhead skylights to let in sunlight when the weather permitted. Watching the animators at work and drawing at their desks, I found it hard to believe that they were drawing the entire film by hand and that the film could be made from start to finish right inside this one relatively small building. During the course of my career I've had many opportunities to visit Disney Feature Animation and Pixar Animation studios. It never surprised me that these were the buildings where *Aladdin* or *Lion King* or *Toy Story* was being made. As at Ghibli there was a palpable atmosphere of extreme creativity, but unlike at Ghibli there were a lot more people and equipment, and a whole lot more space. On my first visits to Studio Ghibli I always wondered where the rest of the studio was.

For a long time at Ghibli, even after the success of *Princess Mononoke*, anybody could just walk upstairs and stand in front of Hayao Miyazaki and watch him work. Miyazaki is an iconic figure in Japan. His usually smiling visage, capped with a shock of snow-white hair and adorned with a full beard and moustache, also white, large squarish black glasses, a wry grin, and a twinkle in his eye, is a face at once recognizable to anyone in Japan—and a lot of people outside it. At work on a film, Miyazaki would sit in a tiny corner of the animators' area at an animator's desk that was identical in every way to any other animator's desk in the room, though the aura emanating from him identified him at a glance as someone unique and special.

Miyazaki would sometimes stop what he was doing, stand up, and shake hands and even chat with a visitor (if he was in the mood). During the production of *Princess Mononoke* I once watched astonished as two local junior high school girls in their school uniforms walked upstairs and interrupted Miyazaki to have their picture taken with him. They made V for victory signs as they posed for the camera. No one objected and they politely left with their mission accomplished.

Ghibli is set in a mostly residential area on the outer fringes of Tokyo. At the time the studio was built, the area's small-plot agriculture was slowly being erased by an increase in single-family housing. Ghibli's was the only commercial building in its neighborhood. The owners of the few vegetable fields immediately surrounding Studio Ghibli were loathe to break with their ancestral link to the land and the over-generous tax benefits of their "farming" status. Most of the local farmers would lovingly nurture their crops to maturity and then pile the produce in a corner and let it rot. It was a quiet, leafy neighborhood, rare in Tokyo. The cicadas sang in the summer. Bats swarmed the streetlights chasing insects in the early evening. Sunsets seen from Ghibli's roof were spectacular. And on those few rare crystal-clear days, the silhouette of Mt. Fuji was visible in the west.

There was little or no car traffic near the studio. Most of the people who passed it on foot or on their bicycles seemed completely unaware of Ghibli's presence and of what might be going on inside the odd-looking building. Most passersby seemed surprisingly incurious. There were no external signs or any obvious indication of what the building was. Sometimes I would stand outside and watch the comings and goings of the people who worked for or had business with Ghibli. For the most part these people in no way looked like anyone who should have any business in the neighborhood, and I often wondered what exactly the neighbors imagined was going on.

Much later I was asked to give tours of Studio Ghibli to visiting foreign guests. It had become my job to explain Ghibli to people, including the heads of all of America's major animation studios, who had much the same reaction that I did on their first visit. Where, they wanted to know, was the rest of the studio?

John Lasseter, the creative head of Pixar (now Disney/Pixar), once sent us a visitor who provided me with the perfect analogy to explain Ghibli to foreign guests. Several of Pixar's board members happened to be visiting Japan and wanted a tour of Studio Ghibli. Over coffee in Ghibli's multi-purpose meeting room, one of the directors, who had formerly been with NASA, told us about a trip he had taken to the Soviet Union to have a look at the Russian space program. He had asked one of his tour guides about astronaut transport vehicles. He explained that in America, in order to deliver the astronauts from their waiting area to the rocket on the launch pad, NASA had developed a special vehicle that cost $24 million. He wondered what the Soviets used for this purpose. His guide responded, "Oh, for that we have used Buick station wagon. Cost us about $7,500."

When I retold the story to visitors, Pixar and Disney Feature Animation would be NASA in the story and Studio Ghibli would be the Russian space program. Ghibli had grown up out of a culture of making do. From wartime Japan, through the Occupation, and through the postwar reconstruction periods, Japanese people had learned how to deal with scarcity. In the animation industry it informed the way they made their art. For Ghibli's animators, having a single brand-new building where everyone could work together was already an unimaginable luxury.

In my quest to learn how animated feature films were made I had the opportunity to study the animators at work drawing, the background artists preparing the sumptuous watercolor backgrounds, the cinematographers turning the drawings into cels, and the color specialists choosing the colors and painting the cels. The first post-production process I got to see was voice recording. Unlike most animation studios, Ghibli would complete the animation first and add the voices later. This is called after-recording, as opposed to pre-recording. Hayao Miyazaki and many of the senior animators at Ghibli whom he trained had an amazing sense of timing. They could imagine a line of dialogue and then capture not only the exact mouth movements it would take to deliver that line, but the timing of each mouth position on screen.

This made things more difficult for the voice actor. He/she would have to strike exactly the right tone and create the right mood or attitude in speaking each line of dialogue while also exactly matching the mouth movements of his/her character as they would appear on a large-format screen in a movie theater. They would also have to say their lines clearly and precisely enough to satisfy the most sophisticated audiophile viewing the film using the most sophisticated state-of-the art audio equipment.

The recording was done one line at a time. After recording each line or each part of the line between ten and fifty times, the voice actor then had to maintain the emotion of the entire speech or scene and match the volume and tone of the lines he/she had said thirty-seven times a half hour earlier. All while exactly matching the lip movements up on the screen.

There was also a fairly long wait between each of the repetitions. After the actor says a line, he/she has to wait while the recording technicians examine every quarter second of the recorded line on a graphic display. The process has been speeded up over the years by the use of computers, but when *Princess Mononoke* was recorded the recording process was still largely manual.

The recording technicians were in a soundproof control room, seated before an enormous crescent-shaped console. The console contained hundreds of dials, lights, toggles, and switches and was identical in every way to the bridge of the Starship *Enterprise*. The director would sit in Captain Kirk's (or Captain Picard's) chair, and his sound designers would sit a half-level below working the dials and buttons. The producer(s) and anyone else involved in the day's recording session would sit in chairs along the back wall. A large viewing screen at the front of the room displayed the part of the film that was being recorded. Monitors displayed a graphic voiceprint of each line and placed it in the context of the film's soundtrack. The actor was in a separate soundproof booth and couldn't hear what was being said in the control room unless someone pushed and held down a large red button of the kind used to launch a nuclear missile.

Each line would be played back and discussed. If the director liked the line, it was examined for sound imperfections, volume level, clarity of pronunciation, continuity with previous lines, and its fit with the screen image. It might be accepted or discussed. The best three or four lines were saved, annotated, and logged in, and one of them would eventually be used in the final mix of the film to become part of the film's soundtrack.

For the voice actor, all of this translated to a fairly long wait between lines. After each line had been examined and discussed, even the most accomplished of actors would invariably hear the director's voice saying, "That was great. Really great. Now can we get one more like that, only this time ..."

My first experience in the recording studio was listening to the very famous, talented, and versatile actress Yuko Tanaka perform the role of Lady Eboshi in *Princess Mononoke*.

The control room of a recording studio may have looked like the bridge of the Starship *Enterprise*, but it also resembled the basement recreation room of a college dormitory. The furniture there had experienced years of use and abuse beyond its natural service life. The hermetically sealed atmosphere reeked of stale cigarette smoke and bad coffee. Overflowing and unemptied ashtrays sat within easy reach of every chair and table in the room. Assorted ceramic and paper cups still held a last quarter inch of coffee and some had become the final resting place for a few dozen stumped-out cigarette butts that the ashtrays couldn't accommodate. Bags of junk food and the remnants of junk food packaging were scattered about the room.

The people in the room looked as if they had been in there for months without sleep. Day after day they would sit there listening to the same lines over and over and over again, hundreds and hundreds of times, their goal being to capture and perfectly record every grunt, moan, breath, and spoken word that would become the dialogue track of the completed film.

Animators at their desks at work appear to be in heaven.

They can't believe that someone is paying them just to draw. They have on headphones and are listening to music. Most of them smoke. All are absorbed totally in the joy of drawing and making their drawings move. They are exactly where they want to be, doing the very thing they want to do.

An animation director in the recording studio appears to be in hell. His stint in paradise is finished and now he is fallen (usually literally, since drawing requires light and occurs above ground, while recording studios are either underground or might as well be). But he's a professional and it's his film, his child, and he is devoted to the process of bringing it into the world. He has his producer to keep him company through the worst of it, and the support of assorted others who show up for various reasons. He makes the best of it. There are brief respites. There are breaks when it's possible to socialize with the actors. But this is real work.

Being an observer of the after-recording process feels at once like a kind of privilege and at the same time like being subjected to a kind of torture. You are listening to the same lines of dialogue, or fragments of dialogue, being repeated over and over and over again. There is no end in sight. You are trapped in a basement with no light and everyone smokes (I don't).

For the voice actor in the sound booth, the challenge, and the thrill of it, is probably a lot like being a hitter in baseball. You want to hit a home run. You want to score. It's much, much harder than it looks, and if you nail a line two or three times out of ten times trying, you're doing really, really well. 70% failure and you're doing very well. Just like a batter in baseball.

Yuko Tanaka was in her early forties but looked much younger. In her public appearances she's perky and lively and projects a kind of girlish charm. But in the recording studio she looked like a different person. She was dressed in jeans and a plaid flannel work shirt, and she looked like she'd spent the day chopping down trees. She looked nothing at all like Lady Eboshi, the strong-willed master of the Tataraba Fortress she was playing in the film. But the voice coming out of her was dense with gravity and authority. So much so that you had to look away to believe that the voice you were hearing belonged to this delicate woman dressed like a lumberjack. After every line she recorded, Hayao Miyazaki muttered to himself about how Yuko Tanaka was teaching him something new about Lady Eboshi, the character he himself had created.

One thing remains indelibly in my mind from Yuko Tanaka's recording session. Miyazaki had her say a part of one line almost fifty times. *"Kunikuzushi ni fusawashii ..."* (It's perfect for bringing down a nation ...). For some reason this line wasn't coming across as he wanted it. I later learned that when a director asks for a line to be done again that many times in the recording studio, it often means that he so respects the actor's talent that he thinks she can get it not just very good but perfect. Usually if the professional recording technicians don't think a line can be done any better, they know after the first dozen takes. Or sooner.

The communication between the director and the actor seemed bafflingly vague. In her fifty attempts to get *kunikuzushi ni fusawashii* perfect, Ms. Tanaka was hearing directions from Mr. Miyazaki such as "do the first part like you did it four times ago but finish stronger the way you did it the first three times." Yuko Tanaka seemed to know exactly what Miyazaki was talking about. Although she couldn't quite do it.

In addition to attending the voice recording sessions, I sometimes attended *Princess Mononoke* production meetings. I sat in the back of Ghibli's large meeting room, which then also doubled as a second screening room and research library, and took notes. During a color meeting we watched a projection onto the front-wall drop-down screen of a line drawing of the tall and powerful lizard-like Didarabotchi hovering over the forest treetops. The discussion during the meeting was about how to color this mostly transparent forest deity. The discussion went like this:

"Over here I think 237 for the main part with 27, 35, and 412 over here. 613 and 89 for the shadows."

"Not 89. 127 or 45 maybe."

"No, 613 is right, but I think 127 and 45 to give it a little more visual impact."

And so on. Everyone in the room but me knew the colors by their pigment numbers and could visualize them on the screen. I attended a meeting on sound effects. The sound effects that went into the film were exquisite in their evocation of nature in all of its moods and guises. The meeting I attended was a kind of catalogue of the different types of rain and of the different Japanese onomatopoeic words to describe them. Should the rain be *dara dara* or *poro poro*? Do we want it *jyan jyan* or *jyaan jyaan*? Or should it be just *peko peko*? Everyone knew exactly what they were talking about. I had no idea.

The final mix, when all of the film's elements would come together, took place in a sound studio as large as a full-sized movie theater. The mixers work with the same console as in the recording sessions, only larger. It's the Starship *Goliath* to the recording sessions' Starship *Enterprise*. The process is even more excruciatingly painstaking than in the recording sessions. The mixers listen to each fraction of each line over and over and over and over again as they try to decide where in the theater's state-of-the-art surround sound system to place each element of each bit of the soundtrack. You admire their skill and their astounding ability to hear minute gradations of tone and volume. You also think that if you have to hear that same little bit of sound just one more time you are going to stand up, scream at the top of your lungs, and kill everyone in the room. Obviously, I'm not a professional.

But seeing these bits of the film played over and over again you do see things that you might otherwise not have noticed. I once repetitively watched a sequence where the heroine San charges into the Tataraba Fortress, leaps up onto the roof, and speeds across it. Then the hero Ashitaka leaps up and goes after her. What I noticed after seeing this again and again was how the tiles on the rooftop react to being stepped on, first by the light and lithe San, barely registering the weight of her compact body and small feet, and then by the heavier and less graceful Ashitaka. Just by how the rooftop registers the tread of their feet you have a sense of the weight, mass, velocity, and physical force exerted by each character.

What I also noticed in the sequence was that when Ashitaka jumps up onto the roof he causes a few of the tiles at the edge of the roof to crumble. Pieces of them fall to the ground. With my newly gained knowledge of animation, I realized that what was unusual about this is that the roof is a part of the background and not something that normally moves in animation. *Princess Mononoke* was the last major feature-length animated film to be drawn by hand and animated on hand-painted cels. In hand-painted cel animation the moving pieces are done in a somewhat simplified style that allows them to be more easily replicated and manipulated. But the elaborate backgrounds on which they move are too detailed, too intricate, and too finely done to be manipulated (animated) in that way. Also, they are done in watercolor and not pencil.

In other words, in order to get those few pieces of roof-top tile to crack and crumble to the ground, Miyazaki would have had to get an animator to specially create elaborate hand-painted cels to match the background image and to painstakingly recreate them in enough versions of crumbling to make the effect work. This sequence lasted on screen for perhaps only a few seconds or less. But it would have taken a large chunk of someone's time (and therefore money) to create. This on a project that was already precariously in danger of not meeting its production deadlines. In a larger studio (a Hollywood studio), the film's producer would probably have told the director that it's a very nice touch and, yes, it would be great to do this but we don't have the time or budget for it and it won't make that much difference to the film so sorry, no, it's out. Not at Ghibli.

This is no doubt one very large difference between filmmaking in Japan and filmmaking almost everywhere else, the US in particular. In America the film belongs to the producer. He/she has the final say. In Japan the film belongs to the director. The

PRINCESS MONONOKE

*The rooftop chase scene that required exceptional attention
to detail using hand-drawn animation.*

director has the final word. At Studio Ghibli the director and the producer were of one mind about the quality of the film (usually). Budget would not be a reason to override an artistic decision (usually). And if Suzuki felt that he had to override any decision that Miyazaki made on a film, he would have to do it with guile and deception and not by fiat.

I asked Miyazaki about that sequence in *Princess Mononoke*. I wondered why, since it was such a relatively large job for just a few instants of effect, and since it happened so fast and in a place when the audience's focus was on the action of the scene, wouldn't it be true that most viewers would not even notice it?

"You don't think you notice it," he said. "You may not be aware of it consciously, but you feel it. You feel it though you're not aware that you feel it, and it does make a difference."

Temporarily Misplaced in Translation

When I first began learning Japanese I was struck by how beautifully it can express certain things in a way that's different from how they might be expressed in English, and by how things that aren't normally expressed in English can be expressed in Japanese. My idol was the Columbia University professor Burton Watson, whose translations of Chinese and Japanese poetry and fiction were the best. My dream was to have a career like his. That was before I learned that he had quit teaching to become a taxi driver. Also before I ever attempted to seriously translate anything.

Translating from Japanese to English or from English to Japanese is very hard. For a lot of reasons the two languages simply don't line up right. Even the best translators are often performing a metaphysical leap of faith. Japanese is very vague. And English, a Germanic language, is more precise.

The scene in Sofia Coppola's film *Lost in Translation* where Bill Murray's translator keeps relaying the director's complex instructions simply as "talk louder" is not atypical. In the movie business translations are never checked by anyone. You're the translator, you say this is how it should be done, and that's it.

One of my Japanese literature professors told me that as a graduate student he once moonlighted doing translations. In an American film he came across the phrase "like a bull in a china shop." He thought the phrase meant "a bull in a store owned by a Chinese person," and that's how it appeared up on the silver screen. Because movie translations in Japan are never checked by anyone, the subtitles of every translated film have at least one bull in a Chinese person's store in them. Whenever I went to the movies to see an English-language film in Japan I always found the audience laughing at something that wasn't supposed to be funny, or I would be the only person in the theater laughing at something that was supposed to be funny but that no one else got because it wasn't translated right.

When I was asked to start translating Ghibli's films into English, I wanted to do better than that, and I was immodest enough to think that I could. As Groucho Marx once said, you should never criticize a person's work until you've walked a mile in his shoes. If he gets mad, you'll be far away and you'll have his shoes.

These are some of the things I learned translating Ghibli's films from Japanese into English:

Rule 1—Don't release your translation until you find out what it's going to be used for.

Toshio Suzuki called me up one day in my office at Shinbashi shortly after I had joined the company and asked me if I would mind translating something for him. It was a summary description of the new film *Princess Mononoke* and was written in very flowery, poetic language. It had been written by Hayao Miyazaki for the composer Hisaishi Joe to help him get a feel of the mood of the film so Hisaishi could work on the film's music. The film was still in production at Studio Ghibli and I had only a very sketchy idea of what it was about.

I immersed myself in the text and let myself feel the atmosphere that it created and then came up with a translation. It wasn't polished or carefully considered. It just more or less conveyed what I thought the meaning of the original was, in English.

I faxed my translation back to Suzuki and for about a week I didn't hear anything more. So I called him up and asked, how about my translation? Was it OK? No questions or problems?

"No," he said it was fine. "Just fine."

"So what was it for?" I asked.

"Oh, they needed it for an art book on the film that's coming out soon."

"WHAT!? It's going into a book? Can I get it back to polish it a little more?"

"No, they're on a tight deadline. The galley proofs are already locked."

About a week or two later I got an advance copy of *The Art of Princess Mononoke* and there, in print, was my rough, awful, crude, awkward, imperfect, first-pass translation, fixed in a published book, there for me to be forever ashamed of.

The studio later decided to use the same English translation as a voice-over for a TV spot for the film. I sat with a deep-voiced British actor in the recording studio as he voiced the lines for the TV spot. After the session the guy said to me, "That was a pretty awful translation. Shouldn't they have polished it a bit more?"

Rule 2—There will be things that just can't be translated.

The Japanese film is called *Mononoke Hime*. The English title is *Princess Mononoke*. The translator (me) has left the two-word title 50% untranslated.

When I first heard the title of the film the word *mononoke* was completely new to me. This is exactly the kind of word that Hayao Miyazaki likes to use in his titles. It is a word that most Japanese rarely hear or see in print or can even reliably recall the meaning of unless they stop and think really hard about it. It is a word that no two people will define or explain in the same way. The dictionary is no help. It provides things like specter, wraith, or supernatural being, but everyone I ask says this isn't it exactly. Any attempt to further explain it takes paragraphs. Japanese is full of words like this.

So I decided to just leave it. I assumed that by the time the film came out in English, someone cleverer than me would have come up with a good word (or words) for it. In the nearly twenty-plus years since the film came out, no one has come up with anything.

Rule 3—Sometimes you just have to let go and leave things out.

As soon as the final version of a Japanese commercial film is approved for release, the translator or translators begin making an English-subtitled version.

Creating the subtitles is very hard. Your translation has to be accurate. It has to sound natural. And you have to be able to read the subtitles in exactly the same amount of time it takes for the character to say the lines on screen.

This is an example:

In the film *Princess Mononoke*, Ashitaka, riding his faithful elk-like animal named Yakul, comes upon a battle. As he watches from a hilltop, several of the samurai fighting below notice him. One of them says "*Kabuto kubi da!*" Direct translation: *kabuto*—helmet, *kubi*—neck, *da*—is. Literally, the samurai has said, "The helmet is a neck."

Though *kubi* may literally mean neck, it also refers to a severed head. So "*kubi da*" refers to a head cut off. *Kabuto* in this case is just a very quick way of saying "that guy wearing the helmet." In feudal Japan a soldier often received a bounty for every severed head he brought back from a battle. Proof of an enemy kill.

So the samurai is saying "That guy wearing the helmet, if

we cut off his head we get a reward." That translation made into a subtitle would take eighteen beats. "*Kabuto kubi da*" is six beats long. Your subtitle translation needs to lose twelve beats. It needs to be 70% shorter.

"Get the guy in the helmet! Take his head!" Ten beats. Still need to lose four beats.

"The helmet guy is mine." Six beats, so it should be OK. But now the translation sounds funny. What's a helmet guy? And you've lost the head being cut off and taken in for a bounty.

"His head is mine." Four beats so it fits fine, and as a bonus, slow readers can follow. It feels right in the context, but you've given up mentioning the helmet. But it's a better line. Japanese speakers get the full flavor. English speakers get an abridged yet acceptable alternative.

Rule 4—Don't take anything for granted.

In the film *Spirited Away* is a scene where it's reported that the character Haku has stolen the character Zeniba's seal. The Disney writers working on the English-language screenplay of the film contacted us urgently because they were puzzled by this. In Japan, a seal (an emblem used as a means of authentication) is a very important thing. Americans routinely affix their signatures to checks, credit card slips, and legal documents, but in Japan everyone uses a seal for this purpose. For legal documents and such, a Japanese person takes out his/her seal, presses it into a pad of red ink, and then stamps it onto the relevant document.

The Disney writers wanted to know why, if Haku had stolen Zeniba's seal (semi-aquatic marine mammal), the seal never appeared in any subsequent scene in the film.

When it comes to foreign cultures, you just never know what other people know and what they don't.

Rule 5—Review everything.

When we got back the first screenplay for *Castle in the Sky* from Disney to review, we checked the dialogue over and over again, but we didn't think to check the characters' names. It was only later when we began to get samples of recorded dialogue that we noticed that some of the characters had odd names. Wishing to impart to his film a slightly international flavor, Hayao Miyazaki had given two of the characters French names, Charles and Henri. These names pronounced and written in Japanese come out as *Sharuru* and *Anri*. Disney's translator, who was a third-generation Japanese-American and had never lived in Japan, and who also didn't believe in asking questions, had decided that the names were probably Chinese. So despite Disney's frequent complaint that the names in Ghibli's films were too exotic and hard to pronounce for an American audience, Disney ended up with characters in its version of *Castle in the Sky* named An-Li and Shalulu when they could have had Henry and Charles.

* * *

After the monumental box office success of *Princess Mononoke*, potential foreign distributors wanted to see English-subtitled versions of all Ghibli's films. Some of these existed but were for the most part very quickly and very poorly done. From both an artistic and a commercial viewpoint, we wanted the films to be as well translated as possible.

Our method at Ghibli of translating the films into English was to do it with a team of at least five people. We figured that with at least two native speakers of English and two native speakers of Japanese, and one person who could go either way, we had a better chance of getting everything right. The biggest problem with that was Hayao Miyazaki. Hayao Miyazaki can say something in Japanese, and five people hearing him will have five completely different ideas about what it was that he meant. And none of them will be wrong.

Our process was an attempt to render the often difficult but beautiful Japanese of the original films into English equivalents that gave the non-Japanese speaker a feel for the original language insofar as it was possible. Making a film is essentially a collaborative undertaking. We thought that the translation of a film should be, too.

Translating a film has other special problems. In the movie business a film made in one country and shown in another is usually deemed to lose commercial value the longer the amount of time since its first release in its country of origin. If your film has a commercial shelf life, as soon as it's completed, or even before if possible, you have to produce an English-subtitled version that you can show to potential distributors abroad. So speed can be important.

Once a film is sold to a distributor in foreign Country A, the distributor will want to subtitle and/or dub it into the language of Country A. If Country A is Norway, say, there aren't a lot of translators who can do Japanese to Norwegian. But there are plenty who can do English to Norwegian.

It turns out that the English subtitles we made for the Ghibli films weren't that useful in creating Country A subtitles or dubbing scripts. The shortcuts we had to take to get the English subtitles to match the length of the dialogue on screen turned out to cause more problems than they solved. So for every Ghibli film we made what we called a direct translation. This was a faithful translation of the film that made no compromises for timing. Then the Country A translators could get their translation right, and it was up to them to figure out how to fit their subtitles to the screen.

Translators are nerds and want their product to be accurate. Because nothing stimulates excellence in the workplace like having someone review your work, we reviewed all the foreign translations where there were people at Ghibli who spoke the language—essentially French, Spanish, and English. If an error was serious enough that we could catch it, it was probably a problem.

But all writers resent criticism of their work. Creating and reviewing the foreign-language screenplays often resulted in heated battles over words and ended with bad feelings. We once had to do Italian subtitles for a Ghibli film that was entered in competition at the Venice Film Festival. We hired a team of Japanese/Italian and Italian/Japanese translators. The work had to be done in Japan at Ghibli for security reasons because the film itself had not yet been released even in Japan. By the end of the project, a stout referee had to be installed in the conference room where the work was being done to keep the translators from physically coming to blows.

The final thing I learned about translation is that if you get it right, no one will thank you for it or praise your work. If you get it wrong you will hear about it, loud and clear. Thanks to the internet, you will never have to wonder where you went wrong. There is no such thing as a perfect translation. Of anything. Whatever you do there will be criticism. And yes, it does hurt.

The Circus

When *Princess Mononoke* was released in Japan, Hayao Miyazaki hadn't been out with a new film since *Porco Rosso* in 1992. The director's *Tonari no Totoro* (*My Neighbor Totoro*) is/was Japan's most beloved film. Much like *The Wizard of Oz* in the US, the Japanese public knew the film through its annual broadcast on TV. Shown every year on the NTV television network in July when schools were on vacation, *My Neighbor Totoro* reliably drew a huge audience share every time it was broadcast. Its theatrical release in 1988 had been only a modest success, though critically acclaimed. But Toshio Suzuki believed that, over the years, every single household in Japan had acquired a copy of the film, which they would have recorded themselves at home off the TV broadcast.

Miyazaki's new film neared its theatrical release bearing the stamp of approval from Disney, a company known in Japan more for its theme park and consumer products, but also a major Hollywood studio and animated film giant of international renown. Suzuki, directing the marketing campaign for the film, went to great lengths to make sure the public was aware of Disney's worldwide stature. The Japanese public often ignores its home-grown talent until it becomes famous abroad. Then suddenly its esteem in Japan grows exponentially.

As part of his strategy to make the Japanese public aware that *Princess Mononoke* would be a huge hit not only in Japan but abroad as well, Suzuki wanted the public to know he had even hired a foreign executive (me) to handle the anticipated worldwide demand for the film. The idea was to position the film as an international hit before it had even been released. At the many press conferences held for the release of the film, I was usually called on to say a few words in Japanese about the plans for the film's international release. There's always more good news to deliver when you're allowed to talk about the possible as opposed to the probable, so my part was very easy.

As the film's release neared, I was regularly invited to be interviewed by the press, and once or twice to do a taped interview for TV. In the 1980s and 1990s there were programs on late-night Japanese TV that featured an ensemble cast interviewing people (celebrities or non-celebrities) or simply humiliating people (housewives wrestling in a ring to win household appliances) or making surprise visits to people's homes or workplaces. Many of the segments featured scantily clad women who were either regulars on the show or guests (an S&M model being tied up naked with heavy rope and hung upside down calmly explaining how the knots were expertly tied to cause pain, reveal the naked flesh just so, but to minimize soft-tissue damage). Many of these shows had big audiences and were taste-makers and trend-setters.

One of the common techniques these shows would employ was to send one of their featured regulars out somewhere and have the audience vicariously experience the visit to the person or the place that was the target. Most of the places visited were restaurants or Japanese traditional inns in famous or out-of-the-way places. To my surprise, one day Suzuki informed me that I was going to be the interview guest on one of those late-night shows.

All I was told about the interview was that one of the show's hosts, a young woman, would be coming to our office in Shinbashi with her film crew and that she would ask me to talk about *Princess Mononoke*. I hadn't watched a lot of late-night television since my student days (aiming then to improve my listening comprehension of spoken Japanese) and I didn't have much of an idea about what kinds of shows were currently popular or who the stars were. I also didn't look into it. I just assumed that someone would come and ask the usual questions and that would be it. But I did notice that when I mentioned to anyone in the office which show it was, the reaction was always a rapid deployment of a hand to a mouth to suppress a laugh. No one would say why it was so funny. What, I wondered, were they not telling me?

By the appointed time of the interview no one had contacted me and I didn't hear anything further about it. I was at my desk late one afternoon when I heard a commotion down the hall. Beams of bright light were steadily approaching the door to our office and the people in their path were leaping out of the way. The bright lights drew closer. In through the office door and bathed in a blazing halo of light came a leggy Japanese beauty dressed entirely in silver. Close behind her came a man shouldering a large TV camera. Behind the camera was another guy holding up an array of klieg lights and one more guy with a large overhead boom mike on a long pole.

The nubile young woman was wearing a silver-metallic high-collared sleeveless jacket over a silver-metallic bra. She had on a very (very) small silver-metallic micro-mini skirt with a slit up its side. Her hair was silver and metallic. She had silver-metallic eyebrows. On one arm was a silver-metallic elbow-length fingerless glove.

The woman in silver strode toward me on silver-metallic six-inch platform boots. Her silver chains and bangles jingled as she moved. She had a silver ring in her nose. And in one hand she held a very large silver microphone.

The interview was beginning even before the silver lady

reached my desk. She held out the mike for me to reply to a question I had not heard. The cameraman bore down on me and the lighting guy fixed me in the glare of his thousand-watt high-beams. I am unusually bad at spontaneous situations. Even if I had heard the question, I would have been too stunned to respond. My staff and a group of people from the neighboring office stood comfortably out of camera range laughing. People from other offices were poking their heads into the doorway.

All I could think of was to ask the silver lady if she bought her clothes on this planet or on the planet she was originally from. But I decided that might antagonize the late-night TV demographic. It was very hard to not just stare at the young woman. A lot of her body parts that were not coated in silver were out and on view. She was very attractive in a way that people whom you normally encounter in day-to-day life are not. And I was getting an up-close view.

I don't remember anything about what the silver lady asked me or what I responded. But I do remember being too distracted to say the things I had been trained to say in an interview. I didn't think the interview went well. But when I saw Suzuki later he seemed to think it had gone just fine. Even if that were true, I understood that I couldn't take any credit for a good performance. 99% of being successful at doing interviews in Japan as a *gaijin* is about just being a *gaijin* and showing up. However, I suppose I did do a good job looking blown away and incapacitated by the presence of the silver lady.

My appearance on TV and at press conferences was obviously only a very minor part of the overall marketing plan. The international aspect of the film's release was but one of its supporting parts, like the little swirl of red syrup on the plate of a fancy dessert that's added to give it a little color but that you don't necessarily eat. The important parts of Suzuki's campaign were the TV spots and theatrical trailers, and the personal visits by Hayao Miyazaki to local markets all across Japan.

The making of the trailers and the TV spots for *Princess Mononoke* was like a lesson in advanced marketing. From the beginning, Suzuki faced stiff opposition to his choice of scenes to be included. Many of these were the same objections Miyazaki had faced from the film's production partners when he announced that his next film would be *Princess Mononoke.* Miyazaki was told that if the film was set in a historical period it would fail because the Japanese were sick of period dramas. Further, if the film took place in feudal times, the Japanese public would not accept main characters who were not samurai but were shabbily dressed villagers. The film depicted heads and arms being severed. That might be OK for a live-action film, but it would be the kiss of death for an animated film. Miyazaki thanked the production partners for their input and went ahead and did what he wanted to do anyway.

When Suzuki designed the TV spots and trailers to promote the new film, he intentionally featured all of these "faults," to the horror of the film's distribution partners. NTV, the film's major production partner, hinted that they might not run the TV spots, though in the end they reluctantly did.

Just before a new Ghibli film opened, Suzuki always made it a point to travel all over Japan with the film's director. It was a ritual that, once their film was finally finished, both Miyazaki and Suzuki greatly enjoyed. They traveled (by train), meeting with the theater owners who would be showing the film and speaking to the local press who would be reviewing it. Miyazaki jovially took questions, drew pictures of the film's characters, handed them out, and signed autographs. The film completed, Miyazaki was usually in a very good mood, and he relished the opportunity to talk to people all over Japan and to sample the odd regional idiosyncrasies that made one part of Japan different from another.

The in-person appeal to local theater owners also made the owners more likely to keep playing the film longer than was normal in the industry. Japanese theater owners were small businessmen with a tough business to run. The expenses of operating a theater were incurred seven days a week, but for the most part the customers only came in on weekends. If a theater was running a film, what the owner wanted to know was, would the film continue to be supported with advertising and publicity as long as it was running?

They success of a film also depended on which theaters it was shown in as well as how long it continued playing. In Japan, which has relatively few theaters and fewer per-capita movie screens than most countries, a theater owner always had the option of dumping a film after only two weeks, even one that was playing well. There were always brand-new releases that common wisdom dictated were likely to play better, and the theater owners knew they could always dump your film for one of those. But they also resented the pressure tactics of the Hollywood studios that tried use their mega-hits for leverage in getting their less popular films into theaters. Suzuki used this to his advantage.

The conventional wisdom among Hollywood studios was that the more movie theaters your movie played in, the more money you would make. Suzuki conceded that in America that might be true, but in Japan it wasn't. Suzuki's strategy was to limit the number of theaters his films played in. The theater owners who played *Princess Mononoke* appreciated this, because that meant there was less competition among theaters playing the same film, and your theater could therefore afford to give the film a longer run.

Americans doing business in Japan would always hear that Japan is different. Savvy American businessmen almost always chose not to believe it. The Hollywood studios releasing their blockbuster films at the same time as *Princess Mononoke* (such as *Jurassic Park*) followed conventional wisdom and urged their local offices to book as many theaters as possible. Suzuki kept his distributor from booking too many theaters, even turning a number of them down.

In the days before digital media, when an entertainment industry reporter in Japan wanted to get an early read on how a big a highly touted new film had opened, he/she got up on a Saturday morning—the day new films are released in Japan—and drove around to look at the bigger movie theaters in Tokyo or Nagoya or Osaka. He/she wanted to see if lines were forming at the box office. If there were lines, the film was a hit. If there were long lines the film was a big hit. A reporter would do this for the first two shows of the day and then write his/her article based on that.

This was another reason that Suzuki made sure Ghibli's films opened in fewer theaters. If the publicity for the film had been successful, there would be many more people wanting to see the film as soon as it opened than there were seats in the theaters showing it. Fewer theaters showing the film made it more likely this would happen. Japanese people have infinite patience for waiting in line. They even seem to enjoy it. For a film that they really want to see, Japanese people are perfectly happy to stand and wait.

For the first showings of *Princess Mononoke*, Suzuki brought in Miyazaki, the film's director, and the famous actors who had voiced the film's characters for live stage appearances. This took place either before or after the film played. The first few audiences for *Princess Mononoke* were treated to appearances of the famous director and their favorite actors. They were also given small souvenirs to mark the event. This increased the desire among fans to attend the very first showings of the film at the big Ginza theaters in downtown Tokyo where these first-day events usually took place.

The TV, radio, and print media reporters covering the film's opening and celebrity appearances and the other reporters driving by to assess the opening box office results would see very long lines of people waiting to see *Princess Mononoke* and conclude, and report, that the film was a huge hit.

In Japan, the film that a Japanese audience most wants to see is the one that they can't see because it's already sold out. If it's sold out, it's popular. If it's popular, everyone is seeing it. If everyone is seeing it, no one wants to be the only one not seeing it. If waiting in line is what you have to do to see it, fine. If you're Japanese, waiting in line is no big deal.

The Kiss

The Walt Disney Company was frequently praised in the entertainment press for having the foresight to acquire the rights to the films of Hayao Miyazaki and Studio Ghibli before the release of *Princess Mononoke*. The Disney executive responsible for the acquisition, Michael O. Johnson, then the head of Disney's Home Video International Division, had extensive business experience outside the US and understood the value of the Ghibli films that had been released prior to 1997.

But neither MOJ (as Johnson was known to his staff) nor anyone at Disney, nor anyone in Japan for that matter, had any idea of exactly what kind of film Hayao Miyazaki was making at the time the Disney agreement to distribute Ghibli films was made.

In early April of 1997, MOJ was in Tokyo and came over to Tokuma Hall in Shinbashi. Toshio Suzuki, the film's producer, had arranged for a screening of the first trailer that had been made for the still uncompleted *Princess Mononoke*. The trailer had not yet been shown to the public, but it was already extremely controversial among the film's coproducers who had seen it. Some of Ghibli's production partners insisted that Suzuki rethink his ideas. MOJ did not know any of this as the lights in the theater dimmed and he settled in to watch the first footage he would see of the film he had persuaded his company to acquire.

Arms were sliced off. A head was shot off with an arrow. Writhing slimy guts spilled out of a rampaging giant boar. The dainty heroine of the film was shown wiping blood from her mouth with the back of her hand. When the lights came up in the theater, MOJ was speechless. He was very careful not to show too much in front of the other people in the room, which included an entourage from Disney Japan, Ghibli production staff, Tokuma PR people, and a camera crew that was filming a long documentary on the making of *Princess Mononoke*.

Only later at dinner with Suzuki and Koji Hoshino, the head

of Disney's Home Entertainment business in Japan, did MOJ beg Suzuki to PLEASE get Miyazaki to add something to the film to at least balance the violence. A romantic scene between the hero and heroine would be nice, or a kiss. Johnson went on to explain that Miyazaki was a great artist whom he respected enormously. He said he understood that an artist such as Miyazaki should not have to entertain suggestions from a mere businessman, and certainly not be seriously asked to make changes to his film. But PLEASE couldn't Suzuki pass along the suggestion and ask him to make just this small change?

Suzuki merely nodded, looking pensive. To MOJ, as to most Americans, the nodding looked like understanding and agreement. To everyone else in the room it just meant that he was thinking. Probably thinking what form his rejection of the request would take.

The trailer that MOJ had seen was actually a work in progress. About a month later when I visited Burbank together with Hoshino, we brought with us the final version of the trailer that would run in theaters and on TV. There was now a line of dialogue in it: "Release the girl, she's human!" To MOJ, that seemed to be a positive addition. MOJ took that to mean that the hero, Ashitaka, was rescuing the heroine, San. This wasn't true, but Hoshino and I didn't disagree.

In a later scene, San is seen bending over Ashitaka and planting what looks like a kiss on his mouth. Wonderful, MOJ said. Now we also have some romance. He looked relieved and asked us to be sure to thank Suzuki and Miyazaki for him. We didn't tell him that it wasn't exactly a kiss.

In the scene in the trailer Ashitaka is near death and barely conscious. San had been chewing up dried meat for him, because he's too weak to even chew it for himself, and she transfers it to his mouth directly from hers. MOJ was happy and we didn't want to spoil the mood. We preferred to let him find out the truth after the film was released. By that time the film had broken every conceivable Japanese box office record, and whatever his concerns had been, nothing says "forget about it" better than a historically record-breaking blockbuster box office release and all of the positive worldwide press that would follow.

The film did prove too edgy for the Walt Disney Company to release it under its own name. Which is why *Princess Mononoke* was eventually released by Disney's new subsidiary, Miramax.

Going Public

Japan likes to find itself featured in the international news media (major earthquakes and nuclear plant meltdowns excluded). When an animated feature film in Japan shattered fifteen-year-old box office records the international press took note. Suddenly, there on CNN was Hayao Miyazaki being touted as Japan's preeminent filmmaker. There were shots of long lines of Japanese people waiting to see *Princess Mononoke* even weeks after it had opened. The foreign press found it odd that adults would go and see an animated film, further boosting its box office numbers. Then people who hadn't seen the film wondered why the foreign press was so interested and decided that they should see the film. The big box office numbers became even bigger box office numbers.

Requests for interviews from foreign (non-Japanese) news agencies began to come in. It began with the entertainment-industry publications that covered most film releases in Japan. Then came the international wire services wanting to know about the big box office numbers, and finally the big American and European networks and print media. They all wanted to know why Japanese people would wait in line week after week to see an animated film that was not targeted at children. CNN, NBC, the BBC, TF1, Arte, and CBS all called. *Time* magazine, *Newsweek*, the *New York Times* and the *Washington Post* called for interviews. The attention was not necessarily unwanted. But it was unexpected. Ghibli had no one designated to handle requests from the foreign press.

I suppose because I spoke English better than anyone else in the company it became my job to field questions from the foreign press. We had assumed that once Ghibli's films were being distributed in foreign countries the film distribution companies in those countries would handle the press there. We didn't expect immediate foreign-press questions about *Princess Mononoke*'s release in Japan. I had not yet learned the all-important art of not answering every question someone asked.

I have always had a respectful but possibly naïve view of the press and of journalists. One of my college roommates became a reporter for the *New York Times*, and no one in the world worked harder at it or took it more seriously than he did. He did exhaustive research. He worked through the night without sleep to finish an article. He never published anything until he was sure of the facts. To me every reporter who managed to get a job with a major news publication or network was like that. I believed that any reporter with a byline must without doubt possess the work ethic, the morals, and the spare-no-effort grit and determination of a Bob Woodward or a Carl Bernstein (as portrayed on-screen by Dustin Hoffman and Robert Redford). Apparently this is not strictly true.

I also learned that though I am pretty good at talking to other *gaijin*, I am not very good at talking to *gaijin* who are members of the press, particularly when I'm "on the record." Being on the record seems to require a certain sensitivity to word usage and the ability to compress a long, difficult, and carefully thought-out answer into a space of fifteen seconds or less. Honest mistakes in speaking are fair game so you have to be careful what you say. Knowing how to *not* answer a question while appearing to answer it is a very important skill. Professional publicists can do this, and that's why you pay them to answer questions instead of doing it yourself.

Some time later, when *Princess Mononoke* began to be released abroad, I had a call from a reporter from the *New York Times*, a newspaper that I still read every day. Stationed in Japan, he was calling to ask for an interview with Hayao Miyazaki. What he actually said was that he wanted to do a piece on "Haiyo Miyazawa" and his new film. He said he had seen the trailers and TV spots for the movie with the boy riding the giant tiger and the alien androids from outer space, and he wanted to arrange a private screening of the new film and then interview the director.

I (politely) explained to him that the director's name was Miyazaki and not Miyazawa, that there were no giant tigers or space androids in the film. Mr. Miyazaki was leaving for a trip to France in three days. I asked if we could schedule the interview for after Mr. Miyazaki's return to Japan.

"Well then," the reporter said, "what about today or tomorrow?"

"Look," I replied, "you don't seem to know much about the director or his films. Mr. Miyazaki really is very busy right now. He really couldn't do an interview until he gets back in two weeks. Wouldn't it be better if we scheduled an interview for then, when the director is back in Japan? In the meantime, we can arrange a screening of the film for you and a meeting with someone else in the studio who can provide a little background before the interview. Would that work for you?"

"Now you look," the reporter said. "This is the *New York Times*, OK. It's not some two-bit local paper. An article in the *Times* will be good for your studio. It's the *New York Times*, so why don't you just tell me what time today or tomorrow I can come over and do the interview."

"You know," I believe I then said, "this is a Japanese film. It was made for a Japanese audience, mainly. Probably no one here in Japan really cares what the *New York Times* thinks about it. The only reason I care about it is that my parents read the *New York Times* and I would love to have them see my name and the name of the film in print in your paper. But the director is not available today or tomorrow or the day after. He might be available in two weeks. Those are just facts. If you can't wait until he gets back to Japan, then don't do the interview."

"May I quote you?" he asked.

"Please, be my guest," I replied. And he did.

This, I can say now, is not the best way to deal with a press request.

An article subsequently appeared in the *New York Times* with an unflattering description of Studio Ghibli and identified me as the studio's publicist. Although the article was generally negative about Ghibli, it contained some information about the film's success based on an interview with a Chinese woman in Yokohama who owned two movie theaters. The article also contained assertions about how the popularity of manga and anime in Japan relate to illiteracy and the difficulty of reading books and articles written in Chinese characters (*kanji*).

A few days later, articles began to appear in the Japanese press with headlines like "*New York Times* Claims Popularity of Manga in Japan Due to Low Literacy Rate." When reached for comment, the *Times* reporter reacted angrily and wondered, for the record, if the Japanese press thought that the *New York Times* was incapable of understanding the UN's literacy tables. He further went on to say that because Japanese *kanji* were so difficult, people reading in a train or subway would naturally rather look at pictures than struggle with difficult *kanji* characters that they are unable to read. When the reporter's responses were printed, the *New York Times* was apologizing for weeks for the article and the reporter's response, and for the angry letters it received, some of which the *Times* published itself.

I have a very high opinion of the films of Studio Ghibli and of the film *Princess Mononoke* in particular. But I've learned that not every reporter who wants to write about a Ghibli film is a film critic looking to understand and appreciate the film or to probe its hidden mysteries or to gain insight from the people who made it. Members of the press have their job to do. And they have no obligation to see the films or understand them in the way that those who are involved in or close to the process of making them do. They have their readers to think of.

After the *Times* article appeared I was surprised when many friends and relatives e-mailed me or even called to say they had seen the article and thought it was great.

"Great?" I would reply. "You didn't think it was negative at all?"

"Well ... your name was mentioned."

"And?"

"I don't know. Maybe I didn't read it carefully. It was negative? All I remember is that your name was mentioned. In the *New York Times*. That's great, no?"

3

~~~~~~~~~~~~~~~~~~

Culture Wars

Minarai (Watch and Learn)

I would often read in a newspaper or magazine article that Hayao Miyazaki hated to travel abroad. Beginning with *Princess Mononoke*, which catapulted him into the mainstream of commercial cinematic success, he was very much in demand in Europe, Asia, and North America for personal appearances whenever any of his films were screened. Part of my job at Studio Ghibli was to help plan these trips and to help the films' producer, Toshio Suzuki, convince Miyazaki to agree to venture outside of Japan.

Miyazaki himself was always quick to point out that this idea of him not liking foreign travel was completely untrue. He said there were places outside of Japan that he did love to visit, had visited, and would happily visit again. Only he would do it on his own time. He hated the idea of having to be abroad in some beautiful or interesting place and have to spend his time there working (promoting his films).

Hayao Miyazaki's way of making a film was particularly stressful, and that was exactly how he thought it should be. He would often say that a person only does his best work when faced with the real possibility of failure and its real consequences. Several times after the completion of one of his films,

Miyazaki would suggest that the studio be shut down and all the staff be fired. He thought this would give the animators a sense of the consequences of failure and make them better artists if and when they were rehired for the next film. No one was ever sure if he was just kidding.

When Miyazaki signed off on one of his films and it was officially done, he preferred to never think about that film again. It was done. There was nothing more he could do to improve or change it. He always wanted to be moving forward and thinking about the next film.

To begin a new project Miyazaki would allow images and ideas to percolate through his imagination, capturing them in drawings or watercolor sketches. Often he had ideas for two or three new films going at once. He would amass the images he had drawn and begin to refine them and work out isolated plot lines to go with them. When he thought he had an idea for a new film, he would confer with his producer, Toshio Suzuki, and they would discuss the possibilities. They would agree on an idea, tell other people in the studio about it, the people who heard about it would enthusiastically approve of it, and a week later the idea would be discarded in favor of another completely different idea.

Eventually an idea would stick and the drawings for it became more fully rendered. Other artists would be brought in to do concept art for the film. A formal decision would be reached and more artists would be hired to do background art, location hunting, and more concept art. One or two of Miyazaki's more elaborate drawings would be chosen to represent the film, and the studio would announce the film. Production would begin, the theaters it would play in would be booked, and almost exactly two years later the final film would emerge.

This process sounds a good deal smoother than it actually ever was. Hayao Miyazaki's reputation in Japan was such that once the film was announced, every theater in Japan already wanted to play the film. The film was almost always announced in December. Year-end was always a good time in Japan to get people's attention. The film would be released to theaters in mid-July two years later, the best time to play a film in Japan because schools would be on vacation. Miyazaki's skill at delivering his films on schedule was what made this kind of scheduling possible. But his process was never easy, or even certain. Miyazaki simply believed that animated filmmakers should always work under the gun. The studio only missed the July deadline once, and this was due to extenuating circumstances beyond the director's control.

Early on in the production process things would proceed at a fairly leisurely pace. Miyazaki drew the storyboards, which Ghibli called the *econte*. The *econte* was a combination storyboard and screenplay, a complete menu for a film that served as a blueprint from which the film could be made. Miyazaki usually divided the *econte* into five parts: A, B, C, D, and E. These were not acts like in a play. Each was just approximately 20% of the expected length of the film.

Miyazaki usually had all of Part A and most of Part B in his head when the film was first announced. The images in Part A would be lovingly and carefully drawn in some detail. For his later films, when he knew the *econte* for all of his films were being displayed in the Ghibli Museum, Part A was executed in delicate watercolor. The drawing in Part B was also done at a more deliberate pace.

Once Miyazaki began drawing Part C, the film would go into full production. The background artists and the composition artists would have already begun, but now the animators were beginning to draw. Miyazaki was both finishing writing the film and beginning to meet with animators to review animation drawings. By the time Miyazaki started Part D, he would begin having doubts about whether the five parts and the length assigned to the film would be enough to contain the story. He usually had no idea how the film would end. He might have competing ideas about how it should end that he couldn't resolve. Or he might have no idea at all. The animators would be catching up to Part D and the writing process would slow to a crawl.

A sense of impending crisis would seep into the studio. Miyazaki would stop writing and spend his time doing things unrelated to the film. He'd chop wood for his studio's Vermont cast-iron stove. Someone would report this to Suzuki, who would go over and try to get him to stop chopping wood and get back to work.

Part E had not yet appeared, and the entire studio would exude an atmosphere of high stress. The theaters were booked. The production was behind schedule. No one knew how the film would end.

And then, a breakthrough. Part E appeared. Following a brief period of elation, the animators and back-end production staff began violating Japan's labor laws and working an illegal number of hours to finish the film. When the animators were ordered to go home and get some sleep, they either pretended to leave and snuck back to their desks, or just outright refused. The production support staff were keeping the same hours as the animators, even those who didn't have any more actual work to do on the film. It was about both solidarity with your comrades who had to work and the unspoken code of traditional Japanese peer pressure: if everyone else is working, so are you, even if you don't have any work to do.

This was Hayao Miyazaki's production process. Once the film was locked he traveled all across Japan to meet with theater owners and the press in local markets. His film was finished, he was free, and the chance to see all of Japan was something he loved. Then he took a month off and retreated to his small house in the mountains with his family. Before long he was already thinking about the next film and starting the whole process over again.

Asking Miyazaki to interrupt the ebb and flow of the cycle that was his creative process for any reason was a seriously unpopular task. The film is finished, the Japan promotional tour completed, the reviews glowing, the box office great, the studio is going to survive, you had a month off, now how about putting yourself in the hands of your well-meaning international distribution staff (and the less-well-meaning publicists hired by the film's foreign distributors) and visit countries A, B, C and X, Y, Z where you will be locked in a small room for eight hours a day to be asked the same questions by journalists in different foreign languages over and over again, and where you will sit and wait for their questions and your answers to be translated? It was a very hard sell.

Miyazaki understood early on that promoting his films abroad was quite different from how it was done in Japan. In Japan the film's producer controlled the process. Outside of Japan he was in the hands of professional publicists.

To a publicist no press interview is a bad interview. Left to their own devices, publicists managing a film promotion would schedule them in rapid-fire bursts of fifteen to twenty minutes each, eight hours a day, for four or five days in a row. On the theory that no available time slot should go unfilled, interviews were often given to reporters who had not seen Miyazaki's films and who did not even know the films were animated. They just knew he was someone famous for some reason.

Most of the reporters in these interviews would ask exactly the same questions and expect to get individualized responses. In this respect Hayao Miyazaki is a reporter's dream, since he almost never gave the same answer when asked exactly the same question. For example:

REPORTER: The main character of this film is a young woman. Do all your films have women or girls as the heroines?

MIYAZAKI 10:00: Yes

MIYAZAKI 10:30: No.

MIYAZAKI 11:00: Half of my films have heroes and half of them have heroines. The split between males and females in the human race is about 50/50 so I think this percentage is about right.

MIYAZAKI 11:30: When I conceive a film I don't really pay so much attention to whether the main character is male or female.

MIYAZAKI 12:00: I wanted to make a film for ten-year-old girls, so of course the main character had to be female.

MIYAZAKI 12:30: Women generally make better main characters so I always try to have the main character be female.

The first time I had to ask Miyazaki to go abroad for a press tour was when *Princess Mononoke* was invited to be screened out of competition at the Berlin International Film Festival. Our US distributor for the film, Miramax Films, felt it would be extremely important for it to be seen in Berlin and that the director's presence would be essential. The film would not be allowed in competition, since the competition then was not open to animated films. According to Miramax, though the film had no chance of winning a prestigious award, there was a positive aura to being associated with and screened at a famous international film festival.

Whenever someone asks Miyazaki to do something, it becomes the one thing in the world he would rather die than agree to do. That's just the way he is. If you asked him to do something he was already planning to do, he would suddenly no longer want to do it. And of course if you just asked him to spend two weeks somewhere promoting one of his films, he would refuse. Only Toshio Suzuki, his producer, knew how to get him to agree to anything.

Most of the requests we got from film festivals or foreign distributors for a visit by Miyazaki we had to refuse because we knew he would say no and because Suzuki couldn't think of any way to persuade him. When we got one that seemed so important that even Miyazaki couldn't reasonably refuse, I first went to Suzuki with the proposal, and if Suzuki agreed with it, we began thinking of what else we could add on to get Miyazaki to agree. Once we had an acceptable schedule for a proposed trip, Suzuki and I and either Haruyo Moriyoshi or Mikiko Takeda would walk over to wherever Miyazaki was and begin the process of convincing him. If Suzuki didn't agree with one of our trip proposals, he would simply tell us to go and ask Miyazaki ourselves, knowing that Miyazaki would say no and that would be an end to it.

The traditional method of learning a craft in Japan is called *minarai*—learning by watching. Like a traditional Japanese *sensei*, Suzuki would not share the secrets of his profession, acquired by long years of trying and failing and then succeeding. Under no circumstances would he simply tell you how he does it. You may only learn by carefully observing him in action.

I had many occasions to watch Suzuki persuade Miyazaki to do something he didn't want to do and had initially refused to do. And having paid the closest possible attention to every aspect of these meetings, I still have no idea how he did it. Sometimes when we would meet for the purpose of getting Miyazaki to agree to something, the topic we were meeting to discuss was never even mentioned. Typically Suzuki and Miyazaki would talk about some person they both knew but no one else in the room did, where he or she was now and what he or she was now doing. They would reminisce for a while, and then Suzuki, without asking the question we had come to ask, or even mentioning it, would signal that it was time to leave, and we would stand up and go. Once outside Suzuki would say, "OK, Miya-san said yes, so go ahead and proceed with your plans."

I always thought that, being a *gaijin*, I had missed something, maybe in the body language, or a phrase or two hidden in the talk about old times. But when I asked the Japanese people who had also been present, Moriyoshi, Takeda, or one of Suzuki's assistant producers, they also had absolutely no idea exactly when or how Miyazaki had agreed. It was a kind of mystery, but whenever Suzuki said that Miyazaki had agreed, even when no one else in the room heard or saw the agreement, he had in fact agreed, and the trip was on.

For that first trip to the Berlin Film Festival, Suzuki had listened to the planned trip my staff and I had proposed, seemingly agreed with it, and sent me in alone to see Miyazaki to make the request. I was still new at the job, and I didn't then quite realize that there was going to be more to it than just explaining the reason for the trip and having him say, "Sure, when are we going?" I now think Suzuki wanted me to fail so that I would later truly appreciate the art of getting Hayao Miyazaki to do something he didn't want to do. But Suzuki couldn't quite bring himself to have me go in and get completely slaughtered, so at the last minute he broke the *sensei's* code of nonverbal direction and gave me a hint. "Miya-san is very interested in Estonia these days," he told me.

Many Americans would be hard pressed to locate Estonia on a map. I was one of them. But before going in to see Miyazaki I did some extensive and detailed scholarly research (limited to what I could find on the then young internet). I unearthed not only the location of Estonia but also some useful facts about it that might interest a history buff like Hayao Miyazaki.

Estonia apparently is full of old castles and fortresses. I knew Miyazaki had been absorbed in studying castles and fortresses in order to design the Tataraba Fortress in *Princess Mononoke*. I knew he was interested in medieval arms and warfare. I looked up all the major historical castle and fortress sites and did a quick check of all of the airlines that flew to the general region from Tokyo. The best way to get there from Japan was to fly to Helsinki and take a ferry across the Baltic Sea. I downloaded photos from the internet, put together an itinerary, and made an illustrated presentation on PowerPoint outlining the proposed trip.

In between films Miyazaki doesn't always keep a regular schedule at Ghibli. So I had to make a special arrangement to see him at his personal studio, and his only available slot was on a Saturday morning. He was in a good mood and very jovial until I handed him a printed full-color set of my presentation slides on a proposed trip to see the fortress castles of Estonia. Before I could present it to him he leafed through the pages quickly and then handed them back to me.

"Suzuki told you to come and ask me this didn't he? He told you I'm interested in Estonia. Ha ha ha. I'm not interested in Estonia. I'm not interested in fortresses or castles. What I am interested in is tanks. There were several famous tank battles in Estonia and I wanted to visit the sites where they took place. But the battles took place in swamps and in the summer. You're proposing to go in February. The swamps would be frozen over in February, so it would be the wrong time to visit. Forget about Estonia. You should be looking at this."

At which point Miyazaki went over to a bookcase and pulled out a huge coffee-table art book.

"Hundertwasser. Ever hear of him?"

As it turned out I had. A college roommate's father had collected his prints, and one hung in our college dorm room.

"Go through this book and study it. It's not so much the prints and paintings I'm interested in, but his buildings. I like his buildings and I've always wanted to see them in person. If we can go to Austria and see some of these buildings I'll make the trip to Berlin."

I reported back to Suzuki and he was visibly stunned. But the trip was on.

Unrepentant Smokers

Mikiko Takeda, the person at Ghibli responsible for publicity outside of Japan, and I spent most of our trips abroad to promote Ghibli films fighting with our distributors about the length and number of interviews Hayao Miyazaki would have to do. Miyazaki insisted on making each trip abroad as short as possible. The distributor wanted to compensate by having him spend every waking moment doing interviews and promotional events. The distributor wanted the film to be as commercially successful as possible. We wanted Miyazaki to live long enough to make another film.

Our first North America distributor was Miramax. Miramax was more used to the reluctance of some film directors to do promotional work. They were flexible and willing to accommodate the whims of artists. When they were told that Hayao Miyazaki would be willing to attend the Berlin Film Festival if he could stop in Vienna to see buildings designed by Hundertwasser, they immediately arranged for a hired van with a guide for three days to search out and visit the sites.

The Hundertwasser buildings in Vienna—an apartment complex, a museum, a power plant fueled by burning garbage, a church, and a restaurant—were all more than worth the trip. They were colorful, undulating structures that stood out from their surroundings and added a lively sense of fun and color to otherwise orthodox neighborhoods of standard European fine architecture. The Hundertwasser buildings incorporated vegetation (trees and grass) into their designs and into the buildings themselves and had uneven floors and irregularly shaped rooms and mosaic-tiled exteriors. Hundertwasser himself had selected the materials for and supervised the installation of the colorful tiles.

The power plant was a marvel of ecofriendly urban infrastructure, recycling garbage and burning it to provide steam heat for the city. Hundertwasser had even designed the garbage trucks that brought the garbage and the busses that shuttled the plant's employees from one building to another. The buildings we saw in Austria provided some of the inspiration for Miyazaki's design of the Ghibli Museum in Mitaka, Tokyo, which was built several years later.

Our promotional trip to the Berlin Film Festival in 1998 was the first of several trips sponsored by Miramax for the international release of *Princess Mononoke*. It came about because the previous October Toshio Suzuki and I had met with Harvey Weinstein in Los Angeles. Harvey and his brother Bob ran Miramax Films, then a part of Disney and the company that would distribute the film in most of the world. Disney's North America film distribution team had concluded that *Princess Mononoke*, a foreign animated film not necessarily designed for children, would be better handled by its new Miramax division,

PRINCESS MONONOKE

The "kiss" in the Deer God's forest scene, which was not really a kiss at all.

whose people were better equipped to deal with foreign films and with edgier films. Miramax was a New York company, but Harvey sometimes set up shop at the Peninsula Hotel in Los Angeles for West Coast meetings.

This was well before Harvey's "Me Too" troubles, and at the time there was no hint at all that the things he's been accused of were taking place. But there was a certain unique feel to paying a visit to Harvey Weinstein at the Peninsula Hotel in LA. The hotel staff seemed to have a particular attitude that could best be summed up as "If you're not rich or famous you really don't deserve to be here." If you arrived at the hotel driving a car yourself that was not a Porsche or Maserati, the valet parker would give you a disdainful glance as he reluctantly handed you a ticket. The people inside the hotel were even haughtier.

Suzuki and I were greeted by the assistant hotel concierge as if we were two homeless persons who had wandered in off the street. We were directed to wait downstairs on a bench in a hallway off the lobby. Harvey had a busy schedule and was running late. Half the people in and around the lobby seemed to be waiting to see Harvey.

When our number was called we were shown upstairs to Harvey's suite. It was magnificent, with a very large, elegantly appointed living room. A roaring fire was going in the fireplace, which I thought odd, since it's usually warm in LA during the day and the air conditioning was also blasting away. There was a bar area and a large terrace with reclining lounge chairs for sunbathing. Harvey himself was seated at one of the sofas in the middle of the room. He was (then) a very large man. He was wearing a polo shirt and a pair of dark wool slacks held up by bright red suspenders. He was smoking a cigarette and the marble counters and coffee tables all had very large ashtrays on them. Suzuki was thrilled. At last, a fellow smoker. America can be hard on the unrepentant smoker. He instantly loved Harvey.

Michael O. Johnson, the head of Disney's international business, was there doing the introductions. First was about fifteen minutes of sequential mutual admiration—Harvey for

Ghibli's films, Michael for Harvey as a caretaker of art and film, Harvey for Michael as a business genius with artistic sensitivity, Michael for Ghibli's films as timeless classics, Michael for Miramax, Harvey for Disney, and so on. Harvey said he had seen "Moan-a-NO-kee" several times and that he loved the film. Was it too long? Would he ever consider cutting it? Never. The music? The music is great. Wouldn't dream of touching it. It's great. But the English translation. Terrible. Way too stiff. That would have to be changed. Needs to be punched up for American audiences. Harvey had a writer in mind. Neil Gaiman. Not that well known now. But he will be very, very big. Soon. Very big. Very soon. Neil will go over the dialogue and make it great.

Harvey went on to explain that "Disney executives, they don't get this film. Except for Michael Johnson here. I love this guy. Michael asked me to distribute this film. If Michael asks me to do something I do it. If Michael says this film is good it's good. Miramax doesn't usually handle animation, but this film is great. It's a great film. Even if Michael had not brought this to us we would have wanted to do it. Miramax is part of the Disney family but we're different. We know about films like Moan-a-NO-kee. We know how to take care of this film. Congratulations Suzuki-san. This is a wonderful film."

After a bit more ordinary conversation and some handshaking Suzuki and I were ushered out and back down to the lobby by one of Harvey's assistants. Suzuki said that he had been watching Harvey's eyes when he spoke, and that they never once stopped moving and were constantly scanning the room.

"This is a very intelligent man," Suzuki said.

It was after this meeting that Miramax arranged for *Princess Mononoke* to be screened at the Berlin Film Festival and for Miyazaki to be invited. Before leaving for Germany, Suzuki and I traveled to New York to meet again with Harvey to discuss the distribution plan for the film. Suzuki knew of a small, hard-to-find store in Tokyo hidden away underneath the train tracks between Shinbashi and Yurakucho. It was where Japanese film studios bought the realistic-looking weapons used in Japanese samurai movies. Suzuki picked out a sword there and brought it with him to New York for our meeting with Harvey. It was a very convincing replica of a Japanese samurai sword. It was realistic in every detail except that the blade was not sharp, which you could not tell unless you got a good, close look at it.

These were still the days when you could bring a samurai sword with you in your carry-on luggage on a commercial flight from Tokyo to New York. Suzuki presented the sword to Harvey in a conference room full of horrified Miramax employees. One of them later approached me and said, "You gave Harvey a *SWORD*? Are you *CRAZY*?"

When Suzuki presented Harvey with the sword, Suzuki shouted in English and in a loud voice, "*Mononoke Hime*, NO CUT!" After the meeting, Harvey arranged for us to have dinner and special VIP treatment at a nearby Japanese restaurant that he part-owned with Robert De Niro called Nobu.

The Big Slaughter

Berlin in February is very cold. It usually snows, but the year we went with Miyazaki it didn't. The hotel we stayed at was in the former East German section of Berlin and very near the Brandenburg Gate, Checkpoint Charlie in the Cold War spy books and films. As we strolled around that part of Berlin we noted that the walk we were taking would not have been possible only a few years earlier. Many of the older buildings were left just as they had been at the end of WWII, including in some cases walls pockmarked with bullet holes.

The official events to which we were invited included an opening-night welcome cocktail party for anyone with a film in competition and specially invited guests. The head of the film festival, a very tall, large, jocular man, came over and draped his arms around Miyazaki and Suzuki and asked me to translate.

"You know," he said, "I have several amusing stories to tell you about your film. It seems when the print arrived, one of the staff members had a look at it and said oh no, this is a cartoon so it must be for the children's film festival. So he sent it over there. Hah, hah! Weren't they surprised! All the heads flying off and arms flying off! What a mix-up! And you know, I myself, I heard the film's director is here, and I see him, but what about the cast? I was looking all over the reception area to find Japanese actors, until I suddenly remembered, yes! It's a cartoon! There are no actors! Ha ha ha ha ha. So funny don't you think?"

On the first day of the film festival there was a press conference for Mr. Miyazaki. Miyazaki sat up on a small stage and forty or fifty of the assembled international film journalists sat on stadium-style tiered rows of benches. There was Japanese-English-German translation.

The translation was something I hadn't thought much about. The festival had said it was providing translators so we didn't worry about it. As the questioning began I monitored the Japanese-English just to see how it was going. To my surprise the English translations of the questions and the answers seemed to be completely unrelated to the Japanese. The more I listened the more I realized there was a problem. The translators seemed to be just making things up. I went over to speak with the festival press coordinator and told him that it seemed that the translations were completely wrong.

"Really?" he said. "No one seems to be complaining."

"Yes, but how would they know it's wrong if all they hear is the translation?"

"Look," he said, "no one is complaining. They seem happy. If they're happy, why stir things up?"

The next day brought an endless string of short press interviews in a small airless, windowless room. Miyazaki was growing frustrated having to answer the very same questions over and over. He was surprised that the questions were brief and formulaic and that no one seemed to want to really discuss the film with him. He also complained that he was having trouble understanding the translator, a young German woman.

He wondered if she actually understood the questions or his answers. Could she be replaced?

I went over and talked to the translator. I asked if she had been doing this for long. She said it was her first time. I asked how long she had lived in Japan. She said never.

"I had two Japanese courses in college and my husband is Japanese."

"Were you doing the translation last night as well?"

"Only the Japanese-English."

"So someone else did the Japanese-German?"

"There's no Japanese-German. Someone translates my English translation into German."

She was employed by the festival and the festival wouldn't replace her. I ended up having to be the translator for the rest of the interviews, and the woman was paid to sit in a corner and read (German) magazines. At least when I had to make up answers to questions I couldn't understand or translate properly, the translation was relevant, if not accurate.

Our Miramax/Disney hosts planned outings for our group to balance out the days of solid press interviews. The first one was an afternoon touring the eighteenth-century palace known as Sans Souci, which was not open to the general public.

Miyazaki dislikes most conventional sightseeing tours and at first refused. But he and Suzuki perked up when they learned our tour guide would be Jan Eric Schluback, the man who had been Stanley Kubrick's art director for the German sequences in his film *Barry Lyndon*, one of Miyazaki's and Suzuki's favorite films. Though the former royal palace and the surrounding gardens were lovely and the palace contained some interesting art, Miyazaki and Suzuki spent most of their time there discussing Kubrick and his films with our guide.

The second outing was to a traditional German restaurant. Miyazaki had for some reason always wanted to try a traditional German dish called *eisbein*. Our Miramax/Disney hosts took us to a restaurant that specialized in it. The restaurant looked very stereotypically old-time German. The dark wooden walls and thick overhead wooden beams were overdecorated with boars' heads, antlers, stuffed eagles and foxes, coats of arms, elaborately framed portraits of nineteenth-century country squires, and the emblems of the brewers of German beer. The unadorned wooden tables were thick-boarded and worn with use. A huge roaring fire crackled away in a very large open stonework fireplace.

The evening began with a demonstration of German beer-drinking technique. We were each provided an enormous pewter stein of lager. One of our hosts proposed a toast, and we were instructed to drain our steins in a single gulp and smack them hard against the surface of the table when done. The last person to smack down his stein had to drink another beer on the spot. And then we all got another round and did it again. More toasts were offered. More steins were drained.

Then the *eisbein* arrived. On the menu, the *eisbein* special had been identified as "The Big Slaughter." *Eisbein* is basically a boiled pickled ham hock. That is, an entire pig's trotter from knee to hoof. The meat is heavily marbled and covered with a thick layer of fat. It's a huge portion and the skin is left on so you have to cut through it and the fat to get at the meat. Seriously sharp, wooden-handled meat knives were provided. The plate the *eisbein* came on was also huge, but not big enough to contain the leg, which hung over the side. There were also roasted potatoes, mashed lentils, sauerkraut, and mustard on the plate.

At a glance there was no question about what kind and what part of an animal the meat came from. Our hosts kindly advised us that not everyone felt it necessary to eat the skin and the fat. You could just cut through and eat only the meat.

Miyazaki commented that this was a cuisine that didn't disguise the thing that you're eating. It's about animals killed by man and laid out upon his table, he said.

Someone else commented that Germans, eating like this and confronting the realities of existence in their everyday dining habits, produced a large number of serious philosophers who thought deeply about life, death, and the nature of existence. The French, whose more prettified cuisine tended to disguise the nature of the things they eat, tended to produce artier, more aesthetic, and less deeply profound thinkers.

Based on my own experience at the *eisbein* restaurant, I believe it's probably better to think less and eat in France. It's what most modern Germans do whenever they can, or so I was told.

First Contact

One of the big differences between the way Japanese people travel and *gaijin* travel is that Japanese go everywhere with more people than necessary. Whenever either Hayao Miyazaki or Toshio Suzuki made a business or promotional trip abroad, we would go *en masse*. My role was trip manager and negotiator for the group. Either Haruyo Moriyoshi or Mikiko Takeda (or both) from the Tokuma International office would come. Suzuki always tried to take one person from Ghibli along to give him/her the experience of a foreign business trip, usually someone he was grooming to be a producer.

Seiji Okuda, from Ghibli's main partner NTV Broadcasting and a close personal friend of both Miyazaki and Suzuki, would always come with us. Since someone from NTV was going, the other major partners that produced and promoted Ghibli's films in Japan would want to send someone. Fukuyama-san from the ad agency Dentsu often came. If Dentsu was coming, the ad agency Hakuhodo couldn't be left out, so Fujimaki-san from Hakuhodo often made the trip. Sometimes someone from the film company Toho and sometimes someone from the conglomerate Mitsubishi/Lawson also joined us. And someone from Disney Japan usually also accompanied us. If Hayao Miyazaki traveled, a film crew might also come along to record the trip. Once we even had someone from Sumitomo Bank, Tokuma's chief creditor.

For our very first Disney meeting in Burbank we showed up

with a dozen people from Japan. The Disney executives didn't know what to make of it and were not pleased. Their program of welcome events and the swag (a technical term) they prepared for the visit had been designed for a group of four. The planned visits to pro baseball, basketball. and hockey games, the Disneyland VIP tours, the dinners at expensive restaurants, and the Disney gift paraphernalia were all hastily, if not graciously, expanded to accommodate twelve. Michael O. Johnson, the Disney executive who was our host, took me aside before the first meeting while his assistant was locating a bigger conference room.

"Who the hell are all these people, why didn't you tell me they were coming, and what are they doing here?" he wanted to know.

I couldn't have told him, because I never really knew very far in advance who would end up joining our trips. The list of attendees had a way of expanding at the very last minute. Toshio Suzuki, who made the decisions about who would come, seemed to think it was OK to just bring people without advance notice.

That first meeting with Disney in the US turned out to be plagued with problems. Movie distribution deals like the one Ghibli had with Disney are usually done by first concluding what is known as a "short form" agreement—also called a "deal memo"—that sets forth the basic understanding between the parties. It's a binding contract, but it's very general, and you can't really conduct business based just on it, or at least not for long. It is used instead to seal the deal so that you can announce it and start making the necessary preparations. Then you start work on a "long form" agreement that contains all of the specific terms and conditions needed to actually do the business. It is also a recipe for dealing with every possible contingency that might come up over the five to twenty-five years that the contract will be in effect.

When lawyers are asked to come up with everything that might occur over twenty-five years, creating a long-form contract may take a while. In our case it took two years. It might have taken less time if I had realized that much of the long-form contract was ignored in actual practice and parts of it were surprisingly unenforceable.

One of the few universally understood and adhered-to conditions in the movie industry is that you do not renege on your word. Not if you ever want to work in the industry again. You can quibble forever about the details of a deal, but you don't go back on a firm agreement. Yasuyoshi Tokuma, the owner of Studio Ghibli, did not completely grasp this concept. For *Princess Mononoke* we had negotiated a very large minimum guarantee, the amount of money that's paid in advance to license a film and is not refundable. That is, it was large for a Japanese film and large for a Japanese animated film. There were plenty of conditionals attached, but Suzuki was happy and Disney was happy. But from time to time Mr. Tokuma suggested that we tear up the short-form agreement and start all over from scratch. Usually Suzuki was able to convince him that this would be a very bad idea and would hinder, not help, Ghibli get its films seen abroad.

It took us nearly two years to finally reach agreement on a long-form contract between Tokuma and Disney, and on one of Michael O. Johnson's trips to Japan he decided to hold a small party to celebrate. The contract hadn't been signed, but all the disagreements had finally been ironed out and a signing ceremony had been scheduled. Mr. Tokuma insisted that the party be held in a private room in the *teppanyaki* restaurant at the Hotel Okura.

The Hotel Okura had been Tokyo's premiere luxury hotel between the 1950s and the early 1980s before the major modern luxury hotel chains started putting up their hotels in Japan. The Okura based its formula for Japanese upper-class elite service on the way it was done in 1950s and, like the Japanese institutions of its era, considered its refusal to change as a mark of its undisputed top-tier ranking. The Okura practiced the Japanese version of Western-style luxury service. All things at the

Okura were done properly, carefully, deliberately, and precisely. Each staff member wore the correct, perfectly pressed uniform for his/her station. The elevator women wore little hats, Hermès scarves, and white gloves, and they bowed deeply as you entered and left the elevator. Women in kimono roamed the lobby, tinkered with elaborate floral arrangements, and bowed guests into the elevators.

Japan has a reputation for the quality of its service. If you are willing to pay, you are cared for with an attention to detail that is legendary. But what most non-Japanese people don't understand about Japanese service is that it is flawless only as long as you don't insist on having it your way. You have it their way, period. No substitutions (please). No deviations from the program. No changes to the menu. Form over substance. Literal adherence to the written word.

When MOJ visited Japan he would always stay at the Okura. The executives from Japan in the Disney division he headed would usually meet him there for breakfast on his first day in the country. The slow and deliberate pace of the breakfast service was conducive to meetings. The overly attentive staff were sensitive to ongoing conversations and never rushed anyone, interrupted, or appeared at the table un-summoned. They hovered in the background ready to be called upon.

At one of these breakfast meetings, after the preliminaries of MOJ's schedule had been reviewed over coffee, the assembled group of ten paused to study the breakfast menu. The waiter was summoned and he went around the table taking orders. MOJ, who ordered last, asked if he could have his cheese omelet with Swiss cheese, and the waiter said "Of course, sir. You wish to have your cheese omelet with Swiss cheese. Certainly."

About half an hour later, as stomachs began to growl and people were beginning to feel seriously hungry, a waiter appeared carrying a tray. On the tray was a selection of about a dozen cheeses. The waiter approached MOJ and addressed him, saying, "These cheeses are all from Switzerland sir. Which one would you like in your omelet?"

That was the Hotel Okura. When Mr. Tokuma had dinner in a public restaurant there was only a handful of places he would agree to go to. All were restaurants with old-style Japanese service and impeccable reputations. All were places where he was known personally. His close friend Seiichiro Ujiie, the chairman of the NTV television network, often traveled to Europe and was a connoisseur and collector of fine (expensive) French wines. If he visited a chateau in Bordeaux he would have a case or two of its best wine sent back to Tokyo. A few of the bottles would be sent over to his friend Tokuma. Mr. Tokuma had the wine kept for him at the Hotel Okura where they knew how to care for it.

There were eight of us present at the dinner to celebrate the conclusion of the contract and the historic alliance between Tokuma Shoten and the Walt Disney Company. From Disney there were MOJ, his chief of staff Greg Probert, a senior corporate lawyer named Brett Chapman, and Koji Hoshino, the head of Disney in Japan. From Tokuma there were Mr. Tokuma, Toshio Suzuki, me, and, in the role of translator for the evening, Haruyo Moriyoshi.

Ms. Moriyoshi had been one of the original members of Tokuma's international division and Suzuki's first choice to represent Ghibli abroad once the international business took off. In addition to her talents and experience in buying and selling films, she was an accomplished translator. She had a unique ability to identify things that should never have been said and to translate them in such a way that they could be unsaid. For example, if you were to say, "We are totally fed up with the morons who work at your company and your pathetic sales results, and if you don't fix the goddamned problems we are dissolving our contract," she would translate it as "Mr. X says he greatly appreciates the excellent efforts of your company and its hard-working staff to promote our products, but wonders if there might not be some way to improve the sales results."

Few business people who travel abroad to do business, especially those exploring new opportunities, appreciate to what extent they are at the mercy of their translators. Americans in particular seem to just assume that anyone who claims to be a qualified translator is a qualified translator. And sometimes your translator is even better than you realized he/she needed to be. Ms. Moriyoshi was a genius at keeping things smooth. During the Disney contract negotiations, when an overly aggressive Disney studio executive told Mr. Tokuma that an important company like Disney would never give a tiny bit-player like Tokuma Shoten a five-year contract and demanded ten years, she translated it as "his company values our relationship very highly and would like to see this as a long-term relationship." Had she translated what the man had actually said, Mr. Tokuma would have ended the discussions immediately and the deal would never have been done. He had a temper.

As the meeting at the Hotel Okura proceeded, and as the hotel's chief sommelier, on loan from the more elegant French restaurant down the hall, stood supervising the proper decanting of Mr. Tokuma's vintage Bordeaux, Ms. Moriyoshi was effortlessly translating light conversational pleasantries. An elegantly dressed hostess was fitting each diner with a paper bib, in order to protect our expensive business attire from the gentle haze of grease that would inevitably drift over from the sizzling teppanyaki grill half-a-foot away. Young women in kimono stood poised to fill the crystal water glasses should their contents be diminished by even a single sip, or to change the linen napkins, rearrange the chopsticks, or attend to any of our needs involving tableware. At each place was a very large wine goblet, appropriate to an expensive French wine, but the glass next to Mr. Tokuma's place was twice the size of anyone else's.

The first few drops of the Bordeaux were poured into Mr. Tokuma's glass by the sommelier, who stood poised to receive the verdict. Mr. Tokuma swirled the wine around in his enormous glass and took a sip. Then, without comment, he held his glass out to be filled. This was a truly serious wine, and the sommelier could not completely hide his disappointment at the lack of reaction as he nodded to a waiter in a black tuxedo and had him proceed to fill all of our glasses. MOJ rose and was about to propose a toast, but Mr. Tokuma motioned him to sit. Then Mr. Tokuma stood and began to speak.

In his gravelly Marlon-Brando-in-The-Godfather voice, Mr. Tokuma said in Japanese without pausing for translation, "We've entered into this contract to make an agreement that will benefit both of our companies. But I'm not satisfied with it. Until now I've allowed my subordinates to handle all the details. That's over. I'm glad that Michael Johnson has come here to Japan. He's here. I'm here. Now it's time to throw out everything we've agreed so far and start all over again. Let's settle it all now. Michael Johnson and me, mano-a-mano."

Then Mr. Tokuma took a firm hold of his large wine glass, gulped down some Chateau Mouton Rothschild (1975), and sat down to wait for the response.

The Japanese contingent, the Tokuma side and Koji Hoshino from Disney, understood the words in Japanese and we tried to keep our reactions to them off of our faces. MOJ, Chapman, and Probert looked over inquisitively, still smiling benignly and awaiting the translation. Hoshino looked at Suzuki to see if he could stop Moriyoshi from translating. Moriyoshi looked at Suzuki to see if he wanted her to translate. MOJ and his guys were still smiling. No one said anything. Suzuki nodded reluctantly, because what else could he do? Moriyoshi translated with, for her, unusually literal accuracy.

MOJ was known to have, at times, a very bad temper. The people who worked for him always tried to avoid getting him angry or getting him into situations where he might get angry. I used to work for him at Disney and was once at a meeting in Tokyo where he called the chairman of a Japanese company that distributed Disney videos a liar to his face, and I thought we were going to have to fight our way out of the conference room (Japanese executives rarely travel with fewer than a dozen subordinates).

MOJ listened to Moriyoshi's translation, and at first he seemed only irritated that his expectation of a pleasant, exclusively social evening had been disrupted. This was ironic since MOJ had always vigorously maintained that the conventional wisdom, that you were never supposed to try to conduct business during a lunch or a dinner in Japan, was complete bullshit.

No one said anything for another few minutes, and MOJ looked around the room to see if (eccentric) old Mr. Tokuma had only been joking, or if the translation had been wrong. And then he started to get angry. Really angry. His face began to redden. The veins on his neck began to throb, and I think steam might have been coming out from the top of his head. He got to his feet and started to shout, argue, and rant. His competitive juices had been engaged. A switch had been flipped and he was in attack mode. He was so mad and so loud that most of the time he wasn't really making any sense.

The restaurant staff discreetly fled the room. No one was translating what MOJ was saying or could translate it. Moriyoshi didn't try and Hoshino didn't want to try. Mr. Tokuma sat serenely in his place and looked completely pleased with himself. Suzuki, Hoshino, and I were thinking that this was the end of the deal that had taken years and a lot of pain to bring into being. Chapman, the corporate lawyer, wore a kind of sinister yet gleeful expression, as if anticipating a really exciting major lawsuit. Only Greg Probert, the finance guy, was calm. Probert got MOJ's attention and said to him in a kind of stage whisper, "Look, they can't do that. Let's just let this pass, eat the dinner, and come back and talk to Suzuki alone tomorrow. We can figure this out and get over it. There's no reason to argue with him now."

For about ten minutes no one said anything. Then Mr. Tokuma began to make random observations about various things that had nothing to do with the Disney/Tokuma business. The restaurant staff returned to the room. Each course came and was joylessly consumed. Hunks of perfectly marbled Kobe beef were sliced and diced and sizzled on the grill. Live abalone and Japanese lobsters were set down on the hot grill and seared to death in front of us for our dining pleasure. Some token vegetables were tossed in for color, and mounds of garlic chips were fried and apportioned out to the diners. The closing course of rice, pickles, and miso soup was served. There were small chunks of wildly expensive melon for dessert and then coffee. No one seemed to enjoy any of it except Mr. Tokuma, who ate everything with great relish. Even the Bordeaux was not properly appreciated, though we did drink quite a lot of it.

The next day we all met again, without Mr. Tokuma. Suzuki proposed that we give Mr. Tokuma every single thing that he had asked for. He suggested that we put it all in the contract, but now that he was more familiar with how American contracts worked, he further suggested that somewhere else in the contract we put in things in the fine print, written in dense legal language, that would completely nullify all of Mr. Tokuma's new demands.

"He never reads the whole contract," Suzuki said. "Just the main points."

The biggest concern for Mr. Tokuma was getting a bigger minimum guarantee for *Princess Mononoke*. The original negotiated guarantee for the US rights had been by far the most ever received for any Japanese film. But for Mr. Tokuma it still wasn't big enough. He had seen all the attention the film had gotten in the international news media, and he had let it go to his head. He wanted to be able to say that he had squeezed more out of Disney. He wanted the minimum guarantee doubled. So we put some language in the contract that raised the guarantee to Mr. Tokuma's figure, and then we added some other language in the fine print to say that the additional amount was contingent on events we were fairly certain would never occur. We made the added amount payable at a later date only if the contingent events came to pass.

Mr. Tokuma never read the fine print and was thoroughly pleased with himself. Then he invited the Japanese press over to announce that he had achieved yet another victory and spelled out for them its terms, disclosing the new minimum guarantee amount, contrary to the agreement's nondisclosure clause.

This caused an unanticipated problem later on when the Japanese IRS picked up on the publicity and decided to audit Studio Ghibli. "You've only reported half of the minimum guarantee," the tax auditors observed. "Where's the rest? Don't tell us you never got it, because we read all about it in the *Yomiuri Shinbun*."

To Russia with Love

In October of 1997 a group of us from Ghibli flew to Los Angeles with an English-subtitled print of *Princess Mononoke* for its first screening in the US, which was also its first screening outside of Japan. A week earlier we had come very close to having the first international screening of the film, using this same print, take place in Russia for an audience that included Boris Yeltsin.

Mr. Tokuma's close friend Keizo Obuchi, who later became Japan's prime minister (1998–2000), was then Japan's minister for foreign affairs. He was about to make a state visit to Russia and wanted to bring a special gift with him. He thought that a screening of the now internationally famous film *Princess Mononoke*, the first to be held outside of Japan, would be just the thing. Obuchi asked that a subtitled print of the film be delivered to his office at the Gaimusho (Japan's State Department).

A "print" of the film *Princess Mononoke* consisted of seven fairly large reels in metal cans weighing in all about 250 pounds. The head of the Daiei film studio and I, with the help of an industrial hand truck, wheeled the print out of our Shinbashi offices and down into a waiting taxi. For two not-so-burly guys, handling a print was cumbersome to begin with, but taking it through the Gaimusho's security screenings and up to Obuchi's office was challenging.

Once we successfully got it up there and were sitting in the inner waiting room of Mr. Obuchi's elegantly appointed government office, we were met by his secretary, a stylishly dressed man in his late forties. In Japan, a major politician's secretary is a kind of chief of staff. He's the guy who, when irregularities or illegal acts are discovered, takes responsibility and does the jail time.

"What's this?" the secretary asked pointing to the stack of metal film canisters teetering on the hand truck.

"The print of *Princess Mononoke* Mr. Obuchi requested," I responded.

"What? This is a print of the film? I thought by now they would have these things on some kind of a small disk you just pop into a machine."

"No, this is what a film is when you project it in a movie theater," I said. "There aren't disks yet. There are a few questions we need to ask if you're going to show this film in Russia. This is a 35mm theatrical release print. Have you checked to make sure that your Russian hosts have a 35mm projector available to screen the print?"

"No, we were planning on screening it at a private dacha outside Moscow where the meetings will take place. Do we need a 35mm projector?"

"Yes. You'll need a professional projectionist and there are a few things about the print he'll want to know. This is a Japanese-language print with English subtitles. Have you checked to make sure Mr. Yeltsin will be able to follow the film in Japanese or English? We understand he has a reputation for . . .uh . . . drinking a lot, and we would hate for him to sleep through the film."

"It's not translated into Russian?"

"No, probably not until sometime next year at the earliest. So, now this may be a delicate matter, but we have to ask about security. Russia is known as a place where intellectual property piracy is not uncommon. If a copy of this print were to get out onto the black market the financial harm it would do to the studio would be great. Before the film has completed at least the first stages of its distribution cycle we usually insist on strict security procedures. Someone from your staff should actually be with the film the entire time it's in Russia. You can't just leave it with the projectionist and pick it up later. You can't leave it unattended in your hotel room. We hope you would give that serious consideration in your planning."

"Minister Obuchi is leaving for Moscow tomorrow morning. Maybe this isn't such a good idea. Wait here, let me go and check with him again."

Fifteen minutes later the secretary was back thanking us for our cooperation and instructing us to take back our print. Hailing a cab while wrestling the stack of film canisters under the suspicious gaze of the Gaimusho security police was tough, but we were very happy to get the only existing English-subtitled print of *Princess Mononoke* back to its secure spot in the Tokuma Shoten Building in our unlocked office behind the meeting room sofa.

It's Magic

Flying abroad with the same 250 pounds of metal canisters was also challenging. Japan Airlines, a one-time coproducer of a Ghibli film, helped out by letting us hand-carry the prints. Having one reel of the film turn up as lost luggage (much more common in 1997 than now) would have been a disaster. The beginning of a film's distribution process outside of its home country begins with screenings of an English-language subtitled print of the film. No distributor will commit to taking the film or scheduling a release date until they have seen it, whatever its reputation.

Princess Mononoke had been such a breakout hit and had been completed so close to its release date that getting all the prints made for its Japan release had required every print lab in Japan to operate at full capacity twenty-four hours a day, seven days a week. We had to beg for a place in line to get even one print to use for making the English-subtitled version. We knew it would be months before we could get another one.

The group that flew from Japan to the US with the print

was so large that hand-carrying was not much of a problem. Seven people each took one reel of the film. The JAL check-in counter staff gave us a hard time about the size and contents of our hand-carry items, but we had been given the name of a JAL executive at the airport to contact if there were any problems, and she was summoned and came by in person to smooth things over.

JAL had imposed one condition in allowing us to hand-carry the film. At least two of our party were required to travel in first class. Suzuki and I were elected. Once on the plane, flight attendants gathered up all the reels (and our small, collapsible hand truck) and stored them in the first-class coat closet.

Though I traveled a lot, I had only rarely experienced first-class air travel, and then only on US carriers. First class on JAL was a completely new experience. After checking in for the flight and explaining to airport security what the metal canisters were, Suzuki and I were personally escorted to the JAL first-class lounge. Once we arrived at the lounge we separated, Suzuki heading to the first-class smoking lounge and me to the first-class non-smoking lounge. I was the only non-smoker in first class on the flight.

Once we boarded the plane I found myself alone at the very back of first class. They still allowed smoking on airplanes in those days, and I considered myself extremely fortunate to have an entire row between me and the smokers because the gentleman directly in front of me only smoked once or twice during the whole flight. I noted that the average age of the first-class passengers, all male, was about seventy. Suzuki and I were by far the youngest, pulling the average way down.

The evening meal lasted a good four hours. There was real silverware and glassware. Each course came individually and ample time was allowed for digestion. By the time the meal was over I was ready to curl up and go to sleep.

As soon as I tried to do that a flight attendant rushed over and took away my blanket. She came back quickly, carrying a featherweight down comforter.

"This is for sleeping," she explained. "The other is just to keep you warm when you are sitting."

As I settled in to sleep, I did notice one odd thing. After finishing their meals, the older male first class passengers stood up in the aisles, removed their trousers, and wordlessly held them out at arm's length. A flight attendant would then wordlessly receive the trousers and come back with pajama bottoms. The men would then get into the pajamas, get back into their seats, and wait for the flight attendants to bring the down comforters, adjust their seats to the sleeping position for them, and tuck them in for the night. In the morning after breakfast, the pants ritual was silently repeated in reverse.

Once everyone was through immigration we reassembled the print and loaded it onto our collapsible hand truck. The US customs people in Los Angeles were not the least bit curious about the film canisters, and we piled into the Hertz courtesy bus for the five-minute drive to the Hertz lot and our waiting rental cars—a big SUV for the film and a minivan for the rest of the entourage.

Although we had the print of *Princess Mononoke* with us in LA, the first screening of the film in the US was to take place at the Pacific Film Archive in Berkeley, a few hundred miles to the north. Security for the print while we were in LA visiting Disney consisted of each person keeping his/her reel in the closet of his/her hotel room.

When we arrived at Disney's headquarters in Burbank, we were met by an extremely angry Michael O. Johnson. Just before leaving for the US, Mr. Tokuma had forced Suzuki and me to have a meeting with Hayao Nakayama, the president of SEGA, known for its video games. SEGA had just entered into a deal with Disney's archrival DreamWorks and Nakayama wanted us to meet with Jeffrey Katzenberg, the head of DreamWorks, while we were in LA. Suzuki had refused (politely), but after the meeting Mr. Tokuma first called Nakayama and told him we had agreed to the meeting, and he then called members of the Japanese press to announce it to them. Mr. Tokuma could always get anything he needed to make public printed in the *Yomiuri Shinbun*, where his good friend Seiichiro Ujiie was one of the Yomiuri Group's most senior executives.

Declining the meeting with Katzenberg was one thing, but not showing up for a meeting that had been agreed to and written about in the Japanese press seemed unnecessarily rude. We had just signed our famous agreement with Disney, and we were not already shopping around for new partners, so we thought it couldn't hurt to just meet him. After all, who at Disney would be reading the Japanese press?

As it turned out, Disney had an outside press-clipping service that provided Disney executives with all mentions in the press of Disney and its related companies and business partners. The Tokuma story appeared on the daily list of press clippings circulated to all Disney executives, and Michael O. Johnson, one of the few executives who read the whole thing, had seen it. MOJ worried that if Michael Eisner found out about the meeting with Katzenberg it would be the end of MOJ's career at Disney. Katzenberg and Eisner were not on good terms.

Before our scheduled Disney meetings could begin it took us the better part of an hour to convince MOJ that there was no harm in our paying DreamWorks a simple courtesy visit. We told him that this is what Mr. Tokuma does. He schemes and he plots and he's never satisfied. So if Ghibli/Disney has a future at all, he should just get used to it, not let it upset him, and deal with it. Because, we told him, this kind of thing is going to happen. Sorry, but that's the guy. When we arrived in Disney's offices, Suzuki was presented with a beautiful leather Walt Disney Studios jacket, and he promised to wear it to the meeting with Katzenberg. MOJ was not happy but told us to go ahead and take the meeting.

Our first working meeting was with Disney's marketing group. When we were arranging and negotiating the Tokuma/Disney agreement, we had been dealing with people from Disney who understood the entertainment business outside of America. In particular, people who were familiar with Japan and Asia. These people considered Ghibli's films to be untapped treasures that should become as popular, or nearly as popular, in the US as they were in Asia. They were certain that the US domestic team would want to release all of Ghibli's films as soon as possible.

This didn't turn out to be true. To begin with, Disney's US marketing team had issues with the films we had never considered. *Castle in the Sky*—someone fires a gun at a young boy; we can't show that to children in the US. *My Neighbor Totoro*—the dad gets naked and bathes with his daughters! We can't show that in the US. *Pom Poko*—the raccoons use their scrotums (!) to do magic. We can't have children looking at animal scrotums. *Nausicaä of the Valley of the Wind*—when she's flying we can see her ass (you can't, actually). We can't have that. *Only Yesterday*—the girl is talking about getting her first period; we can't show that to children. And so forth.

MOJ did his best to persuade them, but the domestic group would only agree to start with a trial release of *Kiki's Delivery Service*, a charming tale of a little girl witch going out on her own (even though you can sometimes see her underpants when she's flying). To them it was the least "risky" of Ghibli's films.

Now we were meeting with the marketing group to see how they planned to present the film in the US. As our large group filed in and more chairs were brought to accommodate us, we could see the Disney marketing team wondering, "Who the hell are all these people?" The simple introductions took about fifteen minutes and both groups ended up having exactly the same question: what is it again *exactly* that these people do?

Introductions completed, we got on with the business. The creative people began by showing us their visuals. Posters, press handouts, print ads, media spots, painted busses, and internet. We listened quietly for about a half hour and then Suzuki asked a question.

"Why did you make Kiki left-handed?"

The Disney marketers seemed stunned. Some smiled, thinking it was a joke. The rest were just puzzled. All of them were clearly thinking, "Why the hell could it possibly matter? This is the guy who's supposed to be Japan's most famous marketing genius?"

Robyn Miller, the head of Home Entertainment marketing who was running the meeting, asked politely, "Suzuki-san, could you please explain what you mean?"

He said, "Well, when we came up with the character and the idea for the film, we spent a lot of time thinking about how a witch would fly using a broom. The idea in the film is, and you see it in all the flying scenes, that the magic goes into the broom and it flies, and Kiki controls it with her hand, and when it's flying she has to hold on for dear life to keep from falling off. When your life is at stake you would probably use your strong hand, or both hands if you don't need the other one for carrying or waving or something. If you look at all of our art, she's always holding on with the right hand, and it's a pretty white-knuckle grip. How did you think she managed to fly the broom? She really doesn't even seem to be holding on at all."

The Disney people looked even more puzzled. Someone finally piped up, "How she flies the broom? It's magic. It's just magic and it flies. It's m-a-g-i-c."

And that was more or less how the relationship with Disney went from there. Many of the Disney businesspeople who then ran the company considered thinking to be a dangerous activity, and they certainly didn't want children doing it.

4

$\sim\!\sim\!\sim\!\sim\!\sim\!\sim\!\sim\!\sim\!\sim\!\sim\!\sim\!\sim\!\sim$

Road Warrior

You Say Potato I Say Starchy Tuberous Plant from the Perennial Nightshade *Solanum Tuberosum L* Family

The main difference between a negotiation in Japan and one in America relates to talking about price. Japanese tend to start off a negotiation with what they think is the actual price. The price they would actually be willing to accept or pay. Typically, in a Japanese negotiation once the price is mentioned it's fixed. No one questions it or tries to negotiate it up or down. Instead what they negotiate is what will be included in the price. What you get or have to give for the price that is now settled.

Americans on the other hand decide the price, and then double or triple it (if selling) or reduce it exponentially (if buying). Then the negotiation proceeds toward getting the price back to something more reasonable, or at least what the parties would be willing to accept.

Thus in an American-Japanese negotiation, Japanese are often at a disadvantage. When I worked as a consultant in New York, a team from our company would go with our Japanese clients to a negotiating session, and as soon as the price was first mentioned they would, despite our best attempts to keep them from doing it, immediately accept it. A hotel for sale in Manhattan that was worth no more than $200 million they were happy to buy for $600 million. And then all they wanted to know was, what could they get included in the deal for that money? When it comes to buying hotels, you have to get a lot of pillowcases, sheets, bars of soap, and minibar refills to make up for overpaying by $400 million.

Financially, Japanese films and TV shows had never done well outside of Japan. People of a certain age can remember growing up watching the cartoon series *Astro Boy* (*Tetsuwan Atomu*). Just about every European adult I have ever met remembers watching the animated TV series *Heidi* as a kid. Every cinephile in the world has seen Akira Kurosawa's *Seven Samurai, Yojimbo,* and *Ikiru*. But despite the unusual popularity of all those properties, the businessmen charged with selling or licensing them had to accept whatever price they were offered, which was usually not much. Even the most famous Japanese animated TV series were typically licensed for as little as $50 an episode.

Not having negotiated contracts with Hollywood film studios the Japanese were not used to or aware of entertainment industry contracts with hidden land mines buried in the pages and pages of legal language. The innocent-looking little clause nesting comfortably in a section of dense verbiage that you didn't realize gives the other party the rights to your film for free and forever after five years. The specialized legal definition of an ordinary-looking word that means the royalties you expected to get will amount to zero. The costs you understood to be almost impossible to ever be necessary but now you have to pay. The language that you were told is standard and necessary in every single entertainment industry contract but really isn't.

Japan for the most part is free of litigation, lawyers, and indecipherable voluminous legal contracts. A Japanese contract is typically only a few pages long. In the American entertainment industry a deal is generally a one-off kind of thing. You make the best possible deal you can for this thing now and then worry about the next one later. Whatever you said in the lead-up to the deal doesn't matter. What matters is what's written in the contract you signed. We have a contract. You don't like it, sue me. More often than not it's that kind of thing.

In Japan a deal is generally about forming a relationship. You do a deal not only for the one thing that's come up now, or for the immediate financial benefit, but because you and the partner you're contracting with are a good fit and can do things together both now and down the road that will benefit both of you for years to come.

The contract itself is usually nothing more than a formality. When Japanese companies reach an agreement with each other they don't need to read the contract to understand each other's motivations or the relationship that's been formed or how the business will proceed. The relationship of the partners is based more on understanding than on trust. You don't need to trust your partner because you understand perfectly how he will behave.

In the American entertainment industry each contracting party is trying to get the best possible deal for themselves, and they're willing to do anything and everything they can to get it. If you don't understand the tricks and the hidden contingencies involved, that's too bad. That's what the expensive lawyers are for, and you are expected to use them, and you had better pick ones with real industry-specific experience.

The Tokuma-Disney long-form contract was originally drafted by Disney's lawyers. It started out as several hundred pages of densely worded, highly specialized legal language. Even the fonts and the spacing and the way it was printed on the page made it unusually difficult to read. It had the look and feel of a document that had been placed in a titanium sphere and left on the moon by a race of genetically advanced space aliens for earthmen to discover at some future date: archaic and futuristic at the same time, its meaning and intent mysterious and obscure.

Although this was a single contract, it contained several riders and addenda that were themselves separate, densely worded contracts, each written in a different font with a different style of organization. There were sentences that were three pages long. Many passages were so difficult and so full of cross-references to definitions and clauses in different parts of the contract that even the lawyers who drafted them couldn't understand them without reading and rereading them at least a half dozen times. I often wondered if it would even be possible to translate certain parts of the contract into Japanese so that Ghibli/Tokuma's legal staff could review it.

It took us the better part of two years to negotiate the final long-form contract. The first part of the process was trying to understand what the contract said. The second part of the process was about getting the language of the contract revised into a version of English that an ordinary person could at least comprehend. Then, once everyone agreed that they understood the contract, the final part of the process was getting parts of it changed.

There were many reasons why all of this took two years. The legal teams for both sides went through at least three complete personnel changes. Each new group of lawyers managed to find new and unexpected things hidden in the language of the agreement, giving rise to new opinions about the need to add or delete this clause, this section, or this add-on rider. The document went through multiple iterations, each requiring a new Japanese translation. And meanwhile the business of releasing Ghibli's films outside of Japan proceeded. As it did, the legal teams discovered yet more things that needed to be changed.

The biggest and most unexpected problem for the Ghibli side was that the contract gave Disney the worldwide rights to all of Ghibli's films but also that if Disney chose not to release the films, Disney could just hold them forever without ever releasing them. For Ghibli, having its films released worldwide, uncut and unchanged (except for translation), was what it cared most about. The Disney executive Michael O. Johnson and the people who worked for him had handled the original agreement and fully intended to have Disney release the films worldwide. But the Disney executives at the head office did not necessarily agree.

Ghibli never imagined that Disney would not release the films and just hold them. When it became clear that Disney intended to not release most of the Ghibli films in most countries, Ghibli offered to buy back the rights or to find and use distributors in those countries that were willing to release the films and let Disney keep the money that was earned. After nearly a year of discussions on this point, eventually, Disney declined. They preferred to hold and not release. The vague language of the short-form agreement that Tokuma/Ghibli had signed allowed Disney to do this.

What changed the situation was the advent of a new technology—the Digital Versatile Disk (DVD). Back in the 1990s, electronic hardware producers and the entertainment industry had been searching for a new technology that would allow an entire movie, complete with trailers and ads for other movies, to fit onto a single small disk and be played in the home with the same or better audio and visual quality than a VHS videotape cassette.

There had previously been the Laser Disk, a two-sided LP-sized disk that was popular with videophiles, but too clunky, expensive, and inconvenient for ordinary mass-market consumers. You had to flip the disk over mid-movie, which was considered a serious drawback, and its size also made storage in the home problematic. SONY, JVC, Phillips, and other companies were working hard to find a way to compress a standard-length movie into a smaller, audio-CD-sized disk that could play it back at a level of quality to satisfy even the videophiles. But for a very long time the most that could be squeezed onto a disk and also maintain the proper sound and picture quality (barely) was a program lasting only seventy-five minutes. The entertainment industry *minimum* for a feature length movie was ninety minutes. A more typical feature would be two hours or even more. Plus ads and trailers.

And then suddenly there was a breakthrough. There was still some debate over the quality, but a disk had been developed that could hold two hours on a single side. Images had an unfortunate tendency to pixilate if they moved too fast or were too complex. But by most standards the DVD was, arguably, ready for the movies. The Hollywood studios' Home Video divisions all changed their names to Home Entertainment.

When the original Disney-Tokuma contract was negotiated, Mr. Tokuma, the company's chairman, took little interest in the technical details in the agreement. But he did insist on one thing. He insisted that Disney be given no digital rights. Tokuma had friends like the chairman of SONY and the president of SEGA, both of whom had advised him to hold on to the digital rights. Toshio Suzuki, who did all the actual negotiating, was sure that Mr. Tokuma did not even know what the word "digital" meant, but he wholeheartedly agreed with the advice, and the Tokuma side had stuck to this position throughout the negotiations.

When putting a two-hour film into a one-sided digital disk finally became possible, all the major studios did studies to see if this new technology would ever be accepted by consumers. Disney's own study had concluded that DVD would never become popular with consumers and would never become an important medium for the entertainment business. So when the subject came up during the contract negotiations with Tokuma, Disney put up token resistance at first but then agreed fairly quickly to allow Tokuma to keep all its digital rights, including DVD. When DVD eventually (soon) did become the most important medium for selling movies, and very quickly began to replace VHS, Disney realized that they now needed the DVD rights for the Ghibli films, at least for the ones that they had already released or were planning to release.

So in exchange for the DVD rights to Ghibli's films, Ghibli was able to get back the rights to the films in countries where Disney had declined to release them. Ghibli was then free to seek out other distributors in those countries. For Ghibli's filmmakers nothing was more important than having all their films seen in movie theaters. Hayao Miyazaki and all of Ghibli's directors and animators think of themselves as theatrical filmmakers. They see their art as meant to be seen on the big screen, in a darkened theater, playing to an assembled audience, and with a sound system that will allow the audience to hear the nuanced and carefully mixed soundtrack.

Ghibli had an intangible goal, and Disney wanted money. So it was an easy negotiation to get back the rights for the films that Disney would not be releasing. Both Suzuki and Mr. Tokuma were quick to take credit for foresight in anticipating advances in technology, though no one could have anticipated that a big Hollywood studio like Disney would study a new technology (DVD) that was on the cusp of wiping out its then single biggest income stream (VHS) and come up with the wrong answer.

California Dreamin'

Beginning with *Princess Mononoke*, every new Ghibli film had been screened outside the US for the first time at Pixar Animation just across the San Francisco–Oakland Bay Bridge from San Francisco. There is no audience that appreciates an animated film better than an audience that itself produces animated films. A great film is a great film and you shouldn't have to know how it was made to appreciate it. But then again, there's something special about being appreciated by your peers.

Living in Japan and working in America or Europe, I found it hard to avoid flying. Flying had been a part of my job for over twenty years, but I never liked it. Even before 9/11 and the security changes it brought I never found flying to be that much fun, and if there was ever any way to avoid it, I did. Traveling between LA and San Francisco you can drive, if you don't mind the seven or eight hours it takes by car.

For our screening of *Princess Mononoke* for Pixar, the thought of trying to make a US domestic flight with seven reels of film (weighing 250 lbs. and irreplaceable) pretty much made the choice to drive automatic. You can go on I-5, the fastest and least interesting way. You can go up the spectacularly scenic Pacific Coast Highway, but it takes two days to do it. Or you can split the difference and take US 101, which is scenic in places and gives you a chance to see firsthand what's going on with California mass-market agriculture.

At 6 am on a cloudless but hazy California morning, Toshio Suzuki, Seiji Okuda from NTV, and I loaded our 250-odd pounds of *Princess Mononoke* into a rented Ford Explorer in front of our LA hotel and headed north. We stopped for breakfast in Santa Barbara at a place called Sambo's. The restaurant was like a slice of frozen time from the 1950s. Southern California Norman Rockwell.

Apparently Sambo's had once been a chain, but now only the original flagship was left (Sambo, as in "Little Black Sambo," a character roughly as PC as a cigar store Indian). The staff wore the same uniforms as in 1957 when the restaurant opened. Bottomless cups of coffee were served in thick white ceramic mugs. All-day breakfast specials included heaping stacks of buttermilk pancakes accompanied by farm-fresh eggs, sausage, and bacon, all for very little money. Frequent diners could earn wooden nickels to be used for future discounts. Only the prices had changed since the 1950s. Coffee was no longer ten cents. Sambo's should still be a great chain with a kind of retro flavor, like Johnny Rockets. Except maybe for the name.

On the road Okuda and I shared the driving. Suzuki saw the road trip as a chance to catch up on some much-needed sleep (in Japan he rarely sleeps). He settled himself into the back seat of the Explorer and was immediately out cold. Every two hours or so he would pop up, look around in a daze, smoke a cigarette (they still let you smoke in rental cars back then), look around again at the scenery, and then drop down and go back to sleep.

When it was Okuda's turn to drive, he placed three large bags of potato chips (sea salt and vinegar, barbecue, and white cheddar with onion) and two quart-sized bottles of Coke within easy reach of his (non-driving) right hand. His average driving speed was about 90 mph. He passed cars on the right or the left as the whim struck him, and every time he reached for a handful of chips or a swig of Coke the car swerved violently. I was afraid for my life most of the time he drove, but we did make very good time. Later Suzuki confided in me that he thought Okuda was the worst and scariest driver he had ever known.

The next day we delivered the print of *Mononoke* to the Pacific Film Archive at UC Berkeley where the screening would take place, and then we headed to Richmond, just a couple miles north, for a tour of Pixar. Ghibli's relationship with Pixar was based on the ongoing friendship between John Lasseter, Pixar's creative head, and Hayao Miyazaki dating back to the early 1980s. Back then a group of Japanese animators, including Miyazaki and Isao Takahata and others from what would later become Studio Ghibli, spent several months in LA working on a project that proposed to make a film out of Winsor McCay's *Little Nemo.*

The concept for the project included the sharing of ideas and techniques between Japan's best animators and America's best animators. There were meetings between the group and Disney's famous Nine Old Men (the surviving ones). And John Lasseter shared his enthusiasm for what he saw as the future of a new kind of feature animation that didn't yet exist—computer animation. From this meeting in LA, John Lasseter and Hayao Miyazaki have been friends ever since.

Lasseter later made his way to Ghibli alone during the production of Miyazaki's *My Neighbor Totoro.* He brought with him clips from the short films he was then working on, "Red's Dream" and "Luxo Jr.," and Miyazaki showed him bits of *Totoro.* It's still a mystery how Lasseter was able to even find Ghibli let alone make his way there without a translator, but somehow he did, and the two men were able to communicate. Lasseter also discovered something else on his visit to Ghibli: that Hayao Miyazaki throws away the storyboards from the scenes in his films that he decides not to use. He learned that when visiting

Ghibli it pays to go through Miyazaki's wastebasket. Fishing out a discarded sheet from the trash he would say, "You're throwing THIS out? Really?"

Lasseter's office at Pixar looked like a kind of toy museum. On my first visit I wondered aloud if it was his actual office and if he had another working office somewhere else. I was told that this was it, his only office. Framed on the wall were the discarded scenes that Lasseter fished out of Miyazaki's wastebasket. Whenever Miyazaki visited and saw his drawings he would sigh and say, "I really should have kept those scenes in the film."

While our group was in LA talking business with Disney, a group of twelve animators from Ghibli was touring Disney Feature Animation. They also joined us in San Francisco for a tour of Pixar. We were at Pixar just before Halloween, and each person's desk, office, or cubicle looked like it had been decorated by the first-prize winner in a nationwide Halloween contest. Everywhere the group went, hobgoblins, ghouls, skeletons (engaged in various activities), witches, jack-o-lanterns, and black cats gazed back at them. Fake spider webs with large fake spiders hung from the doorways. Pixar employees glided through the corridors on flashy silver scooters. Unexpected props appeared here and there, such as an antique barber's chair in the middle of a corridor that Lasseter demonstrated for us, or a fully stocked Roaring Twenties bar.

At the end of the tour the Ghibli animators were asked what they thought of Pixar. They thought it was great. In fact, they said, it had given them ideas for ways to improve Ghibli's facilities, and they were drawing up a list of improvements for Suzuki to consider.

"Everyone has so much space here," they said. "Why can't Ghibli be more like this?"

Suzuki decided on the spot that he would never let the animators tour a foreign animation studio again.

John Lasseter hosted the entire group for dinner at a very nice Italian restaurant in Berkeley and afterward we all went to the Pacific Film Archive for the screening. Just before it started,

MY NEIGHBOR TOTORO

A Japanese family bathing scene that made the film's American distributors uncomfortable.

Suzuki took me aside and asked me to write him a short speech in English, which I did in the semidarkness of the theater's lobby. I handed it to him just as he approached the microphone. He glanced at it briefly, once, and then delivered it, in English, with slight variations, loudly (as he does) and confidently. This became his usual practice at foreign screenings of Ghibli's films.

The screening of *Princess Mononoke* was very well received. More than any other audience, the Pixar animators and staff seemed to enjoy every single nuance of Ghibli's film and fully appreciated the places that, while they might not be apparent to a general audience, represented astounding feats of hand-drawn animation. Many people who see Pixar's films mistakenly believe that the computers do most of the animation. Unfortunately, the art of animation operates at its very highest level when the skills it took to get it there are the least apparent. Which is why Ghibli always preferred to have its films screened abroad for the first time at Pixar.

Tequila Sunrise

After the screening at Berkeley, Suzuki and Okuda and the Japanese contingent flew back to Japan with the print of the film, and I accompanied the Ghibli animators on a visit to the Fox Animation Studios in Phoenix, Arizona. One of the things I've discovered over the years is that animators all over the world deeply respect the work of other animators and feel a sense of kinship that may not always be reflected in the attitudes of their corporate parents. As brothers and sisters struggling at a monumentally difficult task, where the difficulty of some of the things they achieve is often poorly understood and not appreciated, they tend to share their work freely.

With other animators fellow animators are astonishingly open and unselfish. When I discovered this attitude in Ghibli's animators I just assumed they were merely naïve (having surprisingly little contact with the outside world, chained to a desk and immersed in fantasy, etc.). But when I discovered this same condition at every animation studio we visited, I realized it was something else. Something truly admirable.

The group from Ghibli had toured Disney Feature Animation and Pixar just to see the studios and to meet other animators. But they had a more specific objective in visiting Fox Animation. *Princess Mononoke* was the last major feature animated film to be done using traditional hand-drawn, hand-painted cel animation. The colors were hand-painted onto the clear plastic cels, and each of the key cels was photographed individually and put together to make the film. This back-end manual process was now being taken over by computers. The development of new software enabled the coloring of the individual frames of a film to be done more quickly and more cheaply.

But whether it was faster or cheaper was less relevant than the fact that as animation studios worldwide, Japan included, were beginning to adopt this computer technology, the people who did the cel painting could no longer find enough work to make a living and were moving on to other professions. Because it was becoming increasingly difficult to find people who could or would paint the cels, Hayao Miyazaki had reluctantly decided that Ghibli, too, would make the move to computer coloring. Miyazaki famously dislikes computers, and if he could have avoided it he would not have made the change.

During the summer after the release of *Princess Mononoke*, while almost everyone at Ghibli was away for the week-long Obon vacation, the entire ink and paint section of Ghibli was gutted, and the rows and rows of shelves containing a million shades of powdered color in jars were replaced by banks of computer terminals. Michiyo Yasuda, who was usually credited in Ghibli's films as the "color designer," had worked with Isao Takahata and Hayao Miyazaki for about as long as they had been working in animation. In her early sixties, she was now faced with the task of learning commercial computer software even though, like Miyazaki himself, she had never used a computer before. The speed of her learning curve was astounding.

Yasuda had wanted to visit Fox because Fox Animation was the only major studio using the same ink-and-paint software as Ghibli. As hand-drawn animation was becoming increasingly rare, the back-end software supporting it was also being used less. Fox had agreed to meet with us and talk about the way they use the software and share the problems they faced and solutions they had found.

It wasn't completely an exercise in altruism. One of the biggest cost-control issues for animation studios was the nature of the production cycle and its use of specialists. Background artists would only do backgrounds. Animators would only do the moving parts. Most of the back-end work could only proceed once the drawings and the artwork from the other groups were completed. This meant that for stretches of time different parts of the studio would have no work to do. If you only worked 100% on your own films, there would be chunks of downtime when your background artists and your animators and the back-end people would be idle. When the animators were in full production and the back-end was just starting up, the background artists were beginning to wind down. When the animators were finished and the ink-and-paint staff was working full out, the background artists and the animators were idle.

Since Fox and Ghibli used the same ink-and-paint software, it was theoretically possible that the idle ink-and-paint staff at each studio, trained on the same software, could help out the other studio during peaks and give the other studio work during slack periods. Theoretically.

We spent a very enjoyable and exhausting (for me as translator) day at Fox touring the studio, seeing how each department did its job, learning the details of how their films were made, and trading information about the problems of keeping within budget and meeting production schedules. We were also treated to a visit to the top-secret area where animators were working on their next film, which had just begun production. Gary Goldman, one of the directors of the animated feature *Anastasia*, gave us a demonstration of how computer ink-and-paint actually increases, rather than decreases the studio's workload. "There are so many options now," he said, "and what director doesn't want to see them all before deciding? With a click of the mouse the entire color palate can be changed. Show me this. Now show me that. By the time we're done I've doubled their workload."

The trip was highly interesting and informative. We learned a good deal about how Fox created their films and were able to convey something about how Ghibli works. The Fox studio had originally been set up in Ireland, and many of its employees were Irish, so there was an international feel to the place, even though it was in Arizona. We left with a sense that cooperation in many areas would be possible, although nothing ever came of it. What Yasuda-san learned about the ink-and-paint software she never said. But she had asked a lot of questions, and it was clear that she understood the software as well or better than anyone else in the room.

The next morning most of the group was up very early. We had an early flight back to LA for our connection to Tokyo. I wandered outside and found Yasuda with Yoshifumi Kondo, the director of *Whisper of the Heart*. They were gazing up at one of the most beautiful sunrises I have ever seen in my life.

"The colors are just amazing" Yasuda said. "This alone makes the whole trip worthwhile."

5

Young Men, Be Ambitious!

Space Mountain

Yasuyoshi Tokuma was the chairman of the Tokuma Group, the parent company of Studio Ghibli. Among Mr. Tokuma's many interesting qualities was his ability to never let success of any kind go to waste. The idea was not just that you should never rest on your laurels, but that if you ever got any laurels you ought to squeeze from them every last drop of value.

While *Princess Mononoke* was enjoying its ascent to international fame, Tokuma-*shacho* was thinking of new and different ways to put himself into the limelight. His age and the state of his health were such that a trip abroad would have been difficult, but when he heard that Miramax was planning a gala event for the premiere of *Princess Mononoke* in the US, he was ready to hop on a plane and fly to New York. Provided that the event would be attention-getting enough to justify the trip. It was important that the event be held somewhere prestigious, and that people who were famous attend. People, that is, who were famous in Japan.

Harvey Weinstein and other executives at Miramax had been talking of renting the Boathouse Restaurant in Central Park and inviting A-list celebrities. Harvey had connections in the world of politics as well as the entertainment business, and there was talk that then President Bill Clinton might attend *Princess Mononoke*'s US premiere event. Mr. Tokuma let it be known that he would be *very* happy to meet the American president and contribute money toward funding the event if President Clinton came. If it turned out that the president himself could not make it, then he would be happy to sit down for a chat with Hillary as an acceptable fill-in.

That plan was interrupted by the emergence of the Monica Lewinsky affair, and both Bill and Hillary became too busy to attend film premieres. For a while it looked like Al Gore might be willing to come, but Mr. Tokuma was never one to settle for second best. The names of other important politicians were mentioned, but Mr. Tokuma's knowledge of American politics was limited and he hadn't heard of any of the other people whose names were proposed. Eventually the plan for the premiere event ran out of steam and died once the promise of Tokuma funding had come off the table.

Besides meeting with the American president, Mr. Tokuma had also wanted to sit down and have a personal chat with Disney's chairman, Michael Eisner. He believed that since his company and Disney had entered into a deep and long-term relationship, the chairmen of the two companies should sit down and share their experience and wisdom. And since his health pretty much prohibited him from overseas travel, Tokuma thought that Eisner should come and see him in Japan. From time to time Tokuma-*shacho* would call me upstairs to his office to share a cup of Häagen-Dazs ice cream (vanilla) and instruct me to have Eisner visit him in Tokyo.

Whenever I relayed this proposal to the most senior executive at Disney in charge of the Ghibli relationship, Michael O. Johnson, who was then heading up Disney's international business, MOJ tried to change the subject. I did my best to bring it up often, and I explained how much it would mean to Mr. Tokuma. I tried to suggest all kinds of ways that Disney might benefit from having Tokuma Shoten and Studio Ghibli forever in its debt, but it was always nothing doing. Sorry, MOJ would say, just can't do it. It's not going to happen. Eisner doesn't like to travel, except maybe to Europe, and he would just never go for it.

But then suddenly in October of 1998 it was on. Michael Eisner was coming to Japan. He had to be in Tokyo for a ceremony to mark the beginning of construction of a new Disney theme park next to the existing Tokyo Disneyland. Disney was opening up a "second gate" called Disney Sea, a nautical-themed amusement park, including as one of its nautical themes a perfect and detailed re-creation of a part of the city of Venice (Italy). Disney had originally planned to build such a theme park in Long Beach, California, but various problems, including money problems at Euro Disney in France, caused Disney to scrap the idea. As the planning and the development of the technology for the new rides and new shows had been done, Disney decided to convince the Oriental Land Company, the owners of Tokyo Disneyland, to expand their Tokyo park by adding the second gate.

Tokyo Disney Sea was designed to be more of an adult-themed park. The rides would be faster and scarier and the shows would appeal to adults and not necessarily to children. Oriental Land had been reluctant to endorse a second gate with a different theme, preferring, if money was to be spent, more of the child-friendly original Disneyland. But after long and sometimes difficult negotiations, the agreement to build Tokyo Disney Sea was concluded. Now Eisner was making the trip to Japan both to signal the importance of the new park to Disney and to help kick off the publicity that would contribute to the park's success. He was scheduled to be photographed standing next to executives of Oriental Land shoveling out the first spadeful of dirt that would mark the beginning of construction.

That had been the only thing on the Disney chairman's schedule and the only thing he had time to do on a one-day visit to Japan. MOJ made sure that we knew how hard he had worked to carve out half an hour and arrange for Mr. Tokuma to have a meeting with his boss (his boss's boss), one of the most well known and widely respected corporate leaders in America. He warned us not to do anything to make him look bad in front of the chairman of his company. He added that it wouldn't hurt any if Mr. Tokuma told Eisner how much Tokuma/Ghibli valued MOJ's contribution to its business and the Disney business in Japan.

When the news of the hoped-for meeting was delivered, Tokuma-*shacho* bridled at the idea that the meeting would take place in Urayasu—where Tokyo Disneyland was located—and not at his office in Shinbashi and threatened to cancel the meeting. But once he realized that it was really Urayasu or nothing, he gave in. On the appointed day, Mr. Tokuma, Toshio Suzuki, and I piled into Mr. Tokuma's chauffeur-driven town car and headed out to Tokyo Disneyland.

Urayasu, just east of Tokyo in neighboring Chiba Prefecture, is not a particularly attractive area. Much of it was underneath Tokyo Bay until extensive dredging in and around Tokyo in modern times created new land. Like most of Tokyo's waterfront areas, the Urayasu waterfront had grown up as a jumble of functional warehouse buildings with negative aesthetic appeal.

Japanese people (wisely) avoid building houses in areas prone to flooding. But someone at the Oriental Land Company, which owned property there, carved out a piece of the waterfront property and dared to try something different. What if Japan could have its own Disneyland? An exact copy of the actual Disneyland located right outside Tokyo? It was a time when the Japanese economy was evolving from the manufacture of cheap imitation products and transforming itself into a nation of technical manufacturing skill and quality. Oriental Land was sure Disney would agree to building a Tokyo Disneyland.

Two of the most enormous business successes in the history of Japan were initially ridiculed mercilessly in the press and on TV when they were first proposed. McDonald's was brought to Japan in the early 1970s. Its Japanese president, Den

Fujita, was publicly mocked and told again and again that not only would the Japanese people never eat hamburgers, but they would never eat them at a place where you had to walk up to a window and order them. Fujita replied that not only would they eat hamburgers, but their doing so would improve the overall health of the nation. He famously said that "the reason Japanese people are so short and have yellow skin is because they have eaten nothing but fish and rice for two thousand years; if we eat McDonald's hamburgers and potatoes for a thousand years we will become taller, our skin will become white and our hair blond."

He may not have been right about that, but there are now more McDonald's stores per capita in Japan than there are in the US, and in some years McDonald's Japan has even outearned McDonald's in the US. My son, who grew up in Japan, was surprised to see McDonald's in America when we first visited his grandparents in Connecticut. As many Japanese children do, he assumed that McDonald's was a Japanese restaurant.

When Tokyo Disneyland opened in 1983 it was widely believed that no one would come to see an Asian imitation of the real thing. Most of the staff and performers at the park when it first opened were Japanese (possibly because the Japanese government limited the supply of entertainer visas and gave a higher priority to those applying to work as strippers or bar hostesses). If the performers were all Japanese, even though the women wore blond wigs, the lack of authentic American performers would make the park seem so obviously an imitation that the Japanese public wouldn't embrace it.

It was said that if Japanese consumers couldn't experience the authentic thrill or feel of the real Disneyland's exotic American charm, Tokyo Disneyland would surely fail. Even Disney didn't think much of the park's chances for success. Passing up the opportunity to be joint owners of the new park, Disney preferred to act as a licensor and accept royalties. Almost from the start Tokyo Disneyland became hugely popular. It often drew between twelve and thirteen million visitors a year and in some years was ranked as the third most visited theme park in the world. During the summer months it would be so busy that they had to turn people away at the gate.

There are still plenty of warehouses in and around Urayasu, and between the commercial traffic, the Disneyland traffic, the airport traffic, and the normal Tokyo commuter traffic, the trip by car from Tokyo is dependably an unpleasant and time-consuming slog. Two slogs, actually. The highway slog to get from Tokyo to Urayasu and the slog through the streets of Urayasu to get to the area where Tokyo Disneyland and its related resort hotels are located. By the time our car reached its destination, Mr. Tokuma was already in a bad mood.

Our meeting with Disney's chairman took place inside one of the official Disneyland hotels. We had been instructed to proceed to the hotel and wait for Eisner and his entourage to join us. We arrived nearly an hour early in accordance with the established Tokuma company practice of always being at least a half hour early for everything. We were then shown by the hotel staff to our specially reserved Japanese-style meeting room. Mr. Tokuma took one look at the room and said, "Unacceptable. We're leaving. We're going back to Shinbashi."

Mr. Tokuma had decided that the room was too small and an insult to his position. He felt that a small room for an important meeting was a sign of disrespect. I had to think fast and talk fast to keep him from leaving and ruining our relationship with Disney and with MOJ (Eisner would have been pissed at being stood up). I explained that in America it was a greater sign of respect to give someone an intimate interview in a smaller room with fewer people. In a small room the participants can share their real thoughts, whereas in a larger room you would just be hearing the sterilized version of the corporate line. I told him that in America the most important meetings take place in small rooms. It may or may not have been true, but Mr. Tokuma bought it and allowed himself to be shown into the (small) meeting room.

In Japan there are two distinctly different kinds of meeting rooms. There's the conference-room-style meeting room with a table and functional chairs around the table, and possibly a TV monitor or white board at the front—a room that is useful for working-level employees to sit and hash out the (boring and minute) specific details. And there's the living-room-style executive meeting room with comfortable sofas or big armchairs, or both, arranged around a low, usually glass-topped or marble-topped coffee table with plenty of ashtrays on it and no space for much else—a room useful for executives to sit back and talk through the big-picture, blue-sky issues. We were seated in the executive-style meeting room. The Tokuma group sat on one side of the coffee table, as is the custom in Japan, and waited there for Eisner and his guys to show up.

While Tokuma/Ghibli runs on a schedule where everything is always at least a half an hour early, Disney runs on a schedule where everything is always at least a half an hour late. As the appointed time came and went and more time passed, Tokuma-*shacho* threatened to leave once or twice before the Disney group finally arrived, only about forty-five minutes late.

The Disney group filed into the room and before taking seats on their side of the table, Koji Hoshino, head of Disney in Japan, made the introductions. In addition to Michael Eisner and MOJ, Peter Murphy, Disney's head of Strategic Planning, was with the group. Michael Eisner is a tall man, and his hands, when he extends them to shake and be introduced, are exceptionally large and soft. On that particular day he looked to be very badly in need of a nap.

The Disney group took their seats on the Disney side of the coffee table. Eisner sat facing Mr. Tokuma at the far end of the room away from the door. Hoshino was seated next to him and translated for both sides (he is extremely good at it). MOJ sat next to Hoshino and across from Suzuki. Peter Murphy sat next to MOJ, facing me. First there were pleasantries and small talk. Then the obligatory lauding of each other's companies and the importance of the Tokuma/Disney relationship. Congratulations on the success of Ghibli's films. Declarations that a company that does business outside of its home country needs effective and reliable local partners. The importance of Japan, the world's second largest economy, to any company that does business internationally. For the most part, generic corporate platitudes. Not untrue. Just routine.

But things warmed up when Eisner said that to the Walt Disney Company, Japan had always been something of an enigma. Disney seemed to enjoy a great reputation and some measure of commercial success in Japan, he said, but he always felt that the level of accomplishment should have been far greater and that his company was always searching for ways to achieve a higher level of financial success. This opened the way for Mr. Tokuma to explain to Eisner exactly what Disney was doing wrong in Japan and exactly what Disney should do to correct it.

It was a fairly long speech with plenty of examples, but the gist of it was that Disney was poorly organized. The company was split into smaller separate companies that managed only their own slice of the business, and the separate companies neither coordinated their activities nor even spoke to one another, and in many cases they were not even aware of each other's business initiatives and often worked at cross-purposes to each other.

Mr. Tokuma told Eisner that as a business partner you thought you were speaking to Disney, but you were only speaking to a part of Disney, and one that acted in its own interests and not in the interests of Disney as a whole. What, he posed, might Disney not achieve if it could act as a single entity with a single purpose and a single voice? The person who spoke for all of Disney in Japan would have greater power on his own, a power that the separate company representatives could summon if necessary. Provided the person understood how things worked in Japan.

It was a very good speech in Japanese, but from time to time we had to remind Mr. Tokuma to pause, which he did very reluctantly, to allow Hoshino, who was writing furiously in a notebook, to translate. Eisner looked drowsy as the sonorous tones of unintelligible Japanese washed over him, and then would suddenly perk up as a particular part of the translated speech caught his interest. Mr. Tokuma could barely restrain himself to wait for the translation, eager to get on with his prescription for Disney's success.

This pattern of stops and starts with lulls or periods of intensity, depending on which language you were following, continued for a while when MOJ, sitting next to Hoshino, suddenly stood up, walked behind Murphy, around the end of the glass coffee table and over to the Tokuma side, and stood next to me. He leaned down, cupped his hand over his mouth, and in an attempted whisper, which I thought must be audible at least to Peter Murphy sitting just opposite, if not to everyone else in the room, said, "Steve, Tokuma isn't saying anything about me. Can you get him to say something good about me?"

To me it was a kind of surreal moment. It was a small room. There were only seven of us in it. Mr. Tokuma was lecturing Eisner in his deep, gravelly, and resonant politician's voice. Suzuki was following the speech and nodding from time to time as the various points were being made. Hoshino was furiously taking notes. Eisner sat relaxed and sleep-deprived waiting for the English translation to come. He had drowsily followed MOJ's stroll to the Tokuma side of the table with his eyes. Murphy was more alert and his face wore a quizzical expression. I had to wonder if MOJ thought he was invisible or was this just something that Disney executives routinely did and accepted as normal behavior. I looked over at Mr. Tokuma who was still talking and wondered how I could possibly, unobtrusively, un-obviously get that request inserted into his remarks.

MOJ was staring down at me and waiting for an answer.

"Well," I whispered back, "I don't know. I guess I could try."

Satisfied, MOJ straightened up and went and sat back down in his place on the Disney side of the table.

Suzuki turned to me and asked what MOJ had said. I told him. He didn't seem surprised. He only said that it might be hard to explain it to Tokuma-*shacho* and get him to understand what he was supposed to do. When Mr. Tokuma took a break to let Hoshino translate, Suzuki leaned over and passed along the message. Then when Mr. Tokuma resumed speaking, the very next words out of his mouth were about how fortunate we were to be working with such a talented and gifted executive as Michael Johnson. Fumbling slightly over the words in a way he had not while explaining Disney's mistakes to Eisner, Mr. Tokuma added other oddly out-of-context words of praise for the man who was responsible for the two companies being able to have this special, mutually beneficial relationship. Since Mr. Tokuma was very bad with foreigners' names, it was sometimes Michael Jackson and not Michael Johnson who was receiving the credit and praise.

I couldn't imagine how anyone in the room, having seen MOJ walk over and whisper to me and me whisper to Suzuki and Suzuki whisper to Tokuma, would not see the sudden accolades as phony. I couldn't then and don't now understand why fake, orchestrated praise for MOJ (and/or Michael Jackson) would have impressed Eisner. And yet, neither Eisner nor Murphy seemed to react in any way to the oddness of it. When MOJ's name was mentioned and he was praised by Mr. Tokuma, they both just nodded and even brightened slightly and seemed to take it as genuine independent praise. If these guys from Disney were Japanese I might possibly have understood it.

In traditional forms of Japanese theater—Kabuki (elaborate costume dramas where the male and female parts are played by men) and Bunraku (puppet theater)—there are non-actors on stage dressed head-to-toe all in black called *kuroko*. The *kuroko* are like the backstage guys who make things happen or who change the sets in between acts. In the Japanese theater the *kuroko* remain onstage during the action of the play. The audience sees them but at the same time they don't see them. They're the property managers or stage managers who move things around. They're the puppeteers who control the puppets. You're supposed to see them and admire their art, but at the same time you're supposed to view the puppets and human actors as if the *kuroko* were not there. The audience accepts them and ignores them simultaneously. They are there but they are not there. It could have been that MOJ was more sophisticated in his understanding of Japan than I had realized, even though he wasn't dressed in black. The audience seemed to be buying it.

When the meeting wound up, everyone seemed satisfied. Mr. Tokuma got to advise Michael Eisner on how to run his company. MOJ got praised in front of his company chairman. Suzuki and I got one more impossible task removed from our to-do lists. Hoshino again demonstrated his unique ability to translate the seemingly untranslatable and help bridge the culture gap between Japan and the West. On the way back to Tokyo, Tokuma-*shacho* said that when it came to the meeting with President Clinton, well, that probably would have been hard to arrange and he could accept that in the end it never happened. But if the Michael Eisner meeting hadn't happened he would have been truly sorry. After all, he said, Eisner was only a company chairman and really no different from Mr. Tokuma himself.

Technical Problems

Over in New York Miramax was taking the first steps to begin what would turn out to be an epic process, the creation of the English-language version of *Princess Mononoke* that would be seen in theaters in America. Back in Los Angeles Disney was creating English-language versions of *Tenku no Shiro Laputa* (*Castle in the Sky*) and *Majo no Takyubin* (*Kiki's Delivery Service*) for release on VHS. From time to time there would be problems with those productions that we hadn't expected.

The cornerstone of our agreement with Disney was that Disney would absolutely respect and under no circumstances alter or change any of Ghibli's films when they released them outside of Japan. This was not a result of contract negotiations or pleas from Ghibli. Disney, on their own initiative, had opened their proposal with it. Later on, in the process of creating a full-blown contract, Disney's lawyers had laboriously and precisely severed from the definition of "alter" or "change" the act of translating the films. Lawyers are understandably cautious about misunderstandings. But the essential principle of "no change" had remained intact.

Miramax had a certain reputation for altering the films it distributed. But we always felt that the people we worked with at Disney respected Ghibli's films, and we had no reason to suspect otherwise. So, when we received the first tapes of the work-in-progress versions of *Kiki's Delivery Service* and *Castle in the Sky*, we were shocked to discover that Disney had added music, effects, and dialogue. There were quite a few changes throughout both films.

When I raised the issue with Disney's production staff they maintained that nothing had been added and that the English version was identical to the Japanese version except that the dialogue had been translated. This was so obviously untrue that I felt I had no choice but to raise the issue with Disney's legal department, a step you generally try to avoid. You don't like to have to actually fall back on the contract you'd spent two years laboring over, but you do trust that if invoked, a clearly worded contract will protect you.

A few weeks later we were told that Disney's legal department had reviewed the issue with the Disney production staff and was satisfied that no changes had been made to the original version except that the dialogue had been translated. But, they said, even if there had been changes, any and all changes had been approved by Mr. Suzuki. The term they used was "constructive consent." It meant that we were aware of the changes and had not objected.

Disney's lawyers were referring to the time when Suzuki visited LA and was shown clips from the in-progress English-language version of *Kiki's Delivery Service*. He had noticed the changes and reacted only with mild amusement.

He had been curious to see what changes would be proposed and assumed that there would eventually be a formal opportunity to deny approval for any changes that altered or changed the films. After all, it was in our contract.

I called Michael O. Johnson to see if it really was Disney's intent to violate our agreement by making extensive changes to the films and then claiming that Ghibli had agreed to them. After another few weeks MOJ called and said that he had looked into the issue and been assured that no changes had been made to the original works other than translation into English. I told him that this couldn't possibly be true and asked if he had seen the new versions of the films. He said he had been shown excerpts from both films and had seen no drastic changes. But if Ghibli still maintained that changes had been made in violation of our agreement, he suggested that I fly in to Burbank and we review the tapes together with his legal department and the Disney production team that had made the English-language versions.

So I did.

Our meeting took place in a conference room at Disney's offices in Burbank. Ghibli was represented by me. Disney was represented by two of their corporate lawyers, MOJ and two other Disney executives, the head of the Disney Studio's technical department, the head of the Asia-Pacific region technical department, and the Disney producer who was in charge of creating the English versions of the Ghibli films, a woman who I will refer to as X. We all sat at a large conference table facing two large side-by-side TV monitors. One of them displayed the original Japanese *Tenku no Shiro Laputa* and the other showed Disney's English *Castle in the Sky*.

One of the lawyers opened the meeting by asking me which parts I thought had been changed. He wanted to know which parts I wanted to look at first. I looked over at X and tried to imagine how she could possibly have agreed to sit in on this meeting or what she could possibly be thinking. There was not any doubt that things had been added and changed. A few days before leaving for Burbank I had received a note from the man who added the music to the films expressing what a sincere honor it had been to work on and to create new music for the films of Hayao Miyazaki and Studio Ghibli. I had the letter with me.

"You can start anywhere you like," I said. "There's almost no place where there have not been changes made."

"OK then," the lawyer said, "let's start from the beginning."

As we watched the film in short sequences, first a minute or so of *Laputa* original Japanese and then the same minute or so of *Castle in the Sky* English, the changes that had been made were obvious to even the most casual observer, even from the very first seconds of the film. The English version began with dialogue that was not on the original soundtrack. There were numerous added sound effects and more added dialogue. There was added music and added musical flourishes like drum rolls and gongs. MOJ and the lawyers watched the screen visibly aghast. After sampling only several more sequences they put a stop to the demonstration.

"I don't know what to say," MOJ said. "We have clearly made changes to the film. We're going to have to make this right. We will make this right." Then he turned to X and gave her the kind of verbal lashing that makes grown men cry.

When we met the next day, only the lawyers and the technical people and me, we discussed our options. Disney's version of *Kiki's Delivery Service* had already been put into a duplication master and the VCR version of the film had been manufactured and distributed to wholesalers. Disney's practice then was to do this well in advance of the release so that the retailers would all be ready for big in-store promotions on the release date. Recall of the product would have been difficult or impossible and very expensive. But there was still time to repair *Castle in the Sky*, which was being released a few months later.

Most of the Disney team that had created the English versions was replaced, and work on a new version of *Castle in the Sky* began at once. We were assured that going forward, Ghibli would always have final approval over any English-language version of a Ghibli film well before it could be released, and that such approval would always be in writing. Disney further agreed that if *Kiki's Delivery Service* were ever released in a new medium (DVD for example) in an English-speaking market, Disney would make a new version without the additions.

Disney also had an additional request. They wanted to know if Ghibli would consider, with Miyazaki's and Suzuki's permission, letting them work with Hisaishi Joe, who collaborated with Miyazaki on the soundtracks of all his Ghibli films and had composed the original music for *Castle in the Sky*, to create additional music for the English version of the film. I told them that it was very unlikely that Miyazaki would agree, but that I would ask the film's producer, Toshio Suzuki, and if he agreed he would ask Miyazaki.

Suzuki knew that if he simply asked Miyazaki directly he would say no. It was one of his usual ways of killing off bad ideas or crazy suggestions from others. Rather than just say no, he would ask Miyazaki directly, without explanation or expression of support. Miyazaki would look at him in silence for a beat or two and then say no. Suzuki could then say that he had at least asked, but unfortunately Hayao Miyazaki had said no. To our great surprise, when we put the question to him, after a moment or two of deliberation Hayao Miyazaki said yes.

Miyazaki firmly believes when a film is completed there should be no looking back to see what could have been changed because the creative process is endless. Done is done. But that doesn't mean he's not also curious about possible changes to his films. This was a request that gave him the opportunity to see one such change at Disney's expense and required no work or input at all from him. The lush and beautifully performed new music recorded by an orchestra three or four times larger than the original was eventually added to the soundtrack for Miyazaki's review. Miyazaki vetoed its inclusion as expected.

Reality Bites

While we were discussing with Disney exactly how we would go about the process of redoing the soundtrack to *Castle in the Sky* we discovered a new problem. We were informed that the technical materials we had provided for the video release of *Kiki's Delivery Service* and *Castle in the Sky* were defective and that it was going to cost Ghibli nearly a half million dollars to have them replaced.

Understanding and managing the technical materials needed to convert a film shot on actual film to videocassette, DVD, and television broadcast was a nightmare of contending with warring techno-geeks, all of them fiercely convinced that only their way was The Way. Digitalization of filmmaking and film-projecting has made most of those early battles waged over competing technologies completely moot.

In Ghibli's agreement with Disney, Disney had insisted on severe penalties if the videogram materials Ghibli provided turned out to be defective. Suzuki was quick to agree to this because after all, Japanese materials were the gold standard in the industry. SONY PCL, the company that made Ghibli's materials, had invented the process and manufactured most of the machines used to create the technical materials. This was supposedly an area of Japanese technical superiority.

But after Ghibli provided the videogram materials for *Kiki's Delivery Service* and *Castle in the Sky*, we were told by Disney that the materials were defective because they contained certain "anomalies" and that Disney would be exercising their option to re-create them at a cost of more than $400,000.

When we recovered from our shock we had the materials tested by SONY PCL, and they were declared 100% OK. SONY could not understand what possible anomalies there could be. SONY ran test after test and there were no problems. Disney ran test after test and maintained that there were anomalies and "artifacts." SONY had no idea what they were talking about. Disney couldn't understand why SONY failed to see the problem. The international phone bills were mounting.

At this point national pride entered the discussion. The Japan side felt that they were the ones who had created the process and made the machines and that their ability to create these elements was as good or better than anyone else's anywhere in the world. There were not, nor could there possibly be any anomalies. The American side felt that Americans, especially Americans in Hollywood, have the biggest budgets, spend the most money, and have the best access to the most modern and up-to-date technology and expertise, and if *they* said there were anomalies, there were anomalies.

To resolve this disagreement between two of the leading technical giants in the film industry, I was dispatched to LA to sit down with Q, the head of technology for the Walt Disney Studios, to see if we could at least come to a common understanding of the issue. Was there an actual problem? If so could it be reduced to language that ordinary humans could understand and thereby moved into the domain of lawyers who were better than technology boffins at assessing blame and settling the higher question of who pays?

So, on a lovely warm and cloudless southern California afternoon, I and a senior Disney corporate lawyer (B) sat down with Q in a windowless, soundproof chamber surrounded by the most expensive state-of-the-art AV equipment known to man. Q was going to show us exactly what the anomalies and artifacts were so there would be no more doubt.

In the darkened room we scrolled through a section of *Kiki's Delivery Service* frame-by-frame on a very large TV monitor. Q showed us that when you moved from one frame to the next frame, in nearly a third of the frames a very faint ghost image of a part of the previous frame could be detected. Could be detected, that is, if you looked closely and if you had a state-of-the-art giant screen in a darkened room. As we scrolled through the film we all agreed that there were these faint ghostly images.

This is my recollection of the conversation:

ME: Where do these come from?

Q: It occurs as part of the process of turning a film element into a videogram element. These ghost images occur naturally when we convert to videogram format and the only way to remove them is to go in frame-by-frame to delete them. It's a very expensive and time-consuming process. We now do this to all Disney films.

ME: Can an ordinary consumer watching a video at home see these ghost images?

Q: No, that would be impossible. You have to be able to go frame-by-frame to see them. There's no way at all to do that with a VCR.

B: But if you had it on laser disk and could go frame-by-frame, then you could see it, right?

Q: Of course.

ME: But Disney is not releasing these films on laser disk. And even on laser disk, the only way you could see it is by going frame-by-frame right? If you just watched the film normally you wouldn't see it?

Q: No, you wouldn't see it.

ME: So, if you don't mind my asking, why would anyone care if there were ghost images when you went frame-by-frame if you can watch the film normally and not see them? And since these films will only be out on VHS where the ghost images can't be seen at all, why is it necessary to correct the anomalies?

Q: Because it's Disney's policy to correct them for all films. This all started back when the laser disk technology first became available to the public. Certain videophiles were examining films frame-by-frame and they discovered something that had long been a Disney secret. The animators for Walt Disney films, going all the way back to the earliest ones, had ... well, a kind of raunchy sense of humor. I suppose drawing the same images over and over maybe can get a little tedious or something, I don't know, but they started amusing themselves by drawing things in a single frame that they knew no one would ever be able to see.

B: Drawing things? Like what?

Q: Oh, well for example we found a frame where Mickey has his hand up Minnie's skirt. One film had swastikas all over the place. You probably heard about the column in the undersea palace of *The Little Mermaid* that was actually a penis. That sort of thing. And well, technically savvy consumers were discovering these things and writing in about it.

B: Consumers who owned laser disk machines and watched the films frame-by-frame?

Q: Well yes, but some ordinary person with a laser disk might happen to stop or pause the machine for any reason at just the wrong spot. There were an awful lot of these things in the early films. I can tell you it took us a lot of time, expense, and effort to go in and delete them all. I think Disney senior management just felt they didn't want to take any chances and made it a policy to find and eliminate them.

ME: But we aren't talking about that kind of anomaly in Ghibli's films. Ghibli animators don't do that kind of thing. These are just ghosts that no one will actually see when watching the film. Not things that anyone needs to worry about. Even if you were watching on laser disk and you paused and saw the shadow, why would you care?

B: Wait a minute. We've been talking about animated films. Do you mean to say you do this to all of Disney's films? To the live-action films? To Hollywood Pictures and Touchstone films?

Q: Yes.

B: And what does it cost?

Q: In the neighborhood of roughly $200,000 per film. More if there are a lot of corrections that need to be made.

B: You do this to all Disney, Hollywood, and Touchstone films? All of them?

Q: Yes.

B: And to all the films we acquire and distribute? That's something like thirty to forty films a year.

Q: Yes.

B: OK, I think we've got what we need here. Thanks Q for giving us your time. And Steve, I think you make a good point about these anomalies possibly not needing to be fixed. Let's see what we can do.

A few weeks later we were told the issue had been resolved and Ghibli would not be charged for replacing the defective materials. B, I imagine, got a healthy bonus for the money he saved the Walt Disney Company.

6

On the Road Again

LA Confidential

Hayao Miyazaki's first American trip, the trip to promote *Princess Mononoke*, began with a screening of *Princess Mononoke* at the Toronto Film Festival in Canada. The film's distributor, Disney/Miramax, flew Miyazaki and Toshio Suzuki in from Japan on United Airlines. Miyazaki and Suzuki usually prefer flying with a Japanese carrier. Everything is in Japanese and the service is always reliable.

After clearing the long lines at customs and immigration in Toronto, Miyazaki discovered that United Airlines had somehow managed to completely destroy his suitcase. It was one of those very attractive (and expensive) lightweight aluminum suitcases, and it looked as if it had been sat on by an elephant and then tossed around by a team of 800-pound gorillas. The damage was not incidental.

The United Airlines baggage claims agent managed to say with a straight face that the airline's designated luggage vendor would have to examine it to determine what, if any, damage had been done to it. It was Saturday at about 4 pm. The designated vendor would be open on Monday morning. Our flight to LA (on United) would depart on Sunday, the day before the vendor opened for business. Our Miramax escort bought Mr.

Miyazaki a new suitcase. Sometimes it's great to have professional handlers looking out for you.

Besides Miyazaki and Suzuki, our group from Japan included Okuda from NTV, Fukuyama from Dentsu, Fujimaki from Hakuhodo, Moriyoshi, Takeda and myself from Ghibli, and a two-man documentary crew that was completing a nine-hour documentary on the making of *Princess Mononoke*. A Toronto Film Festival screening of *Princess Mononoke* had been scheduled for later that evening, and there were going to be several press interviews, so no down time, Miyazaki having insisted on minimizing his time in Toronto.

We were given a few hours to rest up. Miramax had arranged to have our group picked up in a limo for the ten-minute drive to where the screening and the interviews would take place. It was the first time any of us had ever been in a stretch limo.

Piling into a stretch limo is not easy when you're packing it full of people. The Japanese tendency to worry about seating hierarchy and order of boarding slows things down. The seats inside are uncomfortable, especially if you're only in it to get from A to B. Up at the front with its back to the driver is a bench seat facing backward. Along one side is a very long bench seat facing a fully stocked wet bar. At the back is a bench seat facing forward, more or less in shouting distance to the front of the car. All the black leather seats are low to the floor, making it very difficult to get in or out of the car and uncomfortable to be seated while the car is in motion.

The ceiling of our limo was mirrored and its edges were painted like a starry night (not the Van Gogh version). There was a switch that would bathe the interior in black light. The limo was equipped with a fancy sound system and iced bottles of champagne. Plastic champagne flutes sat out on the counter of the wet bar, ready to be filled. The floor was covered in a thick shag carpet. Probably to get the full flavor of the stretch limo experience you had to be going somewhere that took longer than ten minutes to get to, you had to drink the champagne, rev up the sound system, maybe roll onto the shag carpet, and definitely be in the limo with fewer people.

We arrived at the screening venue. Miyazaki was introduced before the screening and received the wildest and most enthusiastic standing ovation I have ever seen or heard. He seemed surprised at first, humbled even, and it made him much less grouchy, which was a good thing for the interviews that came later.

After the screening we were joined by five of the Miramax PR staff, who treated us to a terrific meal in an upscale French restaurant nearby. At the restaurant the large group seemed to naturally divide into two. On one end of the table the discussion included the role of nihilism in art, fate, karmic predestination, and the value of psychoanalysis and non-Western medicine. At the other end of the table the discussion included the merits of the 1990 Jordan Cabernet Sauvignon.

Several of the PR staff let us know that they had just resigned from their jobs at Miramax. They told us to go ahead and order more wine, brandy, vintage Port, or whatever we wanted because none of them would be around to have to explain the expense. When the Japanese group left the restaurant, the Miramax guys (and gals) were still there drinking.

Thus, when the next round of interviews began the following morning, no one from Miramax showed up to officiate. Roger Ebert was the first interviewer. He came in with a young guy who taped the interview and who we assumed was his assistant. It turned out that the guy was a Ghibli fan who had simply crashed the interview. Since there was no one there from Miramax, we didn't know if a private room had been reserved for the interview, so we just did it in the open lounge of the hotel. Passersby stopped to watch, and many hung around to ask for autographs from Miyazaki, Ebert, or both.

Ebert and Miyazaki hit it off very well. It was one of the few excellent film discussions that took place as part of an interview. All of it was recorded by some anonymous guy who later posted it on the internet. For the rest of the day's interviews, since everything now seemed to be entirely up to us, we decided to move to the hotel's rooftop lounge where Miyazaki and Suzuki could smoke. There was crisp autumn weather outside and a fine view of Lake Ontario. Some of the scheduled interviewers managed to find us up there and some did not.

Late that afternoon we flew out of Toronto and got into LA in time for a dinner with Tom Schumacher, then the president of Disney Feature Animation. Schumacher had requested that we come without the entourage or the film crew. The dinner was at Wolfgang Puck's restaurant Spago, and Mr. Puck himself did the cooking by special request. I was the translator and thus unable to really eat much (sadly).

Miyazaki is not a fan of what might be called high-end fine dining. The first course of our meal was sashimi served in individual miniature ice cream cones and garnished with special herbs and sauces. I was continually having to rack my brains to replace or modify Miyazaki's and Suzuki's running critique of the menu and the expensive wines that accompanied the meal. They knew I wasn't translating what they were saying and that only encouraged them to keep it up. Only when the conversation finally turned to the difficulties of making an animated film and doing it within budget did they cut it out and start saying things that could actually be translated. Because of this, I completely missed out on the last two main courses and three of the dessert courses.

Tom Schumacher had once sent Miyazaki a gift of a bottle of a rare limited-edition California wine from his own personal collection. He deputized one of his division's senior executives to hand-carry the bottle to Japan (back in the days before 9/11 when you could). The executive had found a leather carrying case for the bottle, which contained a nice wine opener and a stopper to preserve the flavor of the wine after opening. When the executive presented it to Miyazaki, Miyazaki removed the wine from the case, set down the bottle, examined the case lovingly, thanked the executive for the gift, and walked off with the case, leaving the bottle behind.

In LA I was also the translator for the next day's visit to Disney Feature Animation. Due to security, the number of people allowed in had been limited. I needed to beg to get Disney to allow the documentary film crew to join the visit inside Disney's feature-animation building, commonly referred to as The Hat (from the outside, the building is designed to resemble the hat that Mickey Mouse wears in "The Sorcerer's Apprentice" part of *Fantasia*). This was where all Disney's top-secret feature films were being hatched and developed and then produced. I had promised on my life that the film crew would absolutely never ever even dream of pointing their cameras at the art on the walls or at the animators at work. If they did, I was given to understand that I would forfeit every penny I owned and my eldest son. They really took security at Disney Feature Animation seriously.

Once we got inside The Hat, I learned a lesson that I now understand very well: documentary cameramen do not give a damn about anything other than getting the shots they want. They don't care who has promised what or what they themselves promised in order to get permission to film. Once they start filming they lose track of all that. To be fair, getting good documentary footage is probably not an easy thing, and their art and livelihood depend on it. Maybe when they are out in the wild filming animals, nature finds a way to balance intrusive harm with expositional value. If the wild lions being filmed take exception to the camera being trained on their cubs, the cameramen will suffer the consequences directly and individually. Lions don't have lawyers who take it out on the producers.

Hayao Miyazaki on a tour will soon ignore the tour guide and wander where he likes. As we were shown the various stages of development at Disney Feature Animation, Miyazaki headed directly to where the animators were at work. In those days Disney was still animating by hand. As Miyazaki ventured into areas we were not supposed to go into and were not permitted to see, he was frequently stopped by Disney animators who wished to be introduced, say how much they admired his work, and in some cases ask for autographs.

The documentary cameraman, of course, followed and also took the opportunity to scan the walls with his camera to get shots of the art being used to create as yet unannounced Disney films. It was only after issuing a credible death threat to the cameraman (and his producer who was with us), and some serious pushing and shoving, that I was able to get the cameraman to follow the guidelines he had agreed to. These guys were members of our own entourage whom we hung out with and shared meals with. But when coming between a documentarian and whatever he is documenting, the normal bonds of human society dissolve.

After the feature animation tour, next up was an unscheduled meeting with a Disney animation director who had a project he wanted to pitch to Miyazaki. We were running late, so Suzuki and the rest of the entourage went to meet John Lasseter for lunch at the Rotunda, Disney's in-house restaurant for its executives in a building supported by the Seven Dwarfs. Miyazaki and I went over to a separate building where we were first shown clips from *Fantasia 2000,* which was then in production. Asked what he thought of the film so far, Miyazaki replied simply "*hidoi ... totemo hidoi*" (terrible ... really terrible), which I translated as "interesting ... Mr. Miyazaki finds the animation very unusual and very interesting."

The project the Disney director wanted to pitch had come from a suggestion made by Miyazaki himself. An executive from Disney had once asked him if he were making a film based on a children's book, what book would be his first choice? Off the top of his head Miyazaki had made a suggestion and Disney had gone out and bought the rights to the book. The presentation they wanted to show him consisted of storyboards outlining how Disney would make that book into an animated film.

In the book, a boy encounters a mysterious monster. The boy lives on a small, dirt-poor farm with his grandparents, who are tough, nonverbal, and don't openly show emotion or affection. In addition to the boy, the other main character in the book is a mysterious talking rock from outer space. Miyazaki had loved the book because it showed how a lonely, isolated youth had both survived and overcome his difficult situation. Were the monster and space rock meant to be seen as real or imagined? Was the author implying that fantasy can have value in helping an individual to overcome hardship? Did the boy's grandparents really not feel affection for him just because they didn't show it openly? That all of this is unclear in the book, and that these kinds of issues were raised by the story, was what attracted Miyazaki to it.

In the Disney version being proposed, the monster had become a cute forest elf. Disney changed the grandparents to an openly loving and understanding aunt and uncle who constantly talked to and reassured the boy. Disney had the mysterious rock crack open to reveal that inside it was a winged fairy princess who needed help to return to her own people. (I'm not making this up.)

At the end of the presentation Miyazaki was invited to come to LA and codirect the film. He (actually) said that he was honored but must decline the invitation on the grounds that he was retiring from filmmaking. He said that even if he were to make another film he had long ago learned that he could only be comfortable working in Japan.

Asses in Seats

I had to leave for New York a day in advance of the rest of the group. The documentary filmmakers following Miyazaki wanted to make sure they captured his on-stage appearances at the screenings of *Princess Mononoke*. For most of the on-stage appearances NTV also sent a camera crew to get footage for their news programs and TV variety shows. Up until the screening at the New York Film Festival at Lincoln Center in New York City, having a crew filming had not been much of a problem. In each case we had agreed to certain limits and restrictions and promised to mention the screening venue on air or in the documentary's credits. Sometimes we paid a nominal fee. But the NYFF was asking for $10,000 for permission to film in Avery Fisher Hall for the two to three minutes Miyazaki would be on stage. Miramax was not able to talk them down. NTV didn't have the budget for it, so Suzuki wanted me to go and see if I could do something to get them to lower their price.

It was Wednesday and the NYFF had given Miramax a deadline of 6 pm that evening to say yes or no to the fee and come up with the money. I had to be out of the hotel by 4:30 am to get a 6 am flight from LAX to JFK. I had let DT, the Miramax liaison with the NYFF (also one of our hosts at the dinner in Toronto), know that I was coming and that once I got to New York we could decide what to do. Meanwhile DT was trying to call in favors from Miramax's New York VIP list to see if he could go over the festival director's head and get the fee reduced. In addition to the fee, the festival had a twenty-page legal agreement they also wanted signed.

The flight to New York boarded on time and was taxiing down the runway for an on-time take-off when the pilot aborted and taxied back to the gate. Many of the passengers expressed their disappointment when the pilot announced a fifteen-minute delay to fix a minor problem. I fell asleep, and two and a half hours later when I woke up, the plane was just taking off. When I got to New York at about a quarter to six I immediately searched out a working public phone (cell phones existed, but they weren't common). I had to shove aside an old lady (I'm not proud of it) to get onto one of the very few working phones. DT said he had got the NYFF down to $8,000.

DT: But they need you to sign the contract.
ME: I can't get there from JFK by 6. That's fifteen minutes from now. Impossible.
DT: OK, let me see what I can do. But you're OK with the eight thousand?
ME: Yes, please do whatever you can. I'm on my way.

When I got outside the terminal, the line for taxis to Manhattan was over two hundred people long. Just around the corner I noticed an attractive and well-dressed young woman screaming at the top of her lungs at the driver of a NYC Yellow Cab. She punctuated her tirade against the driver by slamming the cab door, but the door was stiff and her shove was too girlish. As the cab door clicked closed, all she got from the Pakistani cab driver was the Indian subcontinent shrug. What can I do? Be reasonable. We are all creatures living on this planet together.

As the cab pulled away from her on the sidewalk it slowed as it passed me, and the driver leaned out the window and said, "Hey mister, you are going to Manhattan? Come. I drive you."

He had a very large, neatly trimmed handlebar moustache and was dressed in a brightly colored robe-like traditional Pakistani costume. I looked over at the two-hundred-person cab line. I looked back at the driver's clear, honest-looking eyes. What the hell. I tossed my bags in the trunk and jumped in his cab.

I gave the cab driver the address of the hotel and he gave me the story of his dispute with the angry lady.

"I pick up this lady in Manhattan with two friends. She say go to JFK. OK I'm going to JFK. We arrive JFK and the friends they get out. The lady says wait. She then exits taxicab. Big hugs and kisses. Waving goodbye. That sort of thing. Then lady gets back in cab and she says go to Brooklyn. No way can I go to Brooklyn. My shift ends at six-thirty. Manhattan I can go but not Brooklyn. She says she is going to Brooklyn. I say I cannot. Lady, I tell her, these are New York City taxi rules. Going back from JFK you must go and get in the taxi line. I cannot take you to Brooklyn. I cannot pick up fare from JFK sidewalk. Even it is the same person. Please don't make me call police. This is what I tell her. But sir, you understand me, yes?"

I said that I did. I said I also understood when he pulled off the BQE near LaGuardia Airport into a residential neighborhood in Queens so he could change places with his brother who would then drive me into Manhattan. I said I understood when the brother, now driving the cab, pulled off the highway in the Bronx to fill the taxi's tank with gasoline. In the end it took me nearly two hours to get into Manhattan, mostly because of the traffic. But if I hadn't hopped into that taxi I'd probably still have been waiting in the taxi line back at JFK.

DT from Miramax was waiting for me in the hotel lobby.

"Look," he said, "I signed the contract myself on behalf of Miramax. The festival was OK with that, but they want you to go up there and say in person that you intend to pay the money. The exact amount they want is $8,146.15."

Suzuki had told me to just pay if it came to that so I was ready to agree.

"We'll pay," I said, "but how can I pay and why is it such an odd amount? I don't have checks or anything with me. I'd have to call Japan and have them wire-transfer the money."

"Yeah, that's what I thought, so I assured him that Miramax would pay it. He just wants to hear you say in person that you're good for it. I asked about the amount but they refuse to explain it or to justify it. It's what they want. Take it or leave it."

So the two of us walked the five or six blocks up to Lincoln Center and met with an official from the film festival.

After a very short exchange of pleasantries I asked about the fee.

ME: You have other news organizations shooting footage at the festival. Does everyone pay the same fee?

NYFF: No

ME: So how do you decide which ones you let in and who pays what fees, if you don't mind my asking?

NYFF: We have our criteria.

ME: I see. So you don't think of Japan as an important country where it might be nice to have the festival get a good reputation by letting its news agencies come in and shoot a few minutes of footage of Hayao Miyazaki being welcomed by your audience?

NYFF: Listen, we don't give a shit about the audience in Japan. They don't come to the festival and they don't buy tickets. They know who we are. We had Kurosawa here. We never have trouble getting the films we want from Japan. It's about putting asses in seats. That's it. Are you paying the fee or not?

ME: Yes, we are.

The man thanked me and we left.

On the way back to the hotel DT was sympathetic to my disappointment at the film festival's attitude.

"You still think of film festivals as cultural events run by film lovers with high ideals," he said. "That's not entirely untrue. But they still have to run it as a business. Anyway, look on the bright side. You can toss out the copy of the contract I gave you. I told you in Toronto I quit my job. As of last Friday I was officially no longer a Miramax employee. I probably never had the authority to sign it anyway. You never signed a thing. You should probably still pay them the money, but all that stuff about crediting them and mentioning their name in the broadcast you can ignore. No one from Ghibli signed up for it, so fuck 'em."

Goodfellas

Hayao Miyazaki is an early riser and likes very much to walk before breakfast and explore any new city in which he finds himself. In LA he really couldn't. If you are just out walking in Los Angeles, people will think you're up to something criminal and call the police. Jogging is acceptable but walking is not, so if you really want to walk you have to dress like a jogger (headband, armband with iPod, running shoes).

New York is a great place for walking but out-of-towners hesitate because of its reputation as a dangerous place for those unfamiliar with the city. Our hotel was very near to Central Park and on our first day, a crisp and beautiful early autumn day, the entire group took a walk in the park. I lived in New

York for about ten years and I know Central Park very well. When asked by Miyazaki how I managed to find my way so easily through its meadows, thickets, and wooded paths I made the mistake of sharing the secret: you look up and see where the tall buildings are. Our own hotel was easy to spot.

When Robin Jonas, who was in charge of our press tour in New York and served as our Miramax caretaker during our stay there, arrived the next morning to find that Miyazaki was not in the hotel and out on his own she was terrified. When he returned grinning broadly after having strolled in Central Park by himself and having wandered out onto Broadway to get bagels and coffee, she took me aside and begged me not to let him go out alone again.

There were interviews scheduled for late morning to early afternoon and then a press screening of *Princess Mononoke* at Lincoln Center's Walter Reade Theater followed by a press conference. Everything went reasonably well and Robin took us to a nearby Chinese restaurant for dinner. The restaurant was famous for its Peking Duck.

About eleven courses into the dinner, Robin had a phone call from Harvey Weinstein, the president of Miramax. She clicked off the phone beaming. Harvey was at Martin Scorsese's apartment downtown and Scorsese had invited us all down for drinks after dinner. He wanted to meet Hayao Miyazaki and have the opportunity to discuss filmmaking with him. We translated the news for Miyazaki, and he told us to thank Harvey and Mr. Scorsese but no, he would have to decline the invitation. We relayed this to Robin and she looked concerned.

"Steve," she said, "M-a-r-t-i-n S-c-o-r-c-e-s-e has invited Mr. Miyazaki to his home. Martin Scorsese! Does he understand who this is? Does he understand what a BIG DEAL this is?"

"I think he does," I said. "I think he might just be tired. It's been a long day. End of a long trip."

"Martin Scorsese!" she said. "Please, ask him again. Please."

I conferred with Suzuki. Suzuki was ready to hop in a cab and go down and meet Scorsese. The other six people from Japan at the table were ready to hop in a cab and go and have drinks with Martin Scorsese. Suzuki turned to chat with Miyazaki.

"No, he's not interested," he said. "Tell her to please thank Harvey and Mr. Scorsese but we have to say no."

I relayed the message to Robin. The concern on her face deepened and she reddened slightly. After a few minutes she motioned for me to get up and speak with her off to the side.

"Can't you talk to him? Can't you get him to please do this? I don't want to lose my job."

I told her I would try and then I went back to the table and talked to Suzuki again. He said it was no use. "We would all like to go down there and meet Martin Scorsese but he just doesn't want to. Nothing we can do. You have to tell her to just forget it."

Reversible Destiny Pioneers

Robin wasn't fired and the next two full days of press interviews went off without any problems. Someone from Miramax had called and asked if there was anything in particular Miyazaki might like to do with a free night in New York.

During the entire production of *Princess Mononoke* Miyazaki had been followed around by the documentary film crew, which resulted in a nine-hour film available on videocassette and now possibly on DVD and Blu-ray. Miyazaki doesn't particularly like being on camera, but he had been cooperative if not enthusiastic until this one day in New York. He suddenly refused to be filmed and to be accompanied by an entourage and jumped at the chance to spend an evening in New York on his own.

Miyazaki arranged to meet an old friend, the architect Shusaku Arakawa, for dinner at his loft downtown in SoHo. Suzuki, concerned for Miyazaki's safety, took me aside and said "Alpert-san, you go with him to make sure he doesn't get into trouble. And take Fukuyama-san. He knows Arakawa too and Miya-san likes him. You can relax and enjoy yourself. It will all be in Japanese. No translation."

A Miramax van picked us up at 6 and we headed downtown.

When we got to the address Miyazaki had been given, just north of Houston Street (so technically not in SoHo), we discovered that the buzzers for the several units in the building were unlabeled and none of them seemed to work. Miyazaki went back out onto the street, cupped his hands over his mouth and bellowed Arakawa's name in the direction of an open window. A head popped out and dropped us down a key.

We walked up four flights of rickety wooden stairs and entered an enormous two-story loft. Shelves and shelves of books lined one of the walls all the way up, and there were ladders to help get them down when needed. There were paintings and architectural drawings on the walls, on easels, and leaning up against things. There were models of buildings and building complexes on tables and on the floor in various places. The space was a combination home and workplace.

Arakawa introduced us to his wife Madeline Gins, also an architect, and to his assistant Claudia (she pronounced it KLOW-di-ya), a lovely half-German, half-Indian young woman who was studying architecture at NYU. The conversation quickly turned personal, and since Arakawa and Miyazaki had not seen each other in a while they were rapidly catching up. I assumed the husband would do the translating for the wife, so Fukuyama and I decided to melt into the scenery and explore the artwork. The models of buildings were extremely interesting and extremely unusual. Claudia came over and explained them to us. Everything was removable so you could pull them apart and look inside.

There was a housing project shaped like a gigantic doughnut surrounded by trees and fields and with public recreation space at its center. There was a series of buildings with interlocking compact apartment units. The interiors were all built around sunken living areas with seating and storage space built in at the sides so as to eliminate the need for furniture other than a table and a bed. Some of the designs were oozing rubbery forms and rounded without edges. Others were all acute angles and nothing but edges. Each project had hand-done concept art to go with it, and Claudia pulled out the drawings and sketches for us to compare with the models. All extremely fascinating.

After a while Ms. Gins came over and took me aside.

"You speak Japanese don't you?"

I nodded cautiously.

"Good, then I want you to ask Mr. Miyazaki something. I want you to ask him if he is prepared to become a Reversible Destiny pioneer. Come on, let's go ask him now."

My brain was doing somersaults just thinking about trying to put that into Japanese. Although I knew what each of the words meant, I had no idea what they were up to as a three-some. Gins and Arakawa were known in New York as architects but also as painters and philosophers. The couple had explored ideas about mortality by creating buildings meant to stop aging and preclude death (not entirely successfully, unfortunately), and Reversible Destiny was a part of it. A part that I never understood well enough to translate. I had to explain that I couldn't do it.

When I tuned in to the conversation Miyazaki and Arakawa were having, I realized they were alternately talking about people they knew in common and deciding where to have dinner. After a very detailed discussion on food options and a few phone calls, we all walked down four flights of stairs and boarded the black Miramax mini-bus that was waiting for us outside. We directed the driver to a nearby newly opened Portuguese restaurant that the Gins/Arakawas had wanted to try, their favorite places being all booked up.

The restaurant was the only non-warehouse building on a deserted street near the Hudson River. The front of the restaurant, where there was outdoor seating, opened onto a cobblestone street. The electricity to the restaurant hadn't been completely hooked up yet, and as the evening darkened the wait staff came out with candles and flaming torches to distribute here and there. It was intensely romantic but a little hard to read the menu. The food we ordered was excellent, though by quarter to nine you could barely tell the roasted sea bass from the roasted quail (both delicious).

While the artists talked theory, Claudia was explaining to Fukuyama and me the difficulties of living the artistic life in Manhattan. She said that she and her boyfriend were sharing a small studio with another couple in lower Manhattan, something I was having trouble visualizing. Manhattan was apparently becoming too expensive for anyone just starting out to live there, the four outer boroughs were too far away from things, and if you wanted to live in town (Manhattan), you had to be flexible about your lifestyle.

As the dinner was winding down Miyazaki, who usually doesn't drink (much), ordered a glass of forty-year-old Port after dessert. When it came, and he had tried it, he had me call the waiter over and send it back.

"This is not forty-year-old Port," he said.

I always felt that sending back wine in a restaurant was something that took real confidence. Is the wine really bad, or are your taste buds just not up to the task?

First the waiter tasted the wine and then objected. When I insisted, the manager came over, tasted the wine, and objected. The wine had come from a decanter so they couldn't just show us the label to end the discussion.

"I beg your pardon sir, but this *is* the forty-year-old Port which you have ordered. We will take it back if you insist, but we feel that it would be highly unfair of you to ask us to do so."

I looked over at Miyazaki and he shook his head. "It is *not* the forty-year old Port," he said.

"I'm sorry," I said. "Please take it back."

After about fifteen minutes the owner of the restaurant came over with a stained and dirt-encrusted bottle of Port. He was full of apology. He said that he had looked into the matter and in fact a waiter had poured Port from a younger vintage into the decanter. He ordered up glasses of the real forty-year-old Port (poured from the actual bottle) for the whole table at no charge.

Later, as we eased through the big city's bright lights and sparse uptown traffic on the way back to the hotel, I couldn't stop wondering how Hayao Miyazaki, who almost never eats out in restaurants or drinks much, can tell if a bottle of Port isn't really forty years old.

You'll Never Work in This Town Again

The following day was a Sunday and a free day. Miyazaki had wanted to see what the area outside of New York was like, so we rented a van and I drove. We stopped at Barney Greengrass (the Sturgeon King) to pick up two sacks of typical New York sandwiches for the road—bagel and lox, bagel and sturgeon, bagel and whitefish, and pastrami on rye for anyone who didn't want smoked fish. There was also coleslaw and potato salad on the side with plastic forks and Dr. Brown's sodas to drink. Most of the group had wanted just doughnuts and coffee but I was committed to giving them a real New York experience.

Miyazaki's idea for the excursion had been that we would drive to a typical New England village, stop the car, sit at an outside table overlooking the village green, and sip locally brewed draft beer while enjoying the spectacular early autumn foliage. He was disappointed when I explained that to do this would involve a four-hour drive to Vermont.

My plan was to take the group to the Storm King Art Center, a spectacular outdoor garden of monumental modern sculpture. I knew that Miyazaki said he hated modern art, but I thought that even so he would be impressed by the setting and by seeing the large sculptures each perfectly placed throughout the institute's spacious grounds. Unfortunately I had misplaced the Storm King Art Center in my memory and confused it with another place on the wrong side of the Hudson River. By the time I realized that we needed to be up near West Point on the other side of the Hudson, we were lost in some obscure corner of Westchester County.

With the aid of a map purchased at a local gas station we

were back on track to return to New York City when I made a wrong turn and ended up in the small, picturesque town of Irvington. Immediately after entering the town Miyazaki shouted, "Stop!" His keen eye had spotted something that no one else had noticed. In the window of an antiques shop on the main street was an odd-looking, elaborate nineteenth-century wood and metal machine of some kind, the function of which none of us could even guess at. When we entered the shop we were told it was a factory time clock built by an old New York company that later merged with another company and became IBM.

When Miyazaki discovered that it was for sale and not very expensive, he bought it and had it shipped back to Japan. For a while he had it set up at Ghibli and made the animators punch in and out on it every day until they finally rebelled and refused. Now it sits on the second floor of the Ghibli Museum in Mitaka looking interesting, unusual, and completely unlabeled. Like everything else in the Ghibli Museum, the curious can try to figure out what it is, and the uncurious can pass on by, admiring it without a clue as to why it's there or what it's for.

We got back to the hotel with enough time for a short nap before meeting in the lobby to be driven in limousines the four blocks uptown to Lincoln Center for the premiere of *Princess Mononoke* at the New York Film Festival. Arriving at a film premiere in a minibus is apparently a no-no. Harvey Weinstein met us for the walk down the red carpet and officially welcomed Miyazaki and Suzuki in front of a lot of popping flashbulbs and bright TV klieg lights.

I escorted the NTV film crew inside and in spite of the $8,146.15 we had paid for them to be there, it did not go completely without a hitch. Security held us up and management had to be called. We barely got to our spot in the wings near the front in time to see Miyazaki being introduced on stage, again to thunderous applause. The documentarians and the NTV guys just did get their footage.

After the screening there was a party. Miramax had rented

out a Cuban restaurant nearby on Columbus Avenue called Calle Ocho. It was famous for its mojitos (rum, sugar, lime juice, sparkling water and mint—the secret being less in the list of ingredients and more in the quality of the ingredients and attention to the precise details of preparation). The mojitos came out by the pitcherful and were deserving of their reputation.

The party itself was low key and pleasant. A few members of the press had been invited. Some of the cast members came. Invited guests arrived inside after pushing in through a gaggle of paparazzi outside (ordered by Miramax for the occasion). People were being introduced to each other and quietly chatting away. Neil Gaiman was there and had his chance to speak with Miyazaki. The voice director Jack Fletcher, who had worked on several of the Ghibli films, flew in from San Francisco with his wife. There was a gentle, quiet buzz to the room.

Someone from Miramax caught up with me and told me that Harvey wanted to see me. I joined him and several Miramax executives at a table in the center of the restaurant. Miyazaki and Suzuki were enjoying a chat with Claire Danes at the next table. Harvey seemed to be slightly agitated and began in a low voice that grew louder as he made his point. "Look," he said, "we need to cut this film. I want to cut it down to 90 minutes." (The running time of the film was something like 135 minutes.) I told him I was sure the director would oppose cutting the film.

"Well you'd better fucking talk to him," he growled, "because if you don't get him to cut the fucking film you will NEVER WORK IN THIS FUCKING INDUSTRY AGAIN! DO YOU FUCKING UNDERSTAND ME?!! NEVER!! I WANT TO CUT THE FUCKING FILM!!"

I was about to remind him that I worked in Japan and didn't have any plans to work in New York or LA when Suzuki leaned over and asked why Harvey was yelling at me. I told him and then Miyazaki leaned over and asked Suzuki what was going on and he told him and then Miyazaki said, "I see. OK, let's go

Seiji Okuda, Toshio Suzuki, Haruyo Moriyoshi, and the author, exploring a neighborhood in Vienna with Hayao Miyazaki en route to the Berlin Film Festival.

Hayao Miyazaki, Dentsu's Fukuyama-san, and the author, viewing the Hundertwasser-designed power plant in Vienna.

Hayao Miyazaki and Roger Ebert, at the Toronto Film Festival (September 2002).

Hayao Miyazaki and the author, inside the nursery school he designed being built for the children of Studio Ghibli employees.

Hayao Miyazaki's "desk" at the Ghibli Museum, where he intended to do actual work once a week. He had to abandon the plan when the crowds that formed to watch him ended up obstructing other museumgoers.

A drawing Hayao Miyazaki did for the author upon his retirement from Studio Ghibli. It features the author's favorite Ghibli character, Nausicaä.

Neil Gaiman and the author, in front of Studio Ghibli in Higashi Koganei.

Toshio Suzuki and the author, after completing the voice recording (in Japanese) for the part of Castorp in Kaze Tachinu (The Wind Rises)*.*

スティーブン・アルパート
桜内篤子 訳

吾輩はガイジンである。
ジブリを世界に売った男

岩波書店

This book in Japanese. The title resists translation, but roughly: I Am a Gaijin. The Guy Who Sold Ghibli to the World. *The first part of the title is a reference to a classic Natsume Soseki novel. The second part was added by the Japanese publisher.*

Yasuyoshi Tokuma (center), at the company lunch on the way to the DirectTV satellite uplink station in Ibaraki.

Group photo of the Tokuma department heads at the DirecTV Japan satellite uplink station.

Toshio Suzuki, presenting the Oscar for Spirited Away *to Tokuma-shacho's grave in Aoyama.*

back to the hotel and discuss it. Let's just go now. Everyone else should stay, but the three of us are going."

Suzuki told him that maybe for appearance's sake it would be better to stay at the party for a while and then go back to the hotel, but Miyazaki said no, if he wants to cut the film we should go back and discuss it now. Suzuki tried again to dissuade him because of how it would look to the reporters present, but Miyazaki had made up his mind. Miyazaki had me tell Harvey that we would have an answer for him in the morning, and we arranged to meet him for breakfast at the hotel. Then Miyazaki, Suzuki, and I walked out of the restaurant and got into one of the waiting Miramax limousines and went back to the hotel. There was a kind of murmur that followed us as we left. I heard one of the Miramax PR people say, "Oh my God, what has Harvey done now?"

When I talked to people later it seemed that everyone believed that Harvey had insulted Miyazaki and that Miyazaki had been offended and stormed out of the restaurant. This in fact was not true. When we got back to Miyazaki's hotel room he was in a jovial mood, bemused and not at all angry and very relaxed. Both Miyazaki and Suzuki had huge comfortable suites in the hotel. Suzuki's had a wrap-around view of the Hudson River, and Miyazaki's had a sweeping view of Central Park. Suzuki used his suite as a gathering place for the group from Japan, while Miyazaki ignored most of the rooms' deluxe features and used his as a retreat. For this occasion we settled into the unused living room of Miyazaki's suite, emptied the room's mini-bar, and hunkered down on the floor in front of the big leather sofas to discuss Harvey's wish to cut *Princess Mononoke*.

Miyazaki said, "I really don't understand why he wants to cut the film. They say it has to be ninety minutes long, but which forty minutes of the film do they want me to cut? Is it any forty minutes just so long as it gets to ninety? You can't just make a film forty minutes shorter. Do they have any ideas about where to cut? Do they have reasons to cut certain places? You can have a discussion about a shorter film, but to just say it has to be ninety minutes is ridiculous. It's frustrating. I would like to hear exactly which parts he would like me to cut."

I explained that Harvey couldn't say, because he didn't know. From what I understood, if the film's director said OK, Harvey and some of his people would look at the film, decide where they might make cuts, and then test-screen the film to see how the cuts worked when the film was played. It would probably be a time-consuming process.

Miyazaki continued. "I don't know what to say to him. Alpert-san what do you think? Should we let him cut the film?"

In Japanese meetings it's common to let the junior people speak first so the more senior people can think about what everyone else has said before they give their opinion. I also realized that as the representative of the business side of things, it was my role to advocate letting Harvey cut the film so that it could possibly make more money on its US release. I would make my arguments for the business side and Miyazaki and Suzuki would absorb them and then reject them. This is not to say they didn't want to know what I really thought. I knew what I was expected to do, but somehow I couldn't do it.

If the film was actually cut for distribution in America, which I was fairly certain Miyazaki would never allow, I didn't want to be the guy who said it was OK. It also occurred to me that Miramax would take a lot of time and go to a very great deal of expense to make a ninety-minute version of the film. Though Ghibli would eventually reject it, we would end up having to pay for it. And then the cut version of the film would actually exist somewhere.

"I don't think you should let him cut the film," I said.

Miyazaki and Suzuki looked disappointed with my response. I knew I couldn't explain my reasoning. Instead I went on to say that if Miyazaki said yes, no one was going to give us any guarantees that the film would make more money if it were shorter. No one was providing any numbers as to how much more a ninety-minute film would earn.

If we shortened the film and it still didn't do well at the box office, how would we feel then? I didn't know what Miramax would do to change the film, but from the kinds of things I'd seen them try to do to change the English-dubbed version, I was sure we would regret letting them cut the film. I could tell I was clearly not giving Miyazaki and Suzuki the answer they wanted to hear. What I couldn't say (out loud) was, you guys aren't going to let Miramax release a cut version of the film anyway and letting them go ahead and try is not going to be a good thing for anyone.

I could see that Suzuki in particular was very disappointed with what I had said. There was no chance at all that Miyazaki would allow the film to be cut. He and Suzuki were just very curious about how exactly Miramax would propose to do it. They were probably looking for a way to find out without having to give final permission. Harvey didn't know exactly how he would cut the film, but he would have spent time, energy, and money figuring it out once he had been given the go ahead. And there was no way to find out how he would do it unless he got the green light to do it. I didn't want to open the door by even suggesting that we might say yes to Harvey.

Both men mumbled and grumbled a little and tried to give me a chance to change my position or add to it. When I didn't, the idea of letting Harvey cut the film trailed away as the conversation between Miyazaki and Suzuki drifted back to Japan and to anecdotes about people they knew and had worked with, as it does whenever they meet to discuss things. In a few minutes they were completely off topic for good.

Miramax had gained a reputation for bringing art films from abroad to the US and in some cases getting them both the respect and critical acclaim they deserved, along with very strong box office results. With films like *The English Patient* they had even crossed the line into Hollywood hit territory. And it was often said that the reason for the success had been Harvey's ability to strike a balance between art and commerce, and that making the films the appropriate length for the US audience (cutting them) had been one of the keys.

But possibly the headline successes had been the exceptions. Usually an artistic film is what it is, and at the end of the day it wasn't made in order to make a lot of money. Though it would be nice to make a lot of money, you're not doing yourself any favors by trying to make a film into something it's not.

I learned some very important lessons about marketing films from seeing how Toshio Suzuki marketed Ghibli's films in Japan. He is without doubt one of the most brilliant people to ever market anything, and he does it by not following the conventional wisdom. This is not easy to do when you're under pressure from all those around you wanting you to stick with what is safest. What Suzuki often does is start with the places of perceived weakness, those spots where other people tell him he has an insurmountable problem. Then he makes that problem into his strongest selling point.

The world is telling you that no one will watch an animated film where heads and arms are lopped off. You feature those scenes in the trailers and clips released to the public. The world is telling you no one wants to see another movie set in old Japan with samurai in it. You place that up front in your advertising. The world says the film's heroes can't be from Japan's most despised classes, and you don't hide from the fact that they are. You don't cave in to weaknesses or hide from them. You flip them so that they work in your favor. It's counterintuitive, and not many people are willing to risk trying it. Getting the people who put up the money to make the films to go along with this is no simple matter. And this makes making unconventional decisions all the harder.

Neither Miyazaki nor Suzuki ever had the slightest intention of letting Harvey cut their film. They had both heard all the arguments for a shorter film in Japan while they were making it and heard them made with more conviction and immediacy. Box office failure in Japan for their film could have ended Studio Ghibli. Instead, proving everyone wrong, in Japan *Princess Mononoke* went on to earn more money in its theatrical release alone than anyone had ever dreamed possible. Box office success or failure outside of Japan would not make or break Studio Ghibli. So what possible reason would Miyazaki or Suzuki have to agree to something in America that they had already fought against and won in Japan?

America means something special to most Japanese. To a Japanese baseball fan, a Japanese player making it in America's major leagues, the home of baseball, is the very pinnacle of success. Hollywood is the home of the motion picture industry, and for a filmmaker having a film do well there, though not the pinnacle of success, is big. The definition of success might be a big box office. Or it might be an avalanche of positive reviews from critics.

After our early exit from Harvey's party, Miyazaki and Suzuki were probably hoping for a more spirited discussion about the merits of a shortened version of *Princess Mononoke*. Sadly, on this night they didn't get it.

After a while Miyazaki told us to leave and that he would give Harvey his decision over breakfast in the morning.

The next morning over breakfast in the hotel's restaurant Harvey apologized to me for threatening me in public. He said he knew I understood that he was passionate about the films he distributed and that it was nothing personal. I did understand. Miyazaki then told him that he had made the decision to not allow any cuts to his film. He told Harvey that he wished someone would explain to him exactly how and where to cut the film, but that it really didn't matter because he had made up his mind not to allow the film to be cut. It was his personal decision and it was final.

Harvey said he understood and respected the decision and that the topic would never be raised again. We ordered breakfast and that was that. Later that day everyone boarded the van to JFK and flew back to Tokyo.

7

~~~~~~~~~~~~~~~~~~~~~

Asia

Doing Business in Korea, Taiwan, and China

Non-Asians often find it difficult when they first begin doing business in Asia. Asians have probably been engaged in commerce for considerably longer, culturally and historically speaking, than Westerners, and for that and other reasons their approach to business dealings is more sophisticated and more nuanced. If the Western version of doing business is like solving, say, a difficult *New York Times* Saturday crossword puzzle, the Asian version of doing business is like solving a diagramless crossword puzzle.

Although things have changed and continue to change, generally speaking the rules of doing business are different in Asia. For example, there is no particular virtue associated with telling the truth or any expectation that the parties will always do so. The assumption is that everyone lies. Contracts are mostly ignored, and the parties are rarely embarrassed to have it pointed out to them that they have failed to keep their word. It is assumed that everyone will do exactly and only what is in their own individual best interest, regardless of what they might previously have agreed to, and that therefore the best and only relevant thing to always be aware of is what everyone's real interests are.

This is not to say that there are not rules or functional business norms. It's just that it takes a bit of adjustment on the part of the inexperienced. In Asia you don't hear anyone say, "you will be hearing from my lawyer" unless they are making a joke or being ironic.

Ghibli's original deal with Disney for the distribution of its films had been for the world excluding Asia. Yasuyoshi Tokuma had thought it would be unthinkable to ask Disney to distribute Ghibli's films in Asia. In his view, a Japanese company should not shame itself by asking an American company to handle its Asian business.

Mr. Tokuma believed that if anything, *he* should be advising Disney on Disney's business in Asia. At the time, Ghibli's business in Asia was not going all that well. Korea, Taiwan, and Hong Kong were potentially large markets for Ghibli films. *My Neighbor Totoro* was widely reported to be the most popular film of all time in Taiwan, though Ghibli's licensee there had long been reporting sales close to zero. Animated Japanese films were banned in Korea. Pirated versions of all Ghibli titles were widely available in Hong Kong and China for less than the price of a small order of fries at MacDonald's.

Mr. Tokuma had connections in China's film industry and had produced some films by Chinese directors. His film company Toko Tokuma had put a lot of money into one Chinese film, *The Opium War* directed by Xie Jin. It was an expensive production for a Chinese film at the time. Tokuma's contribution included paying for and having the post-production work done in Japan. In exchange, Tokuma was granted the distribution rights to the finished film in Asia.

The film, an epic historical drama, was critical of the British for their colonial attitudes and activities in China (including the promotion of opium addiction). The Chinese government had been cool to the project until it realized that the release of this film could be perfectly timed with the 1997 handover of Hong Kong from Britain to China. Its theme was perfect for the event. When the Chinese further realized how bad it would look for the film to have a Japanese producer and to be released by a Japanese distributor, they simply reneged on the deal, thanked Mr. Tokuma for his help on the film, and cut him out without repaying his investment.

Most of Ghibli's Asian distributors failed to follow the contracts they had agreed to, including the payment of royalties. The genial people in each country who had negotiated the distribution contracts, fluent speakers of either Japanese or English, soon left their companies once the contracts were signed. Their replacements spoke only Chinese. Working with Disney to expand distribution in the Asian territories would, in contrast, have been comparatively straightforward and stress-free. Disney was well positioned to help Ghibli fight piracy and government bans. I knew the people who ran the businesses there. The Disney subsidiaries in Asia were seeking Ghibli's business aggressively. But Mr. Tokuma had his principles, and we resisted Disney's offers to distribute in Asia. Instead, I traveled to Korea, Hong Kong, Mainland China, and Taiwan seeking better partners and trying to get rid of the old ones.

Korea

Our distributor in Korea was not the problem in that country. The Korean government had been clinging to a ban on Japanese films. The Korean company that had the rights to distribute Ghibli films in Korea worked closely with us to overturn their government's ban, particularly as it applied to Japanese animated films. This company had worked with Ghibli for many years, and there were never any issues of trust with them, possibly in part because they were prevented by law from actually distributing the films. But when the box office and critical success of *Princess Mononoke* became big news everywhere else, we hoped we might gain an exception for the film in Korea. We were sure that many people there wanted to see the film, and it seemed that the Korean government might relent.

Korea had once been occupied by the Japanese military, and

bad feelings from the past still lingered in the minds of older Koreans (government officials). Younger Koreans seemed to have less of a problem and were beginning to enthusiastically embrace things Japanese. The Korean government feared that Japanese entertainment might dominate and unduly influence the minds of younger Koreans, in much the same way that the French government worried that Hollywood would overly influence the youth of France. The Koreans and the French also had their own animation industry to protect from foreign competition. For the release of *Princess Mononoke* the Korean government and its regulators could not be budged.

On my first visit to Korea on behalf of Studio Ghibli I discovered that the demo film being used on every single TV screen in every giant electronics shop in downtown Seoul was a pirated copy of *Princess Mononoke*. Anyone could effortlessly purchase a pirated copy of the film from a vendor selling videos out of the trunk of his car in any part of the city. Some video stores openly sold pirated copies. But *Princess Mononoke* was banned in Korea, and the Korean government was vigorous in its efforts to keep it out of movie theaters, off TV, and from being legitimately sold in stores. When it came to enforcing its own rules on piracy and helping our distributor eliminate even the most blatant transgressions, the Korean government was not interested.

Piracy can tell you a lot about the market for your films. Yes, it robs you of the legitimate revenue you could have earned, but if your film is so attractive to the pirates that they are willing to go to all the time, effort, and expense of reproducing it, and then designing nice Korean artwork for the cover in order to sell it, and bear the financial risk of manufacturing hundreds of thousands of copies of it, then you know for sure that you have a hit on your hands. If the pirates aren't interested or willing to invest in large-scale distribution, then your film might be a flop. You wish the government would enforce its antipiracy laws. But at least your business starts with an established fan base should the ban be lifted and the laws enforced.

On trips to Seoul I visited entire unauthorized Ghibli stores in prominent locations, all selling nothing but fake or pirated Ghibli products. Large electronics and music stores had Ghibli corners selling an array of fake Ghibli goods. On a plane from Tokyo to Seoul, Toshio Suzuki, the producer of all of Ghibli's films, was recognized by many of the young Koreans on the flight and was approached to sign copies of Ghibli art books. When we visited the fake Ghibli stores Suzuki was recognized and asked to sign books that people had bought there. In each case Suzuki obligingly (gleefully) signed, even though I begged him to please not sign pirated copies of our books. But it was an eye-opener to discover that even though none of Ghibli's films were allowed to be shown in Korea, so many people knew them well enough to recognize Suzuki.

In January of 1999 we finally got permission to screen *Pom Poko* and *Porco Rosso* at the Pusan (now Busan) International Animation Festival. Mikiko Takeda, Ghibli's point person for the Korean market, and I were invited to Busan to accompany the films, and I was asked to represent Ghibli and stand up before the screening of *Porco Rosso* to introduce the film to the audience. We understood that this was not a huge breakthrough, but it was at least a tiny opening that might be the beginning of something larger. It was important for us to cooperate and to respect whatever concessions we were offered.

Ghibli films continued to be screened at film festivals and at special events in Korea, always to sold-out audiences. The demand to see the films increased, and eventually the government dropped some of its rules banning new animation from Japan. With normal market conditions more or less restored, Korea became one of the biggest international markets for Ghibli films, and the presence of legitimate Ghibli products in Korea diminished the availability (somewhat) of pirates and fakes. Progress.

Taiwan

My Neighbor Totoro was widely reported to be the most popular animated film of all time in Taiwan. You could buy a copy of the film on video just about anywhere: in department stores, bookstores, drugstores, and night markets or from street vendors. Even so, Ghibli's licensee there had been reporting sales close to zero pretty much from the time the license was first granted. I was determined to find a better distributor.

As a student I had lived in Taiwan for a year and always enjoyed going back to visit. My friends at Disney there understood why we didn't let them distribute Ghibli's films in Taiwan, and they were more than happy to share the information they had on our current distributor. They also generously introduced us to other local distributors. The more reputable ones.

From my own experience at Disney I knew that many local Taiwanese entertainment companies engaged in various forms of piracy even as they carried out some amount of legitimate business. They would report the legitimate sales to the foreign companies with whom they had signed contracts, but not the much larger number of unauthorized sales, which included sales to companies in China, Hong Kong, and Thailand. Some made little or no effort to hide the fact that they were cheating you. If you wanted a reputable partner that would actually honor the contracts they signed, you had very few options. Few options meant that your partner would also be the partner of every other major American and European entertainment company, and that the bigger budget (Hollywood) films would be getting most of the attention.

The company we were introduced to that seemed most promising was headed up by a Chinese man I will call Bill. Bill had been an engineer as a young man and invented a process essential in the creation of VHS videos. He received a small royalty for every single videocassette sold anywhere in the world, except probably in China, Hong Kong, and Taiwan, where patents and copyrights were ignored. With his considerable fortune he had, among other things, built entertainment companies that both produced films and distributed the films of others. He was one of the few honest players in the market, and many of the major studios used his companies.

Bill had two distribution companies. One was run by a woman whom people usually identified as his mistress. The other was run by a younger (male) protégé. Though Bill owned both, the two companies competed with each other.

I first met Bill at a restaurant near Lung Shan Sze, a small temple near Snake Alley in Taipei. Snake Alley had been Taipei's main red-light district until the 1990s when prostitution was made illegal. In actuality, prostitution had been illegal all along, but in the 1990s it was made illegal illegal, a distinction that may only be clear to legal scholars and other connoisseurs of the way laws are enforced in China.

The restaurant that Bill had invited me to for dinner had formerly been a brothel. I have to admit that I have never been to an actual brothel, so I don't know what a real one looks like, and I would guess that neither did whoever designed this one. There were marble statues of naked women, oil paintings of mostly naked women on the walls, red velvet wallpaper, and crystal chandeliers. The furniture was modeled on someone's idea of eighteenth-century France. The food was half Chinese and pretty good, and half Western and terrible. Bill brought the wine with him. One of the first things he did when he came into money, he said, was to learn about fine wine. His doctors had told him that his passion for single-malt scotch whiskey was ruining his health, so he decided drinking wine would be better. When he came across a wine that he liked, he bought large quantities of it and treated his friends to it at dinner.

Our first meeting with Bill had just been a get-to-know-you. At our second dinner meeting with Bill we had a private room in a restaurant that was all done up in chrome, glass, and black leather. Seated at an enormous round table, we could see but not hear our more distant tablemates; we could only from time to time shout monosyllabic pleasantries at them and transmit good will and bonhomie by smiles and body language. I was seated between Bill and his mistress at dinner. Not only was there actually a mistress, but Bill introduced her as his mistress and as the president of one of his companies. I wasn't sure that mistresses liked to be identified in public, but apparently this was not an issue. The mistress lived with Bill and traveled with Bill on vacation. The wife had her own house somewhere else. It wasn't a secret.

Ghibli eventually signed with the company Bill owned that was not run by the mistress. It proved to be a lesson in the importance of heeding the call of common sense. Within six months the company we signed with was absorbed by the one run by the mistress and we were out on the street again looking for a new distributor. But by that time Mr. Tokuma had died, and we were free to hand the business over to Disney Taiwan, where it has blossomed and flourished ever since.

The People's Republic of China

Having Disney distribute Ghibli's films in Taiwan came with an additional bonus. At the time Disney's Taiwan office also handled their parent company's business in China. Disney's senior executives in LA had been trying to figure out how to get their China business off the ground. They were tortured by the thought that if you could get everyone in China to pay a mere penny (1¢) for a Disney something-or-other, you would have just made $13.5 million. It was an opportunity they were missing. They were looking for answers.

An odd thing was happening between China and Taiwan in the 1990s. Taiwanese businessmen and businesswomen were moving to China to help run businesses on the mainland. Relations between the People's Republic of China (Mainland China) and the Republic of China (Taiwan) were not particularly good. To fly from China to Taiwan or from Taiwan to China you had to go through Hong Kong. There were no direct flights. It was illegal in China for a Taiwanese to live there. It was illegal in

Taiwan for any of its citizens to visit China. And yet over half a million Taiwanese lived and worked openly just outside of Shanghai.

One of China's biggest problems as it was ramping up its economy was that it lacked people who knew how to run a business. There were no trained, experienced, or savvy middle managers who knew how to make an enterprise actually run. State-run enterprises that had been used to suckling at the teat of the Chinese state were said to be collapsing right and left.

Taiwan's biggest problems included a lack of space for a growing population and a vast surplus of immensely talented, highly educated, highly capable businesspeople. Despite the laws in both countries, some Taiwanese nationals began moving to Shanghai to manage Chinese companies and to start making them work. Suddenly there were people in China you could talk to and actually do business with. A curious Western businessman might ask if these Taiwanese were ever arrested and deported from China. Of course not, was always the reply. When they went home to Taiwan for Chinese New Year were they arrested there? No, was the reply. Why would they be?

The licensee that Disney was using in China for its films was a joint venture between a Chinese company and a Singaporean company. Foreign companies were not allowed to operate without a Chinese joint venture partner approved by the Chinese government. As a practical matter, foreign companies would never have been able to negotiate the net of government regulations and restrictions, written and unwritten, without a well-connected Chinese partner.

The Singapore partner was owned by turbaned Sikhs with Ph.D. degrees in advanced electronics. Their main business was the manufacture of audio/video products such as high-end TV sets, stereo systems, and DVD players. They also made refrigerators. The distribution of movies on VHS, DVD, and VCD was only a sideline for the Singapore company. The Chinese partner was a small company with few employees and no business operations. Its owner was the then deputy minister of culture. The

Ministry of Culture was the government agency that decided, among other things, which movies would be allowed to play in China and which Chinese companies would be allowed to duplicate movies on VHS, DVD, or VCD (a cheap, low-quality technology that was then very popular in China).

China was changing so rapidly in those days that if you hadn't been back in over a month your information was already out of date. Mikiko Takeda, who worked with me at Ghibli, and I visited our Chinese distributor only once. The company, which I'll call C-T, was headquartered in Shanghai where its operating division was located. They had a smaller office in Beijing to handle relations with government regulators.

At C-T headquarters in Shanghai the engineers told us about their Chinese manufacturing operations. Their hottest product was a DVD/VCD/audio-CD player that delivered extremely high-quality, state-of-the-art audio and video for all new disc formats including HD and was backward compatible with every known type of previous disc technology. This machine sold for about fifty US dollars at the manufacturer's wholesale price. A major Japanese electronics company had contracted to buy C-T's entire production for the purpose of keeping it from competing with the Japanese company's own more expensive machines in Japan. The Japanese company sold the C-T machines in Japan as an off-label brand for about US$500. The C-T managers offered to give both Mikiko and me one of the machines to take back to Japan, but we didn't think we could get them through customs.

One of the C-T company's Taiwanese sales managers took us on a tour of video shops in greater Shanghai. In several of the bigger ones, about three or four times as large as an average American Blockbuster store used to be (or roughly the size of a big Tsutaya store in Tokyo), there were Ghibli sections that ran half the length of the store. There were multiple versions of each Ghibli title featuring Chinese dubbed and subtitled versions. The artwork on their covers ranged from exact copies of the Japanese versions to lurid scenes of passionate lovers in hot embrace (scenes that can be found nowhere in any Ghibli film). None of the versions for sale in any of the stores were legitimate copies of the films issued by C-T.

The C-T sales manager, herself a former Disney Taiwan employee, explained that the only way to combat piracy was to build on what the pirates had already done and try to stay ahead of them on the technology curve. As films became available in new formats, the goal was to own the new formats. It was possible to capture the high end of the market where product was sold in stores known to handle legitimate merchandise, such as department stores and name-brand electronics stores. Marketing and advertising stressed the virtues of owning the real thing.

For lunch we were taken to a pirated version of a famous Taiwanese restaurant, Din Tai Fung. Din Tai Fung is a multi-story dumpling restaurant in Taipei that for years has had people queuing up in long lines outside its doors for the privilege of gorging on the dumplings, noodles, and other dishes for which it is duly famous. They have opened official outposts of the restaurants in many countries, but the Shanghai branch was not one of them.

After Shanghai we moved on to Beijing to see the Chinese-run side of C-T's operations. Beijing is sootier and less vibrant than Shanghai. And it's much colder. The severity of the air pollution is immediately obvious to anyone making use of their lungs.

In Beijing we were not invited to the C-T office, but we were shown a few video stores that were very much like the ones we saw in Shanghai. We also had a chance to wander around a giant state-run bookstore on a wide main street near Tiananmen Square. On our first day in Beijing we had Peking Duck for lunch in a very famous and expensive restaurant where all the other guests were high-ranking soldiers in dress uniform. And for dinner we were taken to the Summer Palace on the outskirts of central Beijing.

The Summer Palace once belonged to the emperor of China

but is now a huge park of landscaped gardens and lakes and a handful of nicely preserved imperial buildings. The site had been an imperial palace since the mid-1100s, but the current incarnation of gardens and buildings date from the Qianlong era in the mid-1700s. The grounds and the lakes and some of the buildings are open to the general public. Our dinner took place in one of the private buildings not open to the general public. Our host for the dinner, Mr. W, was the president of the Chinese half of C-T, the joint venture distribution company, and also China's vice-minister of culture.

We were driven out to the park after dark, so we didn't see much of the lakes or gardens. It was after closing time, so the park was quiet and almost completely deserted. As we were ushered into the closed imperial compound through a secret back door, the icy wind that swept across the vast blackness of the nearest of the lakes made a ghostly whistling sound.

We passed through a series of dark, narrow passageways and emerged into a small courtyard in front of what had been a private temple for the Chinese imperial family. As we stood there, a group of dancers in red silk costumes, faces painted and wearing various types of feathered headdress, filed into the courtyard for a performance of Qing Dynasty dance and music. After that we were shown into a small room with a round table in the middle. It was very cold in Beijing that evening, but the room had been heated to the point where we could probably have baked cookies on the floor.

An unsmiling Mr. W was seated at what could have been seen as the head of the table. Without getting up from his seat, he unsmilingly welcomed us as we came in. Mr. W spoke no English, we were told, and he addressed all his comments to our escort from Disney, who translated for us. When I attempted to thank him in Chinese for his hospitality he ignored me and continued to speak only to our guide from Disney.

Waitresses dressed in Qing Dynasty costume came in and began to serve the meal one dish at a time. As they served they explained each dish. We had been presented with a printed copy of the evening's menu and were told that the meal duplicated one recorded in the imperial archives that had been served to the Qianlong Emperor himself in this very room. There was snapping turtle soup, braised and boiled beef sinew and sea cucumber stew, hot and spicy camel hump, sautéed deer liver with bamboo shoots, chunks of rabbit meat cooked with lotus root and carrot, shrimp heads in hot and sour sauce, fried duck gizzards with scallions, and steamed bread made from chestnut, corn, and wheat flour.

On our last night in Shanghai, Mikiko wanted to buy silk scarves as presents for people back in our office in Tokyo. She needed seven. The hotel's gift shop had only five. The woman in the gift shop offered to have two more made for her. What colors did she want? The factory that made them was only a drive of an hour or so out of town. Mikiko thanked her but said that we were leaving the hotel the next morning at 6 am. The woman said no problem; someone would meet her at the front desk when she checked out in the morning. And so someone did. The scarves had cost about $2 each. We couldn't get over the fact that someone had thought it worth their while to manufacture two scarves and make the round-trip drive into the city before dawn to earn whatever the profit margin is on $4.

Piracy of movies in China eventually did decline markedly. What ended up killing it off was technology. When the technology of home entertainment moved from physical media to digital streaming it bumped into an area of mandatory Chinese government oversight and control. Once the government realized it could earn money while increasing control over content, entertainment product piracy began to die, almost overnight.

Not that it made so very much difference to the foreign entertainment companies looking to increase profits in the world's largest market. As of my last visit to China access continued to be limited. The Disney dream of collecting 1¢ from every consumer in China still remains elusive.

8

<hr>

Spirited Away

Blow Not Thine Own Horn

Toward the end of 2001, Hayao Miyazaki received the following question from a journalist: "*Sen to Chihiro no Kamikakushi* (*Spirited Away*) is the film industry's biggest success in the history of Japan. It is also the only non-American movie which made more than $200 million of box office worldwide. Are you proud of that?"

Hayao Miyazaki responded: "Whether a film becomes a success or a failure, I always try to take the results in stride. I always feel pleased when I hear that the revenue surpasses the production cost, and we can make another film."

I'm a fan of Japanese sumo wrestling. For years I have watched sports journalists from Japanese national broadcaster NHK interview *rikishi* (wrestlers) who have just done something spectacular: a *yokozuna* (Grand Champion) who has just set a new record for number of wins; a junior wrestler who has just toppled a legendary *yokozuna* twice his size. No matter how spectacular his record or how awesome his achievement, the man will suck air for a bit, tilt his head from side to side, look down at his toes, and mumble, "I always just try to do my best." Always the same. Never any variation.

What has always puzzled me is that the NHK interviewers

know exactly what the response is going to be. They seem to take a kind of pleasure in trying to get a different response while knowing that the person being interviewed will only say exactly what he was expected to say, and what we knew all along he would say. To a non-Japanese person the modesty of the response may ring false (or it may actually be false), but that's not the point. In the Western ideal of journalism the reporter is hoping to deliver some new, fresh, special, unique, or individual insight. In Japan, it seems to be about confirmation that things are still as they always have been and will continue to be. You ask the obvious question. You still get the obvious answer. Everyone is happy.

Foreign journalists may not realize that a question such as the one above can have only the answer that Miyazaki gave. Like sumo wrestlers and baseball players, Japanese movie directors are required to answer modestly, and so they do. I always tried to keep this in mind when representing Mr. Miyazaki outside of Japan.

Hayao Miyazaki has always been famously averse to receiving awards in person. Over the course of his career he has won more than a few, and *Spirited Away* accounts for many of them. *Spirited Away* received over fifty nominations internationally, resulting in thirty-six major film awards, including Best Picture at the 25th Japan Academy Awards, the Golden Bear at the 52nd Berlin International Film Festival, and an Oscar for Best Animated Feature at the 75th Academy Awards in Hollywood.

When *Spirited Away* was setting all of its records and garnering all of its awards, I was deputized to travel overseas to accept the non-Japanese ones, to make the acceptance speeches on Mr. Miyazaki's behalf, and sometimes to answer questions from the press. It was all the studio could do to get Miyazaki to take interviews in Japan, but when it came to foreign interviews he would almost always refuse.

For any artist, including filmmakers, there is no higher praise than praise from colleagues, peers, and those whose profession it is to assess the quality of their art. It's not that

Hayao Miyazaki doesn't appreciate the honor of being chosen to receive an award. He just doesn't like to stand up in person and be praised. He can be coaxed into doing it if there is a good reason for it, or if he thinks he can't escape from doing it. Also, like many people who are very good at what they do, he really (really) hates to lose, and if the award ceremony to which he is invited involves sitting in public with the other nominees to see who won, he is unlikely to attend.

Before 2002 no animated feature film had been allowed in competition at the Berlin International Film Festival. The head of Ghibli's European distribution company, Vincent Maraval, suggested that the time might be right for that to change. *Spirited Away* might be the right film to convince the selection committee to let an animated film enter the competition for the festival's highest award, the Golden Bear. It might be time to let an animated film compete against live-action films for the award for the best feature film. When Miyazaki's *Princess Mononoke* had been screened out of competition at the Berlin Film Festival several years earlier it had received very favorable reviews.

I mentioned Maraval's suggestion to the film's producer, Toshio Suzuki, and he told me to go ahead and ask Miyazaki myself, usually a sure sign that he knew already the answer would be no. If a yes were possible, Suzuki would have gone with me to ask. Suzuki also reminded me that if the film were entered, and it lost, he would have to fire me, another reason why I was sent in alone to ask. At the time I didn't realize that he wasn't kidding.

For *Spirited Away* just to be allowed in competition at Berlin would be a huge honor. It would provide Maraval's company with a big boost for the film's distribution in Europe. Europeans take major film festival awards seriously. No one can predict if a particular film will actually win the highest award. There are always several excellent and exciting films in competition at a major film festival.

The Ghibli Museum in Mitaka, Tokyo, had just opened, and

Miyazaki, who usually took off for the mountains to recuperate after completing a film, had put off his well-deserved vacation to stay and help with running the museum. One of its exhibits was a kind of reproduction of the room containing the desk where Miyazaki works to develop his ideas for his next films. Originally Miyazaki's idea had been that he would sit at this desk once a week, and the museum's visitors would actually see him at work as a part of the exhibit.

That never really worked out. Whenever Miyazaki was at his desk, a wall of spectators would form. People would just stand there motionless with their mouths open staring at him. He tried shooing them away and pleading with them to keep moving and allow more people to come in, but to no avail. So he moved to a glass-walled conference room down the hall. On the day that Mikiko Takeda, who worked with me in the International Division, and I visited Miyazaki to ask about Berlin, visitors to the museum had discovered Miyazaki in his glass-fronted conference room and formed a living wall of open-mouthed, awestruck adoration that was again beginning to hinder the flow of traffic.

Mikiko tried to convince me that if *Spirited Away* failed to win the Golden Bear I really would be fired. She also wanted me to understand that though she was helping me persuade Miyazaki, she wasn't planning to share in the consequences if the film didn't win the Golden Bear. Mikiko is a genius at translating my Japanese into the kind of Japanese that's necessary to convince someone of something, and I knew I wasn't going to get Miyazaki's approval without her.

While we were explaining the situation to Miyazaki some of the museum's staff were putting up screens so that the crowd outside wouldn't be able to see into the conference room and, hopefully, would disperse. It wasn't working. Miyazaki was annoyed and in a bad mood. He listened to our request and with little further discussion said, OK, enter the film if that's what you want to do, but I'm not going, so don't even ask.

I checked with Maraval and he said the director's presence

would not only be expected but, if he didn't come in person, the jury might feel slighted and the film's chances of actually winning the highest award would be greatly reduced.

"So you think the film could actually win?" I asked.

"Yes," he said, "I think it can. If Miyazaki won't go at least the producer should go."

I went back and reported this to Suzuki and he agreed to go to Berlin to represent the film.

The Golden Bear

Berlin that February was very cold. It was snowing. When Suzuki, Takeda, and I checked into our hotel, we found its entire ground floor overcrowded with people connected to the Berlin Film Festival. The hotel and the festival were located in Potsdamer Platz, very near to where the Berlin Wall used to divide the city into East and West Berlin. Potsdamer Platz was brand new and full of shiny glass and steel buildings, including SONY's German headquarters, with almost nothing else around the square but empty land. Across from a large park that bordered the square was Germany's parliament (Bundestag). On another side a large concert hall. There were very few stores, shops, or restaurants nearby. All the space just outside the square was still waiting for reunification and economic revival to catch up. The glittering steel and glass mall attached to the SONY building was mostly unoccupied.

Everything connected to the film festival took place in the vicinity of the hotel. The hotel lobby was like a crowded train station at rush hour. There were people sitting or standing on every available surface, most with drinks or cell phones in their hands, or both. After the twenty-hour trip from Japan that had involved a plane change and layover in Amsterdam's airport, negotiating the check-in process against a wall of noise was not easy.

As I was checking in, an argument broke out next to me when the front desk manager refused to cancel a room free of charge. A British couple in leather jackets wanted to move to another hotel because they found their room "intolerable." If the *British* people in the hotel are complaining, you know you have a problem. When I got upstairs I thought I began to understand what the fuss might be about.

The design of the room was exceptionally sleek and elegant. Very angular and swooping. All of the stuff in the room you would actually need to use was either hidden away or disguised. Nearly everything in the room was black. It wasn't easy to distinguish things like light switches or plugs from the rest of the wall. Once you found a switch you had to spend time figuring out what it controlled. There were no drawers at all so I had to keep my clothes in the suitcase. The internet connection, electric sockets, and phone plug were so cleverly hidden in a fold-up panel in the drawerless desk that I had to call down to the front desk to get someone to come up and show me.

The next day there was a press screening of *Spirited Away.* Suzuki took questions from the press and then did interviews over the course of the next two days. Mikiko translated. We sat in on a press conference for the film *The Royal Tenenbaums* and listened to director Wes Anderson and actor Owen Wilson banter with reporters. *The Royal Tenenbaums* was also in competition that year, and Disney was the film's distributor. We had worried that Disney would be upset that Ghibli's film was competing against theirs, but our concern turned out to be unfounded. Disney's head of international distribution, Mark Zoradi, assured me that *Spirited Away* had no chance whatsoever of winning anything. As everyone knew, an animated film could never win.

Zoradi also graciously invited Suzuki, Mikiko, and me to a promotional event for *The Royal Tenenbaums*, a party held at night in another part of town. To promote *The Royal Tenenbaums*, Disney had rented an entire town house and turned it into a replica of the set of their film. When we arrived, the entire building was swarming with partygoers. There were bright lights, music, food, and drink. I never quite understood how spending large sums of money on events like this promoted ticket sales for a movie, but then our movies never made as much money (outside of Japan) as the ones with the big events, so there was probably something there I was missing.

Zoradi introduced me to Anderson and Wilson, who were sitting in an upstairs corner separated from the partygoers by a thick purple velvet rope and a husky security guard. They were eating from a plate of mini-cheeseburgers and looking glum. As I was being introduced, a woman in her forties scaled the staircase wall and tried to climb over the banister railings to get to Anderson but was intercepted by a security guard and removed.

"Organizer of a very small film festival in Los Angeles," Zoradi dryly observed. "There's always one or two. What the guards are here for."

On our last day of press interviews for *Spirited Away*, Suzuki and Takeda and I were having coffee in one of the break rooms discussing our plans for returning to Tokyo when we were joined by Phil Symes, the press agent for Wild Bunch, our European distributor. Phil wanted to know if the film won the Golden Bear would Miyazaki fly in to Berlin, and if not, who would go up on stage to receive it. He was adamant that if the film won, someone would have to be there. It was Tuesday. We were scheduled to fly back to Japan the next day. I asked when we would know if the film might win something. He said Friday. Someone has to stay at least until Friday. If the film wins, the awards ceremony is Sunday.

"But they don't announce the winners in advance, do they?" I asked.

"No," Phil said, "but they leak the names of the winners to the press agents so they can be sure someone from the film attends the awards ceremony. And they release them to the press with the understanding that they won't publish until the awards are officially announced. That way the ones that need to cover it can be here to do it, and the others can get a head start on their articles. I'll get the word by Friday. They don't want to be embarrassed by no-shows."

"If we do win, couldn't they just mail us the award?" I asked.

"Absolutely not," Phil said. "Someone *must* be here to accept it. Someone connected with the film."

Suzuki and Takeda were looking at me.

"It should be Suzuki-san," I said. "He's the film's producer."

Suzuki shook his head. "I can't be away from Japan any longer," he said. "I have too much work to do."

"Then Mikiko," I said. "At least she's Japanese."

"Not senior enough. And your English is better."

Since I had been reassured by Mark Zoradi that the film would not win, I thought about it and decided that I could manage another two days in Berlin. But I wasn't sure about another four.

"Could the film win?" I asked Phil.

"The buzz is that it might," he said.

We were in Europe, and from any place in Europe it can be relatively quick and easy to fly to any other place in Europe. It occurred to me that I could leave for a few days and go somewhere else. I asked Suzuki if there was anything else he wanted me to do in Europe while I was here. He said, "As a matter of fact yes, there is one thing. I want you to go to Aardman Animation and personally invite Nick Park to attend a symposium on animation in Tokyo."

Suzuki is a huge fan of *Wallace and Gromit* and so am I. I did not need to be asked twice. Several of Ghibli's films were being shown in a retrospective at London's Barbican Center, and I knew the head of the center's film department. I called him and asked if he knew anyone at Aardman. I said I wanted to visit that Friday, and he said of course he did know people there and that he would call and see if it could be arranged. Phil had someone take care of the flight arrangements and the hotels in London and then Berlin again, in case I had to fly back.

I spent Wednesday at the film market attached to the film festival and on Thursday I flew to London. On Friday I took an early train from Paddington Station to Bristol, the home of Aardman Animations. I was surprised when the cab driver who took me to the studio from the station had never heard of Aardman, something probably impossible now. But I did get some local history on the twenty-minute ride.

The city's River Avon had been a dumping ground for chemical waste for years but had been cleaned up recently. Bristol was heavily bombed during WWII because of its industry, so there was a lot of empty space for new buildings. The area around the docks along the estuary that flows out toward the Bristol Channel was undergoing a revival, and its gutted factories and warehouses were attracting businesses with lots of space for little money. Even artists were beginning to move in. There was a big university at the other end of town. And a very large cathedral on a hill overlooking the city.

Security at the Aardman reception area was far more lax then than it has since become. The receptionist asked me who I was there to see, I told her, and she had me go on in to find him. To the right of the entrance was a small bathroom whose open door revealed a flea-market-antique mirror and lamp, a handsome oak toilet seat, and lace curtains adorning a fake window. A royal blue velvet rope across the door barred access. When I asked about it I was told that Queen Elizabeth had scheduled a visit to the studio and that the studio's directors had speculated that if the queen had to use the loo, the one used by the staff would probably not do. So they built one for her. The visit was canceled at the last minute, but they kept the queen's WC as a memento of the almost visit.

Kieran Argo, then Aardman's head of promotional events, showed me around the studio. What they do at Aardman is called claymation. Stop-motion animation using clay figures. Except that if you use the word "clay" you are likely to be in for a lengthy lecture. The stuff used by Aardman is called Plasticine. The Aardman characters are made of Plasticine and not clay, and there is a lot of Plasticine-not-clay modeling going on there. Really good, skillful Plasticine modeling.

I was amazed to see that everything else that goes into a scene in an Aardman film is manufactured right there in the

studio. Every single thing is made right there in perfect miniature reproduction. I was shown the sets where the photogra-
phy takes place and watched part of an episode of *Wallace and
Gromit* being made. Seeing the sets where the action is filmed
was a thing of wonder. It was like a day spent at the North Pole
watching Santa's elves at work, except real. The process of making an animated film by moving the characters bit-by-tiny-bit
and individually photographing each move requires nerves of
steel and the patience of Job.

I was introduced to Peter Lord, one of the studio's founders,
and later shown some of Nick Park's drawings done as part of
the planning stages of a *Wallace and Gromit* feature film. Nick
Park was locked down with his development team in another
location, and I met his assistant and passed along Suzuki's invitation. Kieran knew of the Ghibli Museum and asked if Ghibli
would be interested in staging an exhibit of Aardman sets in
Japan, and I said I would pass along the question.

When I got back to London there was a message waiting
for me at my hotel from Phil Symes. *Spirited Away* was going to
be awarded the Golden Bear. It was about 5 pm in London so
about 2 am in Tokyo. I knew Suzuki would still be up, because
he almost never sleeps, so I called him with the news immediately. He seemed happy and said he would tell Miyazaki in the
morning, and they would e-mail me his comments to be translated for the acceptance speech.

I called Phil, who had flown back to London for an event.
He said he would fly back to Berlin with me to help me manage
the acceptance speech. I asked if I needed to dress up for the
awards ceremony. He said smart casual would pass, barely, if
that was the best I could do. Others would be wearing suits and
some of the ladies would wear gowns. I said I had a sports jacket
and a shirt and tie with me, but the only shoes I had were the
ones I was wearing; hiking boots. Berlin is cold in the winter. It
snows, and I like to walk during my down time. I wasn't expecting to go on German TV to accept an award.

"Absolutely unacceptable," Phil said. "When you get back to

Berlin, buy the shoes and the clothes that you need. You need to look presentable when you accept the award. What else do you have to do there on Sunday? You'll have the whole day."

Phil met me at Heathrow Airport the next day and had a look at my clothing. He judged everything minimally acceptable except for the shoes. You absolutely need to buy shoes, he said. And then he suddenly remembered something.

"Oh my God, we're going to Germany. Germany doesn't allow stores to open on Sunday. We won't get there in time for you to shop for shoes. You have to buy them here in the airport. Now!"

Our 3:30 pm British Airways flight would arrive at Berlin Tegel Airport just after 6 pm. Heathrow is a huge airport, and the terminal that serves Europe has lots of shops in it, including, as it turned out, a shoe store: Clarks Shoes.

We located Clarks Shoes on one of the airport maps and rushed over to it. With twenty minutes to go before boarding, I ran to the airport terminal shopping mall and found the shoe store while Phil trailed behind with the luggage. I grabbed the first pair of black loafers I saw that looked like they might fit me and dashed up to toward the cash register. There were about ten people ahead of me in line.

Though I'm not proud of it, for the first time in my life I elbowed and shoved my way to the front of the line. A Chinese couple at the very front were holding calculators and trying to bargain down the price of some running shoes. The British sales clerk was patiently trying to explain that stores in civilized countries, stores such as Clarks Shoes, do not bargain. The price that is marked, she said, is the price for which the item is for sale. I listened to the exchange for about thirty seconds, and then I shoved the Chinese couple out of the way (it's how people in China behave in malls, so they must have been used to it). I told the sales clerk to please ring up the shoes right away.

The sales clerk gave me a look of stern disapproval. "Sir," she said, "please proceed to the end of the queue and wait your turn."

"Look," I said, "I have a plane to catch, and I really need you to do this right away."

"Sir, everyone here has a plane to catch. This is an airport."

"Would you *please* just ring up these goddamned fucking shoes and let me get out of here!" I heard myself say in a loud voice.

It looked like it was going to be nothing doing, but at that point Phil caught up with me and came over and said something in British to the woman and she rang up the shoes, reluctantly. Then we were off to the boarding gate.

At the gate Phil received a phone call from Mikiko. Phil handed me his phone. Mikiko passed the phone to Suzuki who said, "Miya-san wants to speak to you." He handed the phone to Miyazaki who said, "Golden Bear ... good ... it's ... a good thing ... I guess ... good...." He seemed happy, but it was hard to tell because we were boarding the plane and the BA gate agent was shouting at me "Sir, sir ... sir, I need to see your boarding pass. Sir, your boarding pass!" And then the connection was breaking up and I have no idea what else Miyazaki was saying. It was just after midnight in Tokyo. I guess they were happy back in Japan.

The Twilight Zone

The awards ceremony was choreographed in minute detail. Each awardee had an official aide from the festival. He or she would come over to explain the order of things at the awards ceremony and what was expected of the award recipient. My aide met me at my hotel for the ride over to the ceremony in the festival's limo. Phil was also there to guide me, but they wouldn't let him sit with me in the awardee's section of the huge theater where the ceremony took place. Instead, Phil had to crouch in the aisle at the end of the row and give me advice and encouragement in a stage whisper. After a while an usher came over and made him go back to his seat.

This was a big-deal televised ceremony like the Academy Awards with big movie stars and breaks for commercials. It was entirely in German, and I had no idea what was going on most of the time. The guy sitting next to me was Italian and translated for me, but only occasionally. The festival's director served as the evening's MC. There was a printed program, so from time to time I could recognize a film clip or a person and more or less keep up with how things were progressing.

When the first award was announced the person receiving it was not present. The presenters, two attractive women in evening gowns, stood smiling on stage for several minutes (live on German TV), and the MC became visibly upset while fumbling with his notes. Finally a guy in a tuxedo walked up and whispered something in his ear. The MC said something and moved on. According to the guy next to me it was something about hell freezing over and the mail.

When the next award was announced, the person named stood up in the middle of the audience and shouted something. My seatmate told me that he was saying that he was not associated with the film mentioned and was refusing to come forward to accept the award. A brief dialogue between the man and the MC ensued (apparently hell was mentioned again), and the MC moved on. Next was an apology that Catherine Deneuve, scheduled to receive an award on behalf of the ensemble of actresses in the film *Eight Women*, which had also been in competition at the festival, had been delayed in Paris and would not be appearing after all. He held up the award she was to receive and then passed it along to a smiling woman in an evening gown and moved on. Germans have a reputation for precision and reliability. The other Europeans in the audience, especially the French, seemed pleased by the unbroken string of glitches.

The next thing that happened was that the order of awards presented became different from what was printed in the program. *Spirited Away* was supposed to have been next to last, but for some reason they decided to move it up to first among the major awards. Since I don't speak German, I didn't realize that I had just been called. I thought I still had plenty of time. I was rememorizing Miyazaki's acceptance speech that Suzuki had e-mailed me when I heard Phil stage-whisper-shouting at me.

I got to my feet and pushed my way to the aisle from the middle of my row. A spotlight caught up with me as I stepped on people's feet. The new loafers were a little too large and walking in them was not comfortable. The spotlight followed me as I mounted the stage.

The award was being presented by the Indian film director Mira Nair, chairperson of the awards committee that year. As I approached she stood on stage radiating grace and beauty in a shimmering, fairly low-cut evening gown and holding the Golden Bear in her right hand. When in Europe and not being European it is never clear how you will greet a person in a formal situation. Americans shake hands (or hug). Brits kiss the air next to one cheek. The French kiss the air next to two cheeks. Some Europeans kiss both actual cheeks and go back again to the first cheek for another kiss.

My instinct was to start with a handshake. But Ms. Nair had the Golden Bear in her right hand. She was going for an air kiss and had to shift slightly to avoid the handshake. So on live German TV, amidst the deafening din of congratulatory applause, I grabbed on to her left bosom. It was an uncomfortable moment, but she seemed to be an understanding woman, and somehow I did end up with the Bear and not a slap in the face.

When I turned to deliver Miyazaki's acceptance speech (short, as always) I couldn't see the audience through the blinding bright klieg lights. I also couldn't tell where the end of the stage was, and I was worried about falling off. Someone behind me was translating the speech into German as I spoke and there was more applause. I'm not sure how it happened, but a few minutes later I was back in my seat holding a heavy golden statue of a bear and watching the rest of the ceremony.

This was my first time receiving an award on behalf of Hayao Miyazaki. It felt strange to be treated like an award-winning honoree. I felt proud and honored on behalf of Mr. Miyazaki and Studio Ghibli, but also like an imposter because I wasn't the person being honored, only his stand-in. I took the questions and tried to think how Hayao Miyazaki would answer them. On behalf of Hayao Miyazaki I was very honored to be holding a Golden Bear, but I tried to suppress my enthusiasm. We are happy when our films are appreciated, but we try to take our success in stride. Who was I kidding? I was holding the top award from a major film festival in my hands, a Golden Bear, and I was thrilled to death.

My instructions from Toshio Suzuki were that on my return to Japan I was to proceed immediately from Narita Airport to the Imperial Hotel in Hibiya, where there would be a press conference for the "Kinkuma-chan" (the Golden Bear). There would be no going home first to shower or change. Someone would meet me at the airport and escort me directly to the hotel. The press conference would begin immediately after I arrived there.

I like to get to the airport early, so I arrived at Tegel Airport a good three hours before my Monday 9 am flight was scheduled to depart. I was taking KLM1822 to Amsterdam, where I would lay over for four hours before catching KLM861 to Tokyo. That got me into Narita the next morning, a Tuesday, at about 9:30 in the morning, a trip of about eighteen hours .

When I got to the Berlin airport at 6 am there wasn't much activity. Only a few flights were leaving that early and things were slow and quiet. I found my gate and proceeded to check in. Each gate had its own security screening. I received my boarding pass, removed my coat, shoes, belt, and watch, and emptied the change from my pockets. At the reception dinner I had been given a specially made hand-crafted box for the Golden Bear. Kinkuma-chan was wrapped snugly in its purple velvet polishing cloth and nestled comfortably in its wooden travel box. I was taking no chances and would hand-carry it the whole way.

I expected to have to remove the bear from its box and show it for the security screenings in Berlin and Amsterdam, and for customs in Tokyo. But there was no way I would entrust it to baggage handlers. The Japanese nation takes awards to its countrymen very seriously. If someone Japanese wins a Nobel

Prize or other major international honor like an Oscar or an Olympic medal, the nation as a whole accepts it as if it were an honor for all Japanese people. In effect, I was carrying a Japanese national treasure, and I felt the responsibility for its safety very keenly.

The top of the golden bear's box had little doors that conveniently flipped open so you could push aside the polishing cloth and show the bear's face. Security screeners at Tegel had seen these bears before, so I didn't have to open the box and take him out. But when I proceeded through the metal detector it beeped and a security guard came over to check me out. For years I had been carrying on a keychain in my pants pocket two things: a *kotsu anzen* (safe travels) amulet from a Buddhist temple in Kyoto and a very useful and very small miniature Swiss Army Knife. I had always managed to get through security with both. But someone a month or so earlier had tried to set off a bomb in his shoe on a flight to the US, and European airport security had tightened up.

The security guard pulled me aside and said I had two options. Toss the little knife in the trash now or go back outside and mail it to myself in Tokyo. There was a post office in the airport and they had everything that would be needed. The security guard offered to hold on to and watch my things for me, including the box with the Golden Bear in it. He said the flight would be boarding soon so I'd better hurry.

I dashed back through security and out of the gate area and all the way to the other side of the airport and found the post office. I bought an envelope and a stamp and mailed my little Swiss Army Knife to myself in Tokyo. It was a limited edition, super-thin, silver-metallic version of the knife that I had never seen before (and have never seen since). I didn't want to lose it.

I dashed back to the KLM gate, went quickly through security, since I was no longer carrying anything, and made my way over to the security guard. When I asked for my stuff back the guard looked at me blankly. When I repeated to him three or four times how he had told me about the post office and mailing and said he would look after my things he just shook his head and said he'd never seen me before in his life. No he didn't have my things. No he wasn't holding anything for me. I could look for myself if I didn't believe him.

It is impossible for me to describe the kind of out-of-body experience I was having. I was in shock. The Twilight Zone music was playing in my head. This can't be happening, I was thinking. I had somehow managed to lose a Japanese national treasure. I had actually *lost* the Golden Bear. Lost it. I wandered out of the gate area in a daze. Could this really be happening? How could it have happened? What could I do? How could I explain to Miyazaki and Suzuki that I had lost their Golden Bear? I was about to become an enemy of the Japanese people.

After I calmed down I decided to retrace my steps. When I got to the KLM gate, I felt there was something odd about it. I couldn't quite put my finger on it, but there was something. All the gates in the airport were identical. The only differences were the names and logos of the airlines. The KLM one looked like the one where I had gone through security, but was it? Could I have been at a different gate? But how? How could I have been? I had checked in and received a boarding pass. I had a boarding pass. I took out my boarding pass and looked at it. I had a boarding pass for a Lufthansa flight to Chicago.

I found the Lufthansa gate and went through security again. I found the guard and got back all my stuff. The last passengers were just boarding the plane. It occurred to me that had I not been carrying my Swiss Army Knife I might well be on my way with the Golden Bear to Chicago. Possibly security at Tegel Airport could still use a bit more fine tuning.

It took some explaining to get a boarding pass for my actual flight to Tokyo via Amsterdam. For the rest of the journey to Tokyo I never let the bear out of my sight. Not even once. The envelope I had mailed from the Berlin airport arrived at my home in Tokyo a few days later. The knife was not inside it. I really loved that little knife.

When I arrived at Narita Airport I got through immigration

and customs without any problems. Ishii-kun from Ghibli, Suzuki's assistant and producer-in-training, met me just outside the arrivals door and drove me directly to the Imperial Hotel. He was driving the same beat-up Toyota sedan he used to drive Hayao Miyazaki around when he was up for an award and Suzuki didn't want him anywhere near a radio or TV.

At the Imperial Hotel someone from NTV escorted me from the car to the VIP waiting room, where I was introduced to the chairmen of Dentsu, Hakuhodo, and NTV, all extremely famous business icons in Japan, and to the Governor of Tokyo. Most of what I remember about the blur of activity leading up to my handing over the statue of the bear to Hayao Miyazaki in front of popping flashbulbs and TV cameras and an audience of journalists is wishing I could have showered and changed my clothes first before going on national TV and having my picture appear in every newspaper in Japan the next morning.

When I was asked at the press conference, on live TV, what it had felt like to receive the Golden Bear, all I could think to say was that it was much heavier than I thought it would be. Whoever had asked the question did not hide his disappointment, contempt even, with my answer. "You've had in your hands a sacred award that few people have been privileged to hold," his look seemed to say, "and all you can think of to say is that it was heavy?"

What I might have said, had I been able to express myself more completely, was that the statue seen up close and held in your hands, was finely made, artistically crafted, and had a very solid feel to it. In an age when awards for all kinds of things have proliferated, and the crafting of them has become less individual, and the workmanship less fine, this lovely statue, even if seen by someone who had no idea what it was, would convey the feeling of excellence recognized and rewarded. It was a wondrous thing, and entirely equal to the task of calling out special praise for a marvelous film as a unique and special achievement.

I wish I'd been able to say that.

The 75th Academy Awards

The Golden Bear was only the first of the thirty-six awards won worldwide by the amazing film *Spirited Away*. Hayao Miyazaki remained steadfast in his position of not appearing in person to receive an award. He felt, or at least he said he felt, that a film was a work of art, and artists didn't create works of art to win prizes. Claude Monet didn't expect to get a prize for best haystack or best lily pond. Miyazaki also felt that standing up and receiving awards and prizes meant you were at the end of your career, and his career was far from over.

Sending me to receive these awards became partly a matter of superstition. Miyazaki wasn't going, and someone from the studio had to go. Whether or not Miyazaki cared about winning, everyone else in the studio did care, and now I was like a good-luck charm in addition to being the best-qualified to deliver an acceptance speech in English.

This is both a great honor and a great burden. You're thrilled to be somewhere special, bathed in the applause and connected to a studio and a director who have created a great film. You're also facing an audience that's very disappointed that you're not Hayao Miyazaki. Like the audience that has just paid top dollar for a ticket to that play that's been sold out for months hearing that that the world-beating actor who plays the lead won't be performing tonight. You're the understudy's understudy and you're not even an actor.

At an awards ceremony everyone in the front three rows is famous. There's George Clooney right in the very front, impaling you with his crystal-clear brown eyes. There's Claire Danes or Cameron Diaz looking gorgeous in a gown or cocktail dress waiting to hand you a plaque or Lucite disc on a stand. You're completely out of your league. You don't deserve to be there. You're the walking shadow, the poor player that struts and frets his two minutes upon the stage and then is heard no more. You do your best not to come off as an idiot or ask for autographs.

The very last award ceremony I attended on behalf of *Spirited Away* was the only one where the result was not known in advance: the 75th Academy Awards in Los Angeles. The nominees were announced on February 11, 2003.

John Lasseter, the creative head of Pixar, called his friend Hayao Miyazaki to congratulate him on the nomination. About a week later John called me to ask if Miyazaki would attend. I told him I didn't think so, but I would ask again. Miyazaki had said he doesn't attend award ceremonies, period, and not to ask him again. Toshio Suzuki told me not to bother trying to get him to go because Miya-san had made up his mind.

I relayed this information to John, and for the next month John called me several times a week with a new idea to get Miyazaki to change his mind. Each time I trundled over to Miyazaki's atelier where he was designing exhibits for the Ghibli Museum and pitched the new idea. The answer, as expected, was always no.

John wanted to know why. Was it the jet lag? If so we could schedule the flights so that he could board the plane in Tokyo, go to sleep on the plane immediately, be picked up at the airport, and be driven directly to the Oscars, accept the award (John was sure *Spirited Away* would win). Miyazaki could be driven right back to the airport, get on a plane to Tokyo, sleep on the plane, and be home by morning. He wouldn't even feel he'd ever left Japan.

Would he go if John went with him? Miyazaki could fly to San Francisco and stay at John's house in Sonoma. Then John would go to the awards ceremony with him. He'd be with John the whole time. He could bring other people. He would really enjoy it.

Was it the flying? The hassles and inconvenience of air travel? John had spoken to Roy Disney and Roy was willing to lend Miyazaki his plane for the trip. A Boeing 737. Built to carry over 120 passengers. Very comfortable, and Miyazaki can take as many people with him as he wants. He'll love it.

Was it the formality of the event? The publicity? He's really

SPIRITED AWAY

The amazing cast of characters in the most commercially successful Japanese film ever.

not coming? Really? Miyazaki should at least come to the nominees' lunch. There's no press coverage and you get to meet and talk to all of the other nominees. It's fantastic. He really shouldn't miss that.

Each time I brought John's new idea to Suzuki. If there's anyone who can change Miyazaki's mind once he has made it up it's Suzuki. But no matter how appealing the new scheme was (Roy Disney's 737!), or how much Suzuki himself wanted Miyazaki to say yes, the answer was always no. Miyazaki wasn't going and that was it. But Suzuki wanted to know if he, as the producer of the film, could go and accept the award.

Ever since 1973 when Sacheen Littlefeather accepted Marlon Brando's Oscar for his role in *The Godfather* and delivered a speech protesting Hollywood and television's treatment of Native Americans, the Academy has not allowed anyone but the actual Oscar recipient to come on stage and accept the award. The only exception is if the recipient has died. I called the Academy and someone from Disney's PR department called the Academy, and we were told that if Miyazaki didn't go, and continued to be alive, no one else could come up on stage and accept the award if he won.

John refused to give up on convincing Miyazaki to go. But if Miyazaki still refused to go, he thought that at least Suzuki, the film's producer and Miyazaki's creative partner, should be able to go up and accept the award. The Walt Disney Company petitioned the Academy to let Suzuki accept the award. John petitioned the Academy. Ghibli petitioned the Academy. At first the Disney PR person was optimistic that we would be given an exception. In the end the president of the Academy called and said he was very sorry but they just couldn't bend their rule. Suzuki and one guest could be invited to attend the ceremony, but he couldn't go on stage to accept the award.

And then the United States invaded Iraq. Antiwar sentiment in Japan was very strong. Suddenly the question became, *should* anyone from Ghibli even attend the Academy Awards ceremony? Suzuki took the question very seriously. He called numerous meetings to discuss the issue. Most of the meetings began at around 10 pm.

Hayao Miyazaki had already emphatically refused to attend. This had already been reported in the Japanese press, so Miyazaki was unable to refuse even more emphatically. For everyone else at Ghibli it was a more nuanced issue.

While soldiers were fighting in Iraq, no one wanted to be seen in public immersed in the trappings of excess, sipping champagne and enjoying miniature hot dogs and chocolate Oscar statues fashioned by Wolfgang Puck while surrounded by gorgeous and partly naked women in lavish evening gowns and men in designer tuxedos. People were about to lose their lives for what seemed like no good reason, especially to people who were not Americans. The Japanese government was issuing warnings to its citizens about travel to the US. The Japanese news media were making a trip to Los Angeles sound as dangerous as a trip to Iraq itself.

There were commercial reasons to be represented at the Academy Awards ceremony. Studio Ghibli wanted its films to be successful in America. Disney was convinced that winning a Best Animated Feature Oscar would be the key ingredient in achieving the box office numbers that the Ghibli films deserved. *Spirited Away* had had only had a limited theatrical release in the US. If it won the Best Animated Feature Oscar, it would get a brand-new wide release. If it didn't win, the film would end its run having earned only $5 million at the US box office. Snubbing the Academy Awards would not help. The film had a very good chance of winning the Oscar.

Studio Ghibli's way of resolving difficult problems can be Zen-like. Zen monks in their quest for enlightenment ponder an esoteric question called a *koan*. The most famous *koan* is: "What is the sound of one hand clapping?" Zen monks are supposed to spend most of their waking hours thinking about their *koan* and coming up with a response that will please the *roshi*, the spiritual head of the Zen temple. The *roshi* rejects these answers, urging the monk to continue thinking ever more deeply about the question. In a few years the monk may have developed the necessary frame of mind to move on to the next stage in his quest for *satori*, enlightenment.

As an American I feel skeptical about this process, though I respect it. Zen temples and Zen art are wonderful, so if the *koan* is an expression of Zen thought, there could be something to it. But to me, to clap means to strike the palms of the hands together repeatedly, typically in order to applaud (or to summon *koi* in a *koi* pond). One hand by itself can't clap. So there is no sound to one hand clapping. Why would you spend years thinking about that?

Similarly, as a *gaijin* at Ghibli I didn't see the problem with attending the Academy Awards. It's the Academy Awards. If you're invited and you're up for an award, you go. Football players taking a knee during the singing of the National Anthem aren't asking for the game to be canceled.

After many (many) late-night hours of meetings and deliberations, it was decided that I would attend the awards ceremony to represent Studio Ghibli. Since I already bore the taint of being the business face of the studio, and an American, there was no further threat to Ghibli's reputation. Someone had to do it. In case there was another statue to bring home.

Seiji Okuda from NTV and Koji Hoshino from Disney Japan went with me. Okuda was thrilled to be going and felt fortunate that his company, Japan's number one TV network, took a different view of commercialism and warfare in general. The Ghibli relationship in Japan was important to Disney, and Hoshino had been instructed to look after whoever went to the Oscars from Ghibli. Thus the three of us were able to claim that we really hadn't wanted to attend the Oscars but were forced to by our companies.

In most of the Northern Hemisphere it's cold outside in February. But in LA it's summer. Everything in LA seems mellower than anywhere else. The traffic is very bad but somehow manageable if you arrived expecting it. The days when the city was completely enveloped in brown smog seem to have passed.

As you sit stuck in traffic in your rented car you can see majestic purple mountains in the distance. Temperatures drop at night and the sky is full of stars twinkling brightly in the dry desert air. The sunsets are usually magnificent.

Disney had taken care of our hotel reservations. Okuda, Hoshino, and I stayed at the Four Seasons in Beverly Hills, generally considered Oscar headquarters for that weekend. It's almost impossible to get a hotel reservation there at that time. But Disney books rooms years in advance, so when the nominations are announced they can turn them over to whoever has been nominated for a Disney-related film and doesn't already live in LA.

The hotel that weekend was packed with Oscar nominees and attendees. You couldn't leave your room without bumping into someone famous. If you were an actual nominee (or nominee stand-in, as I was) you had three or four overflowing sacks of swag waiting for you in your room when you arrived. Champagne, chocolates shaped like the Oscar, and cookies spelling out the word "congratulations." Strawberries dipped in chocolate, hair crèmes, expensive perfumes and cosmetics, designer sunglasses, expensive leather bags, sweatshirts, T-shirts, and more. There were flowers in vases. What I didn't eat, I gave away to people I knew in LA.

Oscar

When it came time to leave for the Oscars ceremony there was a massive rush-hour traffic jam as the celebrities, essentially the entire hotel, all left their rooms and rang for the elevator at exactly the same time. Limos were stacked up around the block and beyond. Horns were honking. People were screaming. It was a chaos of black limousines, uniformed drivers, and passengers in tuxedos and ball gowns, all being photographed by a crush of professionals and amateurs surging against the police barriers for a better shot.

Disney provided an enormous stretch limo for just the three

of us (until the very end they thought that Miyazaki, Suzuki, and a Japanese entourage might still arrive, because who says no to the Oscars?). After waiting only thirty or so minutes, Okuda, Hoshino, and I, dressed in tuxedos, hopped into our limo and headed for the Kodak Theater, a mini entourage minus its stars. Everyone in LA runs late, but being from Japan we were trained to be on time, so we actually got out more quickly than most of the others.

On the way to the awards ceremony and in the vicinity of the Kodak Theater there were organized protests against the Iraq war and against having this kind of a celebration when soldiers were fighting and dying. That year there had been cancelations because of the war, and for the most part the women had toned down their dress out of respect for the troops. The gowns were in darker colors and there were fewer acres of naked female flesh on display. Okuda, Hoshino, and I found this a little disappointing. I had once seen Salma Hayek in person in an evening dress at an awards ceremony in New York, so I had a good idea of what was being sacrificed for the sake of the troops being sent to fight in Iraq.

Even the limos that the biggest stars arrive in are not allowed into the red-carpet area. Everyone is deposited about a block from the theater and has to walk the rest of the way. We made our way back to the theater in the company of Will Smith and Jada Pinkett Smith, and Zhang Ziyi and her mother. Attendees are issued colored tickets to the ceremony. At the entrance to the red carpet those with red tickets are diverted to one part of the carpet and everyone else to another. Red ticket holders make their way into the theater by passing through the press line. They are stopped along the way to be interviewed and photographed.

An NTV crew was waiting in the press bleachers to interview me as I walked the red carpet. Okuda-san had drilled me on the way over with the questions I would be asked so I could respond in Japanese spontaneously. But when we got to the red carpet I wasn't allowed onto the interview side of it. I wasn't the actual nominee and didn't have a red ticket. I had a blue ticket. I tried to explain to the guards that a Japanese TV crew had camped out on the red-carpet press bleachers since 6 am in the morning just to interview me. He wasn't having it. Will Smith wouldn't help us, and Zhang Ziyi's mother hustled her daughter away once it was clear we were troublemakers.

The back part of the red carpet is visible from the press bleachers, so the NTV guys were able to shout their questions across at me, which I could barely hear, and I shouted back my rehearsed answers, which I am sure they couldn't hear. The NTV crew had been there in the red-carpet bleachers all day, and their entire and only assignment was to capture my appearance on the red carpet and ask me a couple of questions. I had to wonder how, in the twelve hours they were sitting there, they had failed to confirm the details of how the thing worked. What were these guys doing there all day?

We went through security twice and had our credentials scrutinized and matched to a master list. We had any electronic devices in our possession confiscated and consigned to lockdown to be returned at the end of the ceremony. That accomplished, we were handed glasses of champagne and offered some Wolfgang Puck canapés by waiters in tuxedos circulating with trays. Someone gave us each an official program. If you want to keep your program you have to hold onto it because people steal them if you ever set them down. Okuda found one on a sink in the men's room and kept it to give to someone in Japan.

The entrance lobby, which is tier 1 of the theater, was swarming with celebrities. There were many more people around wearing black tuxes and non-designer gowns who were not famous, but everywhere you looked there was someone very famous. Sean Connery in a kilt. Jack Nicholson, Meryl Streep, Julianne Moore, Nicole Kidman, Michael Caine, Daniel Day-Lewis, Julia Roberts, and many more. All standing around sipping champagne, eating little hot dogs and chatting.

The colored tickets corresponded to the tiers of the theater. If you had a red ticket you were in the first tier with all the celebrities and most of the nominees. Tier two was for people connected with nominated films but not nominated themselves, and for senior studio executives and nominees in the non-televised categories. The upper tiers were for the Academy members, studio employees, and other guests who were lucky enough to get a ticket and willing to put on a gown or tuxedo. A ticket to the Academy Awards could be hard to come by.

Once we went up to the next tier we discovered that you couldn't come back down until the ceremony was over, unless you had a ticket for a lower level. I was in tier 2, Hoshino was in tier 3, and Okuda was in tier 4. When we had almost had our fill of ogling famous movie stars, we decided to move up a level and check out the action there. That was when we discovered that we weren't allowed back down until the ceremony was over.

Each level had its own bar where you could order free drinks and eat the same free hors d'oeuvres as the movie stars on tier 1. The bar stayed open through the entire ceremony. You could come out of the theater at any of the (numerous) TV commercial breaks, get a drink, and go back to your seat at the next commercial break. John Lasseter was seated downstairs, but he came up to find me and gave me tips on how to enjoy the ceremony. He was sure *Spirited Away* would win and had smuggled his cell phone inside. "When it wins I'll come up and we'll call Miyazaki," he said.

When I went in and found my seat I discovered I was surrounded by animation people and Disney executives. Two of Disney's films had been nominated for Best Animated Feature; *Lilo & Stitch* and *Treasure Planet*. Not everyone at Disney had been happy to see *Spirited Away* nominated.

The award for Best Animated Feature was almost the first one presented. As Cameron Diaz came forward with the Oscar and the envelope I could feel everyone sitting within two rows of me, all people connected to one of the nominated films, tensing up and in some cases praying. I tried to be as cool as possible about it, but as the words "and the Oscar goes to ..." were spoken I had somehow blanked out and did not hear a ed.

thing. I only realized *Spirited Away* had won when hands from behind were slapping my back and hands from the front and side were reaching over to be shaken. Wow. *Spirited Away* just won an Oscar. Try to take *that* in stride.

Sadly, no one went up to accept the award, and Cameron Diaz took it backstage with her. At the next commercial break I went out to the bar, and John Lasseter was there waiting. He called Suzuki to congratulate him, and of course Miyazaki. It was about 9 or 10 in the morning in Tokyo. Suzuki had dispatched Ishii-kun, his assistant, to go and pick up Miyazaki at home and drive him to the studio. Ishii had received strict orders to make sure Miyazaki wouldn't hear the result until he had been properly prepared, just in case he didn't win. The studio begins its day at 10 am. Ishii-kun was supposed to delay his arrival as long as possible.

But Ishii had forgotten to fill the car's gas tank the night before and had to stop for gas on the way. The gas station's PA system was tuned to a radio station that was just then playing the news. Miyazaki's Oscar was that day's top story. According to Ishii, Miyazaki had to work very, very hard to look unmoved by the news.

When I left the hall I was handed more souvenirs and invited to dip into a basket of tiny gold-leaf-covered chocolate Oscar statues, also by Wolfgang Puck. I had to figure out how to find my exact black limo among an ocean of identical ones, while the limo drivers had to navigate the chaos of all those important people descending on them at once for the same purpose. The magic of the evening might have begun to dissipate with this sudden cold-water plunge back into the real world. But not when you're with a film that just won an Oscar.

The next day Hoshino, Okuda, and I walked over to the Academy itself, which was only a few blocks from our hotel, to collect the golden statuette. Disney had arranged in advance for visitation rights. The actual Oscar, as it was explained to us at the Academy, had to be returned by the end of the day so they could have Hayao Miyazaki's name engraved on it.

The people at the Academy also pointed out that Miyazaki himself would not own his Oscar. It had been leased to him for $1 (Disney paid), and it would remain the property of the Academy of Motion Picture Arts. It could not under any circumstance be sold or otherwise disposed of. We were told of cases where a famous actor had died, and his/her estate had tried to sell his/her Oscar(s). We were assured that the Academy had lawyers who would prevent this from happening. We were also told that Mr. Miyazaki could send his Oscar back at any time to have it professionally cleaned and polished. We said we would let Mr. Miyazaki know and thanked them.

Then we took the Oscar out and played with it. We showed it around. We took pictures of ourselves with it. An NTV film crew came over and I was filmed holding it on the street outside the hotel. "How did you feel being in the audience when the award was announced?" I was asked in front of the TV camera.

"Whether a film is a success or a failure," I said, "we try to take it in stride. We're just happy to have our films appreciated and look forward to being able to make the next one."

By now I was able to say this with a straight face. Nobody would believe it, nor should they. It was an interview for Japanese TV. The show of modesty isn't about fooling the people watching. It's about reminding yourself how lucky you've been, and that the world as you know it hasn't changed a bit.

9

My Ass Is a Chicken

The Rest of the World

Spirited Away was the most artistically and commercially successful film in the history of Japan. It set box office records and records for garnering awards that will probably never be matched. Expectations for the film's release outside Japan were high. There was a well-publicized deal in place with Disney. But previously, when *Princess Mononoke* had been released outside of Japan, Disney had given the film only lukewarm support in most countries. At Ghibli we worried that the Disney release of *Spirited Away* would suffer the same fate.

Spirited Away was brought to Pixar in the fall of 2001 for its first screening outside of Japan. Everyone at Pixar who saw the film thought it was a masterpiece. At that time the most successful Japanese film ever to play in America was Akira Kurosawa's *Ran*. We expected *Spirited Away* to do better.

Hard as it may be to believe now, Pixar's earliest films followed the same path as Ghibli's to determining how they would be released in the US. There would be a screening of the completed film for Disney executives, and then the executives would decide how much of their marketing muscle (and money) to put behind it. Many of Disney's key executives had expected Pixar's first feature film, *Toy Story*, to bomb at the box office.

John Lasseter provided me with his insights on how to best approach the Disney executives. Lasseter advised that audience reaction would play a big part in how the executives would evaluate the film. He told us we should make sure of two things. First, that the screening take place in one of Disney's larger screening rooms. And second, that we pack the screening room with animators from Disney Feature Animation.

According to Lasseter, in the smaller screening rooms the executives tended to be more relaxed and might pay less attention to the film, even bringing other work into the room with them. With a bigger audience they would be more focused on the film. The larger screening room would impart more of a sense of importance. The animators, he said, would completely get and adore the film. They would be enthusiastic about it, and show their enthusiasm, and the executives would get the sense that the audience loved it.

Through the people we worked with at Disney we were able to make John Lasseter's suggestions happen. We got the screening moved from one of the smallest rooms, where it had originally been scheduled, to one of the biggest ones. We extended invitations to Disney's animators and animation directors, who were thrilled to be able to see the film. Disney's most senior executives, including chairman Michael Eisner, were invited to the screening as a matter of protocol, and as expected they all declined. Only the actual decision-makers were signed up to be there. The rest of the seats would be filled by the most ideal audience possible, Disney animators and animation directors.

But then something happened. All the publicity about the huge box office records in Japan began to reach the US. Eisner himself took note and decided that he wanted to see the film everyone was making such a fuss about. When other senior executives learned that Eisner was attending the screening, they didn't want to look bad by ignoring something the chairman thought important. They also changed their minds and decided to accept the invitations to the screening. The executives who worked for these senior executives didn't want to look bad to their bosses, so they also decided they needed to be at screening, too.

In a kind of cascading chain reaction, the screening of *Spirited Away* suddenly became a must-attend event for every senior, middle, and junior executive at Disney. The animators were informed that there was no longer any room for them at the screening. All the seats were taken up by studio executives, most of whom had no interest in or no connection at all to the distribution of the film.

I always attended these screenings. That is, I wasn't allowed inside, but waited outside to get an initial read on the verdict. When the screening was over I anxiously awaited my meeting with Mark Zoradi, Disney's head of international film distribution.

"Steve," Mark told me, "we saw the film, and *we* all loved it. But to be honest, everyone thinks it's too Japanese, too ... esoteric, and nobody in the US will get it. Europe too. A tiny art house film maybe, if even that. Sorry, but that's just how it is."

The Disney executives in charge of worldwide distribution for Japan's most commercially successful film ever had decided that its commercial potential in North America and the major European film markets was approximately zero. Disney's team in France, long fans of Ghibli's films and Ghibli's best foreign distributor, was the sole dissenting voice to their parent company's estimation. Jean-François Camilleri, the head of Disney distribution in France, and his team loved the film and urged us to let them release the film there. And because of our relationship with John Lasseter, we reluctantly decided to stay with Disney in North America.

As a result, Disney passed on the film everywhere except for France and North America. This turned out to be good news for Ghibli, since we were now free to seek other distributors. We continued to manage the distribution in Asia directly, thanks to chairman Yasuyoshi Tokuma's fond memories of the Greater East Asia Co-Prosperity Sphere. That left to us the territory we called "The Rest of the World" in which to find distributors for the film.

Big Girls Don't Cry

The general public probably doesn't realize that there are two separate parts to the Cannes Film Festival. There is the festival itself with lavishly attired film stars mounting the red carpet for premiere screenings of their films, nubile starlets sunbathing topless on the beach, billionaires' yachts anchored just offshore, and boozy parties lasting until the wee hours of the morning. But the Cannes Film Festival has a twin event taking place simultaneously and completely out of the public eye: the Cannes Film Market.

The Cannes Film Market is the largest and most important international venue for the buying and selling of films for release in theaters and on TV and video worldwide. Film buyers and film sellers from all over the world gather to buy and sell the rights. There are by far many more people in Cannes for the film market than there are for the festival. If you don't have a distributor to release your films somewhere in the world, this is where you need to be.

The Cannes Film Festival is still huge. Big movie stars and famous film directors make the pilgrimage there every year. The big names come to act as judges on the panel that chooses which films will receive awards, including the coveted best film award, the Palme d'Or. They come to walk the red carpet at the (European) premieres of their films. They come to do press interviews and promotional events and to attend the famous invitation-only parties that last until dawn and where formal wear is absolutely required. If you haven't brought your tux or evening dress, you won't be rubbing elbows with the glitterati.

Cannes is a very small town with a single main street along the beach where almost everything happens. During the festival it becomes so dense with filmgoers, film reporters, paparazzi, movie star gawkers, random publicity seekers, PETA protesters, accidental tourists, and lowly movie industry business professionals that wherever you go you find yourself mired in a crowd of people trying to get somewhere. Just getting from place to place can be a challenge. Vehicular traffic is perpetually and hopelessly snarled despite the efforts of the infinitely patient police officers dressed in crisp blue uniforms.

The French citizens of Cannes take pride in their festival but also make no attempt to conceal their contempt for the foreigners who attend it. Prices for anything and everything are raised by about 400% for the duration of the festival. The town's hotels and restaurants cannot even remotely begin to accommodate the crowds that arrive. If you haven't booked your bed or your table a year in advance you are out of luck.

If you are invited to one of the many beach-side luncheons for the press, usually held to promote a film, you can at least eat extravagantly for free while gazing out at the gleaming white sands, the emerald blue sea, and the enormous white yachts and full-sized cruise ships anchored alarmingly close to shore (the ocean there gets very deep very fast). The women bravely exposing their naked bosoms to the chilly sunshine either don't want tan lines interfering with the look of a low-cut or backless evening gown or are Americans who mistakenly think that this is how it's done on the French Riviera. It's not warm in the month of May. Even when the sun is out.

Here and there along the main avenue are huge video screens set up to display the day's main events: red-carpet premieres or interviews with movie stars. Brad Pitt and Angelina Jolie might be standing no more than five feet away from you having a chat with reporters. The crowds surrounding them are so dense you have no idea who is there or what's going on. But you can glance up over your shoulder and see it in full digital HD on a giant outdoor screen. In other words, you, standing a few feet away, have exactly the same vantage point as someone sitting in Osaka or Philadelphia or Liverpool watching it on TV. Except that they're comfortable and at home and you're in the middle of a jostling crowd trying to get from A to B.

You Know You're in France When...

On my first trip to the Cannes Film Festival to seek out a distributor for The Rest of the World, I found my hotel about a half-hour drive past Cannes to the west. I discovered that it was not actually a hotel. It was an enormous apartment block called the Cannes Beach Residence. When you make your reservations less than a full year in advance, this is what you get. A friend in Paris had once explained to me that Cannes and the Côte d'Azur, despite the smattering of giant yachts anchored offshore and the pricy hotels, is no longer the fashionable beach destination it once was.

My friend explained that the French are still very class-conscious. French business executives and other more well-to-do or fashion-aware individuals do not wish to share a beach with their bakers, butchers, dry cleaners, and mailmen. Cannes and the area west of it are now destinations where the working class go to enjoy their holidays at the beach. And the Cannes Beach Residence is one of the places they stay while doing so.

The Beach Residence was a minimally staffed complex of about a dozen cheaply made ten-story apartment buildings. The overall impression was of a minimum-security prison. You reached your apartment by a small elevator leading to an external passageway along the back of the building. The front sides of the buildings had balconies facing each other across an amoeba-shaped common courtyard.

My own unit was about six stories up, so I could take the stairs up or down when the long wait for the arrival of the extremely slow elevator seemed the less desirable option. The hallways leading to the front doors of the apartments were lit by bulbs attached to timers so as to not waste electricity. The ones on my floor were good for about thirty seconds. You flipped on the switch as soon as you got out of the elevator, and then heard the loud ticking reminding you that you had to be quick with your key before you were plunged back into darkness. You can usually figure it out after two or three tries.

Once inside my unit, a compact one-bedroom affair with a separate kitchen and living area, I discovered that everything in it was made of molded plastic. Plastic bed, plastic furniture, plastic plates, glasses, knives, and forks in the kitchen. Fortunately the plastic beds were very light and there were quite a few of them in the bedroom, so it was possible to push four of them together to make one regular adult-sized bed. Although the invoice (paid in advance) specified that the suite would be fully furnished, "fully" apparently included sheets and pillow-cases but not towels or blankets. Areas near the beach can be chilly at night, but if you wear all the clothes you brought with you to bed you will probably be all right.

When I stepped outside on my balcony to survey the set-ting I was greeted by a view of a wall of balconies ten-stories high. Here and there a shirtless figure sucked on an unfiltered cigarette and blew smoke into the French night. Laundry hung from the railings of some of the apartments, and through the windows of others I could see men in their underwear eat-ing solitary dinners from plastic containers. The sounds from inside the apartments were mostly audible, and unseen people shouted or murmured into their phones in a variety of foreign languages.

At some point during the night my arrangement of beds drifted apart and I found myself wide awake at 3 am. I went back to the balcony for some air. The only other human in sight was a rather attractive woman on a balcony just opposite mine in a white terrycloth robe having a cigarette and staring up at the moon. A white-robed guy emerged from the shadows and in one graceful swoop had the woman in his arms and her robe off. She was naked except for a tiny pair of those fancy little underpants they advertise in Paris bus stop posters.

The lovely woman's underpants shimmered faintly in the pale moonlight, and the guy was just working them off when suddenly a harsh yellow light snapped on in the room behind them. In a flash they disengaged and were dressed again in their robes and leaning on the balcony railing and staring up at the moon. A second man walked out onto the balcony, lit a cigarette, and also stared up at the moon. The first man and the woman also lit cigarettes. I watched them for a while, three figures in white terrycloth robes. I wondered in what order they would depart but felt sleepy and went back to bed without finding out. I did feel satisfied that I was most definitely in France, and not just because everyone was smoking.

The next morning I made my way into Cannes proper to attend the Cannes Film Market. In appearance it is somewhere between a normal industry market and a gigantic flea market. The booths are organized to sell their products to seasoned professional buyers. Many of the booths seem to be manned by disorganized, improvisational, but enthusiastic amateurs. Some sellers have large booths with glossy printed booklets about the films they represent and clips playing on a loop and DVDs to hand out. Others have small booths with nothing but posters and single-page handouts on their films.

Buyers stroll the aisles looking for films of interest that they might otherwise have missed, or glance in and make mental notes on their way to and from meetings or screenings. Each booth has a space for appointments with buyers. The bigger ones have small conference rooms in the back. The smaller ones have extra folding chairs that can be squeezed in between the stacks of surplus handouts.

I had made appointments with all of the big European film distributors that have departments specializing in the more artistic films, and with a few of the American independent film companies that do nothing but artistic films. All of them knew about the films of Studio Ghibli, so the appointments were very easy to set up.

There was a separate section of the film market where the bigger companies had booths that resembled small offices. These had receptionists and multiple conference rooms with four walls, tables, and chairs that all matched each other, and doors that could be closed. You showed up for your appointment and the astonishingly good-looking receptionist, dressed for a day at a Paris fashion show, would treat you with contempt and then dismissively direct you to sit and wait for half an hour until the person with whom you had an appointment would see you. Half an hour is the minimum wait for an appointment for which you have arrived on time.

On the one hand it was encouraging that so many of the best-known distributors were interested in Ghibli's films. On the other hand there was something off-putting about the extravagant way the companies' buyers would effuse praise for the films, and for the legendary greatness of their film-maker, while assuring me that they were offering me the very best financial deal available ever, the details of which they were not willing to share. I was told again and again by different people at different companies that this was a deal so good that "even Steven Spielberg doesn't get it. If he finds out we have offered it to you he will be very angry." I heard this so many times and always with reference to Steven Spielberg that when I finally met him I thought of asking him if he realized that everyone in the film business was getting a better deal than he was.

I left all of these meetings simultaneously encouraged by the interest in Ghibli's films and discouraged by the falseness of the conversations. There was something about the expensively slick atmosphere and smooth talking that didn't seem right. The conversations had never quite left the realm of metaphor and hyperbole. Offers were made but nothing about them made any real sense. There was a kind of disconnect between what was being said and what I knew of the practical realities of commercial film distribution.

During these meetings there was one particular French phrase that would run through my head. When I was in junior high school my best friend Donnie had a French exchange student living with his family. She was a year older than we were, chronologically, though being from Paris and female, it seemed like a lot more than one year. Often when you told her something she would express her skepticism. She seemed to doubt just about everything anyone told her. The phrase she used was *"Oui et mon cul c'est du poulet"* (Yes, and my ass is a chicken). That was the phrase that ran through my head as the big film distribution companies made their offers.

My final meeting of my first film market was with the head of Wild Bunch, a division of the French giant StudioCanal. Wild Bunch handled independent films, and I had low expectations for this meeting because bad feelings remained after certain legal problems between Tokuma and StudioCanal that had occurred well before my time at Tokuma/Ghibli. Tokuma had licensed the French rights to a Ghibli film to a Japanese woman who lived in France and was the daughter of a famous Japanese politician, a personal friend of Mr. Tokuma. The woman had managed to sublicense the same film, *Porco Rosso,* to two different French distributors. One of them was StudioCanal, which released the film and was then successfully sued for $2 million by the other distributor.

My meeting with Wild Bunch was with the head of the division, Vincent Maraval. It took place outside of the film market in a seedy and rundown corner of Cannes where the festival-goers usually do not venture.

Maraval met me in an open-air seafood restaurant that wasn't quite open for business but was serving coffee at the few tables up front that did not have chairs stacked on top of them. Maraval was dressed in a rumpled soccer club T-shirt and seriously distressed jeans. He hadn't shaved in a few days and appeared to have just got out of bed to come directly over to meet me, though it was already past two in the afternoon. Wild Bunch people had a reputation for being hard partiers who seldom went to bed before 4 am (if at all) but were also great film lovers and astute (and more importantly fair and honest) businessmen/women.

I listened to Maraval's casual yet very specific and detailed explanation of how Wild Bunch distributed its films and who its people were and what their distribution philosophy was. He listened to my explanation of the difficulties involved in getting

Disney to give up control of rights that they had no plans of actually using. For each of Ghibli's films Maraval gave me an idea of where and when each one might be released and how. He seemed knowledgeable about each of the films and its commercial potential and limitations. I mentioned the past difficulty between Ghibli's parent and Wild Bunch's parent over the Ghibli film *Porco Rosso*. Maraval acknowledged it might be a problem.

We finished our coffee, shook hands, and agreed to pursue the discussions about licensing Ghibli's films at a later date in Paris. A year later Wild Bunch became the licensee for all of Ghibli's films in The Rest of the World and continues to be so to this day.

We'll Always Have Paris

The first commercial release of *Spirited Away* outside Japan was in France in January of 2002. Miyazaki had said yes to traveling to promote the film in Paris, provided that we keep the stay short and throw in a side trip to Alsace. He wouldn't explain why Alsace, though we later discovered he had been wanting to see a certain kind of building unique to the area. One of the French Disney marketing managers was from Alsace, and the trip was easily arranged.

We arrived in Paris as a relatively small group of five a week before Christmas. Miyazaki, Suzuki, Takeda, and I from Ghibli were joined by Seiji Okuda from NTV. Okuda's daughter was the model for Chihiro, the main character in *Spirited Away*. I violated the prime directive of Japanese business etiquette by having my wife and son join me a few days after we arrived. I had convinced Suzuki that the Christmas vacation was so sacrosanct to the American family that my (Japanese) wife and son would secede from the family if I deserted them for Paris at the end of December.

Disney had offered to put the Ghibli group up anywhere in Paris, including Paris's most deluxe hotels. We opted for a small inn in the heart of the Latin Quarter near Saint-Germain-des-Prés on the Left Bank of the river Seine: the Relais Christine. This small, traditional hotel on the rue Christine in the 6th Arrondissement has since become popular and exorbitantly expensive (and renovated somewhat), but at the time it was merely charming and uniquely old-fashioned.

The rooms in the Relais Christine were small and without certain amenities such as closet space or places to sit other than the bed. The tiny elevator could handle only two people at a time, or one person with luggage. But the place was overflowing with classic charm and ambiance. The staff were extremely pleasant and helpful. A fire glowed warmly in the fireplace in the downstairs sitting room where there were comfortable chairs and an honor bar stocked with hot coffee, chilled champagne and Perrier, and bottles of good French wine. The breakfast in the ancient cellar (dungeon) was superb. Across the street was a small movie theater that showed only black and white American and British movie classics, many of which were rarely seen in the USA because of the delicate (puritanical) sensibilities of American censors.

The rue Christine is exactly one block long and narrow. There were several restaurants on the street. At one end was an older Michelin three-star restaurant where the prices on the wine list had the same number of digits as the vintage of the bottles. There were also three smaller, relatively reasonable, less formal restaurants.

As soon as the group had unpacked, Miyazaki and Suzuki wanted to get something to eat. This, I have to confess, I always dreaded. All Miyazaki and Suzuki ever really want to eat is Japanese food. But Miyazaki is sensitive to the fact that foreigners think that all Japanese people can only eat Japanese food, and that he himself dislikes non-Japanese food. He goes out of his way to prove them wrong. Suzuki on the other hand doesn't care what anyone thinks, but he dislikes menus with more than three choices. Okuda will eat anything and appreciates fine dining, as do I. Takeda thinks that a business trip is about business and that your private likes and dislikes shouldn't come into consideration even when deciding where to eat.

No decision on what to eat or where to eat is ever reached; the only requirement is that it be close by and simple. Both Miyazaki and Suzuki stipulate no elaborate courses or anything fancy. I suggest one of the three fast food sushi places down the street and around the corner. Miyazaki objects. No Japanese. I suggest the mid-market rotisserie chicken place across the street recently opened by a noted French chef. Suzuki objects. Too fancy. We finally settle on the family-run, cozy little bistro at the far end of the street. We enter. We sit. We study the menu.

Miyazaki decides all he wants is soup. Suzuki can't find anything he wants to eat so he decides he'll have the beef stew (Beef Bourguignon on the menu). Okuda and I want to eat full courses, but we realize that once Miyazaki and Suzuki are finished they will be pissed off if we are still eating, so we order main courses only. Takeda orders nothing, saying she knows Suzuki won't finish his and she will finish it for him.

Now the hard part. I'm doing the talking for the group so I have to order. It's dinner time. We are five, taking up two of the small restaurant's tables pushed together. The waiter registers his displeasure as I relate Miyazaki's order of soup only. Mademoiselle is having nothing. Monsieur and monsieur and monsieur are having main courses only. No one is drinking. With each successive order I have been earning the waiter's unreserved Gallic contempt, directed exclusively at me, the mouthpiece for the group. Fine, he thinks. It would be illegal for me to refuse to serve you. And, I am French so I must respect your order. If I were Chinese I would tell the chef to spit into your food as he cooks it. But we are French and civilized. We don't do this. But never come in here again you asshole. You fucking piece of shit.

The French are so good at conveying this wordlessly.

To add insult to injury I pay by credit card. As I'm doing this the rest of the group leaves. Not only do I have to assume all of the contempt for the group alone, but I have to leave hungry.

The little restaurant is not bad at all, but now I can never go in it again.

To be fair, as it turned out, the excellent cuisine of France did severely test Hayao Miyazaki's ability to show appreciation for being treated specially and superbly.

Because Miyazaki had insisted that his stay in France be as short as possible, the schedule we had booked for him was very full. In addition to the long days of interviews with print and TV media, he was invited to speak on a panel one evening at the Forum des Images, France's national Cinémathèque. On each night of our stay a different group had vied for the honor of hosting a dinner for Mr. Miyazaki. In France, a spectacular dinner is the highest honor that can be bestowed on an esteemed guest. As Hayao Miyazaki rarely appears in France, where his work has long been highly appreciated, there were many different people who wanted to honor him by sitting down to dinner with him.

The first night's dinner at a really excellent two-star Michelin restaurant was hosted by the head of Disney in France, Jean-François Camilleri. Jean-François had long been a fan of Ghibli's films and had arranged for even the earliest Ghibli films to have first-run theatrical releases in France. The restaurant he chose for us took great pains that we should know we were having a very special meal completely appropriate to the season and made from the season's finest ingredients.

There was champagne to start, and an amuse-bouche. A first course of fresh foie gras d'oie (goose) was followed by a fish course of poached trout in a sauce made from its own roe. The main course featured wild venison with winter vegetables, and dessert was an apple tart bathed in Grand Marnier–accented crème fraiche. The foie gras was accompanied by a rare Alsatian Gewürztraminer, the fish by an excellent white Bordeaux, the venison by an esteemed Burgundy, and the tart by a vintage Sauternes. We were made to understand that the sex of the deer had been female and the apples imported directly from Normandy. The sex of the goose was not mentioned.

Jean-François had been informed in advance that neither Miyazaki nor Suzuki embraced the concept of dinners that began at 10 pm and lasted until 1 am, nor were they fans of the leisurely pace of a formal French meal. The dinner had begun late because of the panel discussion, and Jean-François had asked the restaurant to speed up the service. Even so, by the time the post-dessert desserts with coffee were being passed around, the gentlemen from Japan were more than ready for bed. It helped that smoking in the restaurant was still allowed.

On the very next night we were hosted by the Forum des Images, the French cultural institution that both archives and showcases artistic films and where Miyazaki had joined a panel discussion the night before. The meal took place at an ancient and very exclusive classical French restaurant directly facing the Seine. We were ushered upstairs into a private dining room with a very eighteenth-century ambiance. The organizers of this dinner had gotten the memo about their guests' aversion to a late start and slow service. But being more truly French than Jean-François, who worked for an American company and had lived in LA, they ignored it.

Thus we experienced authentic traditional French fine dining in a meal that began at 10 pm and proceeded at the same pace it would have two hundred and fifty years earlier. At least an hour passed between each course, leaving plenty of time for film- and philosophy-related conversation. The pace of the meal was so slow that even the translators had time to eat. Both Miyazaki and Suzuki, who were again delighted to be able to smoke, bore the honor of it with grace and near enthusiasm, almost through the second main course.

The meal we enjoyed that night again consisted of the very best special seasonal food with dishes created from the season's finest ingredients. There was champagne to start and an amuse-bouche. A first course of fresh foie gras d'oie was followed by a fish course, a main course of venison with winter vegetables, and an apple tart bathed in Cointreau-accented crème fraiche. The foie gras was accompanied by a rare Alsatian

Gewürztraminer, the fish by an excellent white Bordeaux, the venison by an esteemed Burgundy. and the tart by a rare vintage Château d'Yquem Sauternes. We were made to understand that the sex of the deer had been female, that of the fish, having roe, female, and the apples imported directly from Normandy. The sex of the goose was again not mentioned.

The next day we headed off to Alsace in the northeast of France. We flew out of Paris's Orly Airport on exactly the same day that Richard Reid, known in the annals of modern history as the "Shoe Bomber," was boarding his flight just up the road at the much larger Charles de Gaulle Airport. As we flew to Alsace, Reid was failing to blow up his flight to Boston (not the plane's original destination). Our destination was the town of Colmar.

Miyazaki had wanted to see Colmar because of its famously well-preserved Old Town in which there are many noted buildings in the Germanic/French style of the region. Throughout its history Alsace had been a contested area seized like a ball in a rugby scrum by whichever political or military group was then attempting to consolidate power in the region. The civilian population had become fluent in the languages and cultural mores of both the German and the French sides, possibly because they were never quite sure in whose jurisdiction they might end up. The good news here was that the land was fertile and the climate pretty good, or it wouldn't have been worth fighting over, and the dual culturalism produced terrific buildings, great food, and really nice wine. As an added bonus we were there in time for the town's annual Christmas fair.

Alsace was having an unusually cold December that year. We arrived into a very icy winter landscape. Miyazaki's books had been translated into French, and his literary translator had volunteered to be our guide in Alsace. He met us at Colmar's tiny airport when our plane landed, and we piled into a minivan and drove into the center of town. We spent the afternoon touring the Old Town, where we saw buildings of sandstone and age-darkened timber that had survived the French Revolution. These are the buildings Miyazaki had wanted to see; some

of them are lovingly reproduced in the backgrounds of Miyazaki's 2004 film *Howl's Moving Castle*.

Our hotel was located in the tiny town of Riquewihr, about
a forty-minute drive back up north on the Route du Vin. Upon
arrival in Riquewihr we dumped our luggage and walked the
half block up the street to La Table du Gourmet for dinner.
Not only did the restaurant have one Michelin star, but also
three crossed spoons and forks, a sign that the ambiance was
also very nice. For dinner that night our host had insisted that
we have, of course, the very best seasonal food available at the
moment.

The meal began with poached Alsatian Foie Gras with apri-
cot and black garlic, proceeded to lightly sautéed Vale of Orbey
Trout with cucumber gel, horseradish, and parsley juice, a main
course of grilled venison steak, and an Alsatian apple tart for
dessert. Miyazaki objected to the foie gras, saying if he had to
eat foie gras one more time he would become foie gras (the
expression has more punch to it in Japanese). But Disney was
paying and running things here, and our guide had been given
strict instructions that he said he dared not deviate from. He
made the sign of the guillotine with one hand and the protests
died down. Appropriate information relating to the sex of each
course was duly provided.

The next day we did some walking around Riquewihr and
some shopping in its local crafts shops. Miyazaki bought a
bunch of handmade witches on brooms, some of which he gave
to people as presents back in Tokyo and some of which are now
displayed in the Ghibli Museum. As a parting treat, the hotel
made us pitchers of hot mulled and spiced red wine to fortify us
on our way back to the airport.

Back in Paris it was Christmas Eve and we were invited
to the home of long-time Ghibli fan Michel Reilhac, who had
recently retired as the head of the Forum des Images.

You don't know what a home in Paris can be until you are
invited inside one. The older buildings are structured around
internal courtyards that can't be seen from the street. Once

inside the outer gate we passed through the courtyard to an inner building, where a wide flight of stairs spiraled up toward the sixth-floor entrance to Michel's apartment. There were dozens of lighted candles arranged along the way leading us to our destination. Michel and his wife were there to welcome us along with his kids and his brother and wife and their kids and their parents as guests. The large duplex apartment was decorated with traditional Christmas stuff. A fire roared away in a large fieldstone fireplace. The table was set for the traditional Christmas Eve dinner.

As we drank champagne the parents explained that on Christmas Eve the children are allowed to stay up until the fire burns down, and then they go to bed to wait for Santa. Apparently Santa can't get down the chimney if the fire is going. Each of us received Christmas Eve stocking stuffer gifts along with the children. I still wear the boiled-felt house slippers I received that night. As we sat and watched the fire, Hayao Miyazaki took requests from the children and made them each a drawing of his/her favorite Ghibli character. This is something he enjoys doing, and the number of drawings he made exceeded the number of children in the room. Suzuki made Japanese character calligraphy for the adults.

The conversation at the table (grandparents, uncle, aunt, cousins) was almost entirely about food: how hard it had become to get the perfect oysters we were eating that come from that one special place near Mont Saint-Michel because only two stores in Paris now sold them; how only one kind of truffle could go into the sausages Michel's mother made to go with the wild boar meat that was the main ingredient; how only just the right potatoes would go with the sausages; where the goose came from for the foie gras made by Michel's wife's mother; and the sex of the main course, an amazingly delicious stewed and roasted free-range neutered rooster. Several home-made desserts closed out the dinner, including a Bûche de Noël, a really tasty concoction of sponge cake, chocolate buttercream, and pure chocolate shaped like a log. It was an astonishingly fine meal. It was so good that Miyazaki did not even think to complain about having to eat foie gras again.

After coffee we adjourned to the street for the ten-minute walk to the Cathedral of Notre-Dame to attend midnight mass. Midnight Christmas mass at Notre-Dame is popular, and the gigantic cathedral was crowded. As we entered the cathedral, people on their way out handed each of us a lighted candle that we in turn handed to someone else as we left. There was music. The cathedral was bathed in bright lights. Gently falling snowflakes danced in the high-wattage beams as they drifted gently earthward. For once there was hardly any car traffic on the surrounding streets, and we walked back to the Relais Christine through the hushed back alleys of the Latin Quarter.

And that was it. Paris shut down between Christmas and New Year's. The group from Japan stayed another day but almost nothing at all was open, and the city appeared to be nearly deserted. Seiji Okuda from NTV is fascinated by trains, and we walked all the way to the Gare Saint-Lazare to look at some. Near the Opera we found a street of mostly Japanese restaurants. All were open for business, and Miyazaki and Suzuki were finally able to enjoy the food they really wanted to eat: real Japanese soba, udon, and ramen.

On the day after that my wife and son and I left France. The new European currency was being introduced on January 1, and if you went to a bank in December you could purchase a Euro starter kit, a selection of coins and bills to play with and get used to just before they became actual money. In the airport I bought a bag of Euro coins for future use, and to this day I've never used them. They are sitting in a jar on my desk in the company of coins in the currencies they replaced.

In a world where more and more of the little things that make one place different from the next are disappearing, it's somehow comforting to hold on to a few bits of the past.

10

Princess Diary

Lost in Translation

The Japanese can be bad at translation. Books have been written illustrating the biggest bloopers. The main problem in the film industry is that no one checks the translations. Another problem is that Japanese people love English and are too comfortable with their version of it. They are far more tolerant of linguistic errors than a native speaker would be. Sounds OK to me. What could be wrong?

I was determined that the translations of the films of Studio Ghibli would be done properly. I have an academic background and always wanted to be a translator (of poetry and novels). Seeing it done right was a matter of personal pride. Also, the language in the scripts of Ghibli's films has the kind of depths of meaning and artistic beauty that deserve a proper translation. But then the question arises, what exactly is a proper translation?

At a minimum of course you want to avoid outright mistakes. Beyond that, you want the translated dialogue to sound natural to a native speaker who doesn't know Japanese. That's doable, though native speakers don't all agree on what sounds natural. But what about the things Japanese people say that nobody else says and that there just aren't equivalents for in other languages? Or the Japanese words that even Japanese people have trouble defining that Hayao Miyazaki likes to use in the titles of his films?

Disney was our distributor in the US. One problem we hadn't anticipated was that Disney would use the translations to "correct" perceived problems with the films themselves. To Disney, translation meant an opportunity to change all of the things that they didn't think would appeal to a commercial audience in America. They filled silences with dialogue that wasn't in the original script. They added plot points to fill out storylines they found unclear. They changed names to make them sound more American. And they made the kind of translation mistakes that review by a native speaker would have corrected.

Heated discussions took place on how the translations of Ghibli's films would be made. The discussions included the participation of lawyers. Disney and Ghibli agreed on a process. Guidelines were established and made contractual. The first English-language version of a Ghibli film that was made under the new guidelines was *Princess Mononoke*.

The process of making the English-language dubbed version of *Princess Mononoke* began in New York with a meeting at Miramax. I had heard that Miramax was very interested in learning how to dub foreign films into English. Miramax was then the main importer of the very best foreign-language films into the US. They thought their films would be more widely distributed and more widely viewed if there were well-made dubbed versions of them, not just the subtitled versions favored by arthouse audiences.

Several people at Disney told me that they'd seen Miramax's first and only attempt at dubbing in English, the 1994 Italian film *Il Postino*. The award-winning and Academy Award–nominated film is a fictional story about the Chilean poet Pablo Neruda and his relationship with a local postman during his exile in Italy. I was told that the English-dubbed version of it came off as somewhere between an episode of *Mr. Ed* and Woody Allen's

What's Up Tiger Lily? Princess Mononoke would be Miramax's attempt to do better. Dubbing a live-action film with human actors in it is very difficult. Dubbing an animated film with animated characters should have been less difficult. In theory.

The production team that was assembled to produce the dubbed version of *Princess Mononoke* met for its first script meeting in New York. No one on the team had any actual experience creating an English-dubbed version of a film. The author Neil Gaiman had been hired to write the English-language screenplay. He flew in from his home in Minnesota. Miramax had screened the film for him and had made him a rough working-copy video that he had watched many times and studied in order to arrive at the meeting familiar with the film. The Miramax staff assigned to the film had also screened the film several times to identify the issues they wanted Gaiman to address in his script.

Hayao Miyazaki had given me a short list of things to be aware of, or to do or not do, in making our dubbed version. I related these to the group. Miyazaki's comments ranged from casting advice to concerns about certain details he was sure no one else would care about or even notice. These were some of the things he told me:

- Don't bother trying to translate the title; it can't be done.
- No contemporary language or modern slang.
- Choose good voices; the voices are important.
- Ashitaka is a prince. He's well spoken and formal; old-fashioned for his time.
- The Emishi are a people that never made it into modern Japan: wiped out and gone.
- Lady Eboshi's people are very low class; outcasts; former prostitutes, hustlers, crooks, and reformed pimps; lepers. But she's not; she's from a different class.
- Jigo Bo says he works for the emperor. The emperor is not how we think of him now. He would have been

living in poverty and making a living selling his signature. Who does Jigo really work for? We don't know. He has a document signed by the emperor. Doesn't mean anything.

- The things that look like rifles are NOT rifles. Rifles are a different thing. These are more like portable cannons. Do NOT translate them as rifles. They are not rifles. Do not use the word "rifle."

Then there were questions from Miramax.

"This guy Lord Asano, who is he? Is he a good guy or a bad guy? Who were the samurai working for? Why were they attacking a village? Why were they attacking Lady Eboshi? She's a bad guy, right? Who is this guy Jigo and who does he work for? Why does he want the Deer God's head? Is he a good guy or a bad guy? Why is the Deer God a god? Is that a Japanese thing? Is he a good god or a bad god?"

I explained that Miyazaki really doesn't have good guys or bad guys in his films but tries to take a more nuanced view of human nature. I told them that I didn't know exactly if there were clear answers to their questions and that part of Miyazaki's intent was for us to think about it or to be satisfied with the uncertainty of not knowing for sure.

One woman with a pronounced Brooklyn accent asked, "So why do they call this Ashitaka guy a prince?"

Neil Gaiman answered, "Because he *is* a prince."

"Yeah," she said, "but, how do we *know* he's a prince? He lives in this crummy dirt village. His clothes are rags. His tiny village is in the complete middle of nowhere. How can he be a prince?"

"We know he's a prince because everyone refers to him as Prince Ashitaka," Gaiman said. "He's a prince because his father was king and he will be king when his father dies. The filmmakers have told us he's a prince. He's a prince. He just is."

Maybe because Gaiman is British he's more comfortable with the concept of a real prince or princess and not tied to the Disney Sleeping Beauty version. I would have thought that Americans, especially New Yorkers, who know the Anastasia story from the movies, and who have dry cleaners, restaurant owners, and language teachers who used to be royalty in one country or another, would have been more receptive to the concept of a former member of a royal family down on his/her luck and reduced to lesser circumstances.

The discussion between Gaiman, maintaining that a prince can remain a prince despite his reduced circumstances, and the Miramax woman, who argued that audiences would not accept a prince with a village kingdom and bad clothes, continued.

> GAIMAN: Look, his being a prince is important to the story. It's part of his character. I believe it's what Mr. Miyazaki decided. We're supposed to be adapting this film for an American audience, not changing it.
>
> MIRAMAX: But the audience won't *get* it, that he's a prince.
>
> GAIMAN: Of course they will. The audience isn't stupid. If they were, they wouldn't get the rest of the film either.

We moved on.

Neither Gaiman nor the Miramax production team had ever written an ADR script (a script for recording voices) and had not discussed the process to create one. Gaiman's idea was that he would first write his best version of a script based on the English-subtitled version of the film. Initially he wouldn't worry about timing or the fit of the lines to the characters onscreen. Gaiman would create his best version of the dialogue in an ideal world where there were no restrictions on his writing.

The next step would be for Gaiman to watch the film line-by-line against the script he wrote and do a rough edit of the lines to fit the timing onscreen. Finally he would hire temporary actors to deliver the lines to try to further tailor the dialogue more precisely to the faces of the characters and their mouth movements. How an actor reads a line can change the way it fits into the film. Read one way it might not fit. Read another way the same line could fit perfectly. Or the read of the line can show the writer how a line could be changed for the better or how to correct lines that don't work when read aloud.

This was not a bad plan. But since it hadn't been discussed, and since no one on the team had ever seen an actual ADR script, we wrongly assumed that the first script Gaiman sent us for comments from his home in Minnesota, although not a final version, was what he had in mind for eventual use. The consensus was that it was much too long to fit the film.

We received Gaiman's first draft of the script in May 1998. It was written in standard screenplay format (there are software programs). It had the dialogue and speaker clearly set out, stage directions (Ashitaka climbs the old man's lookout tower), and performance notes (groaning with the effort). What it lacked, and what no one on the production team knew at the time, was what an ADR script requires: each line of dialogue has to be numbered and precisely matched to the film's time code. Every single sound that a character in the film makes (word, sentence, grunt, sigh, laugh, cry, sob, deep breath, groan, hiss, cough, sneeze, etc.) has to be precisely matched to its place in the film.

This is a time-consuming and exacting process done by experienced professionals. The recording technicians need this information to display the exact corresponding piece of the film for the actors to record to. The sound mixers can't place the recorded lines in the final mixed version of the film without it. Errors in matching slow down the recording time, eat up time in the recording studio, interfere with the actors' performance of the lines, and add greatly to the cost of dubbing.

Gaiman's original script was terrific. The dialogue flowed smoothly. Things that were awkward in the direct translation from the Japanese were given back the power and the flow they had in Hayao Miyazaki's original version. Things that worked fine in Japanese but not in English were tweaked to restore the liveliness that direct translation had robbed them of. For example, in one scene Jigo Bo complains that the *okayu* (rice gruel) he just paid for tastes like hot water. This sounds forceful enough in Japanese, but flabby in English. Gaiman rewrote the translation as, "This soup tastes like horse piss. Weak horse piss."

Gaiman also made changes to satisfy Harvey Weinstein, the head of Miramax. These were changes that the Miramax production team felt would help an American audience understand things that were not clear in Miyazaki's original version. Jigo Bo's mysterious motivation, left unspecified in the film, was cleared up for the English-dubbed version by adding the line "The Emperor promised me a palace and a hill of gold for the Deer God's head." The relationship between Jigo Bo and Lady Eboshi was also given some clarity by adding the lines "The Emperor has ordered you to kill the Deer God at once. He doesn't want to wait anymore. Do you think the Emperor cares about your pathetic little ironworks?" There is nothing even remotely close to these lines, or what they imply, in Hayao Miyazaki's original version of the film.

Gaiman's script was also being reviewed by people at Ghibli, a slow process because it involved reading English. But curiosity about how Gaiman and Miramax might change the translation was running high. Ghibli wanted the English version of the film to be good and to appeal to Americans. But they didn't want it altered in material ways.

Some of the things that were added clearly clashed with Miyazaki's and Ghibli's ideas about filmmaking. Ghibli didn't want the motivations of the characters unnecessarily simplified or for some of them to be made into good guys or bad guys. Not conveying all the facts in any given situation is a filmmaker's artistic choice. And the concept of an emperor in Japan is probably different from what most Americans think of when they hear or read the word. Ordering people to go out and kill a forest god (even a made-up forest god) is not the kind of thing a Japanese emperor would get involved in (and suggesting it could earn you death threats from Japanese right-wing extremist groups).

Not that Gaiman didn't understand any of this or wasn't sympathetic to keeping faithful to Hayao Miyazaki's work. He had his marching orders from Miramax, and Harvey Weinstein's main concern, or one of them, was to make the film accessible to a larger American public. Gaiman's problem was having to walk the line between what Harvey wanted and messing with Hayao Miyazaki's film.

In the first version of Gaiman's script Miramax got the artistic side of what they wanted. Gaiman didn't realize that to get the rest of what they wanted Miramax would take the script and make changes to it without consulting him. Gaiman and Miramax were independently revising it with no communication between them. Ghibli had final say over the completed script, so we were getting both versions as they were being revised.

The Stars Align

Recording sessions to dub *Princess Mononoke* had been scheduled to begin in June, but the voice actors who had signed on— Minnie Driver, Claire Danes, and Billy Crudup—all had conflicts and had to be rescheduled. A voice director, Jack Fletcher, was hired. Jack was a classically trained theater director who had extensive ADR experience.

The Miramax team wanted more changes to Gaiman's script to clarify the film and boost its appeal to the American audience. Everyone agreed the script had to be cut down to fit the film, but no one could agree on how. Jack Fletcher recommended a guy who did this kind of work and proposed that we give him the English subtitles for the film and let him create a technical ADR script. The result would be a script that had every line and every utterance spotted with the exact time code matching the film. Each line would be deliverable by a voice actor within the time allotted. And the words in the script would at least approximately match the on-screen "mouth flaps" (the technical term).

The idea was to start with a technically exact script as a baseline and put in Gaiman's more elegant dialogue wherever possible. Miramax liked that idea, and production of a second script began independently of what Gaiman had created.

In the meantime Gillian Anderson, who had signed on to play Moro the giant wolf god, had a schedule change that required her to record earlier than planned, before the ADR script was ready. Hers became the first voice added to the film's English version. The recording took place in LA.

The voice director and the recording staff all got into the studio well in advance of the actual recording session. The clips from the film that correspond to the lines being recorded in a session have to be preprogrammed into the computer that keeps them in synch with the recorded voices. The sequences are reviewed again and again so that everyone at the session is familiar with them and their placement in the film. An actor's availability to record in the studio is usually limited, so you want everything to go smoothly in order to finish the recording in the time allotted and avoid having to call an in-demand actor back for more sessions, which might not be possible for weeks or months later.

When Jack Fletcher got into the studio and discovered that the ADR script for Anderson to read from wasn't ready, a kind of panic set in. The good news was that she had relatively few lines. The better news was that she was running about four hours late, and a morning session had become an afternoon session. We got to work and created a handwritten ADR script on the spot.

People from the business side of Disney who knew about the recording session began making up excuses to drop by. Everyone wanted to have a close-up look at the famous movie star. Since we hadn't updated anyone on the delays and the change in schedule, the drop-by visits stopped by early afternoon.

No one in the studio had ever worked with Gillian Anderson so no one knew what to expect. Some of the actors come with an agent. Some come alone. Some have an entourage to keep them company. Lauren Bacall came with her dog. Sean Combs came with a posse and Jennifer Lopez. Jada Pinkett Smith came

KIKI'S DELIVERY SERVICE

The heroine's exposed underpants in some scenes made the film's American distributors uncomfortable.

with her infant son and her agent. Some actors want to discuss the character and talk about the film. Some just want to stand up next to the microphone and get on with it.

We were huddled in desperation still trying to get the script finished, typed, and printed out when Gillian Anderson arrived. She came by herself, dressed in faded jeans and a tank top. No make-up. She said, "Hi, I'm Gillian. Where do you want me?" Without looking up and assuming it was yet another Disney person looking to get a close-up look at a movie star, Jack told her to just have a seat over by the wall. A few minutes later he realized the mistake.

"Was that ... ? That wasn't ... Oh God. Steve, go over and tell her about the movie."

Anderson was well prepared for the recording session and had studied her parts of the film. She wanted to know if she needed to make her voice sound like the one in the Japanese version. I told her no and mentioned that the Japanese actor who did the role in the original version was male, middle-aged, and a transvestite.

"Oh," she said, "you needed someone to play a middle-aged Japanese transvestite and you thought of me?"

After that Jack came in and took over explaining the part.

Being the first to record when all the other voices you hear are in Japanese can be difficult. Your script has the English translation of the lines you are reacting to, but you have to imagine the tone and the nuances of meaning in the Japanese you hear on the soundtrack. There may be clues in the way the original Japanese lines of your character are delivered, but you may not pick up the inherent femininity in the voice of a fifty-year-old Japanese man.

Asked to be the voice of an angry nine-hundred-pound, twelve-foot-tall wolf god, Gillian Anderson did pretty well and handled the recording session with considerable grace. Miyazaki had conceived the voice for this character as an older male with female aspects, but he is always willing to entertain different interpretations from the actors he selects, and sometimes he is moved to change his mind. Anderson working with Jack Fletcher, an accomplished voice director, tried several different directions for the role, and in the end they made the character more female and a touch warmer than the Japanese original.

More recording sessions were scheduled, and at the same time the ADR script was being rewritten and re-rewritten. Since Miramax was paying the writer(s), they controlled the process. They wouldn't release the latest version of the script to anyone outside of Miramax until the Miramax marketing and distribution executives had submitted their "notes" and had all the corrections made that they deemed necessary.

When I finally saw the script I was surprised that a lot of new material not in the original Japanese version of the film had been added and that there was almost no trace at all of Gaiman's work. When I called Neil to ask about it, he said he had submitted the revisions requested by Miramax and had not heard back. He didn't even know there was a new version of the script in circulation.

For a period of months, even as the actors recorded their lines, a battle over the script was being waged. Miramax was adding new plot points never imagined by Hayao Miyazaki. Gaiman was trying to shorten the script while preserving the beauty of the one he had written. Ghibli was trying to delete changes to the film. The ADR guy was trying to make everything fit.

Minnie Driver came in to record her lines in LA. She had her own ideas about what her character would say and showed us how different versions of her lines would work better. Gaiman was flown in to LA to meet with Jack Fletcher, who was based in San Francisco, to re-revise the script for the recording sessions for the major roles. Claire Danes would be doing San and Billy Crudup would be Ashitaka, and the recording would take place in New York. The cost of the production was mounting.

Because of all the arguing about what would be in the final script, the scripts the actors used had multiple versions of many of the lines of dialogue. Miramax insisted that we record them and then decide later which ones would be used in the final version of the film. This meant doubling the time the actors would be in the recording studio and doubling the time the recording technicians would have to work on mixing the film, greatly increasing the cost of the project.

Jack Fletcher convinced everyone that it would be better to just record everything and then settle the disputes in the final mix. Asking the actors to record alternate versions of most of their major speeches made their job more difficult, but it was better than making them wait in the recording booth during the recording sessions while Fletcher, Gaiman, Ghibli, and Miramax attempted to resolve their disagreements over the script. So all arguments were postponed until the final mix.

It took both Claire Danes and Billy Crudup a full week of all-day sessions to finish their parts in New York. Billy Bob Thornton and the other voice actors recorded their parts back in LA.

For Love (Not Money)

When we finally began to mix the recorded voices for the English version of *Princess Mononoke* together with the music and effects in preparation for laying them down on the film, Miramax raised a new issue: what to do about the sound effects? I was shown a nine-page list of sound effects that Miramax wanted to add to the film. Where there was little or no ambient sound, or where the effects had been used sparingly, the Miramax team wanted to add more sound. The Miramax list was a cornucopia of heavy footsteps, animals snorting, birds flying, birds singing, fire crackling, chickens cackling, drums drumming, cymbals clashing, magical tinkles, insect chirps, howling wind, flowing water, and loud animal-god footsteps. Some of the suggested effects were difficult to imagine, like the sound of a cloud passing.

I was invited to meet with Miramax's chief sound effects

expert in one of their downtown New York offices known as the "Cutting Room." It was in an older building shared by Miramax and other tenants. The elevator in the building was the smallest passenger elevator I have ever seen, and very old. Reluctantly I stepped inside with two people from Miramax, and the three of us had to squeeze together and stoop down to fit in it.

I have a fear of elevators. I have had recurring dreams involving elevators. If I had known we were only going up six floors I would have walked.

The door closed in slow, jerky motions. There was a little window in it the size of a child's fist, just big enough so you could see how slowly the elevator was moving. The elevator inched up unsteadily and hesitantly. As we progressed slowly upward one of the Miramax people asked me if I minded small, enclosed spaces. I said no.

"Good," he said, "because this elevator gets stuck between floors a lot. Yesterday there were people stuck in here for about forty-five minutes."

The elevator finally released us on the sixth floor after about ten minutes that felt longer. I suppressed an urge to kiss the seriously worn oak flooring of the hallway. Our discussion on sound effects was ongoing, and on subsequent visits I discovered a freight elevator in the back that the people who worked in the building usually used. It had a flat platform with no walls and was manned by a full-time elevator operator. He sat on a stool smoking a big cigar, and the cup next to his ashtray gave off the aroma of coffee mixed with whiskey. He got you approximately to whatever floor you requested, but at alarming speed. You had to hop down or step up to the floor where the elevator had failed to align with it.

"Got to work this lever very carefully," the operator told me. "This thing ain't got no safety brakes or all that."

The sixth floor of the building was where Miramax's technical staff worked. Here they cut the films they distributed to make them more audience-friendly or spiced them up for the American audience by enriching the films' original soundtracks.

Miramax wanted to demonstrate to me how they would use the soundtrack to make *Princess Mononoke* a better film. They wanted me to then convince Ghibli to allow Miramax to add sound effects and more music. The Miramax production team believed that the soundtrack was much too quiet. The sound effects technicians played several sequences of the film to show me what they had in mind.

In the scene where Ashitaka first approaches the Deer God's pond deep in the dense, lush forest, the original version is bathed in an eerie blanket of quiet. In the proposed Miramax version of the same scene even the movements of butterflies now had sound. There were magical Tinker Bell–like sounds whenever the little white *kodama* (imaginary forest sprites) appeared. The Deer God had his own Deer God theme music and two other accompanying sound effects called "Aquacool" and "Unknown Territory." They were the kinds of eerie sounds you hear in science fiction or space alien movies.

Additional birds and insects were added. More tree rustling sounds were added. Yakul, the elk-like animal that Ashitaka rides and treats like a cowboy treats his horse, though silent in the original, now had a voice. The effects manager proudly informed me that it was a combination of horse, donkey, camel, ostrich, and llama. An underlying track of moving air was placed throughout so that at a minimum any scene would at least have the sound of wind.

I was stunned by the changes but also relieved. I was afraid that if I thought the changes sounded OK, or at least supported the theory that Americans absolutely will not tolerate silence and that something like this would solve the problem, then I would have to go back to Ghibli and try to convince them to let Miramax Americanize the soundtrack by adding more effects. But the added sounds had made poignantly beautiful scenes comic. The additions were terrible.

Setting aside the fact that the Miramax team really thought that the changes had improved the scene, they insisted that if we didn't make the changes, people in the audience would jump up and yell back at the projectionist "SOUND!!" People would fidget in their seats and be uncomfortable. Some of the audience would even walk out.

I mentioned the no-cut clause in our contract. One of the producers from Miramax mentioned Harvey Weinstein. The sound manager from Miramax mentioned his respect for Hayao Miyazaki. The Miramax producer explained it was her job to keep pushing for what Miramax knew would be best for the success of the film. I mentioned my respect for Miramax and my responsibility to the filmmakers. The Miramax producer mentioned her degree from the NYU School of Film. We all said how much we loved *Princess Mononoke* and how much hard work had gone in to making the English version of the film the best it could possibly be. No decisions were reached and I walked down six flights of stairs and went back to my hotel.

Mixmasters

The final mix of *Princess Mononoke* took place in New York at a sound studio located inside a gorgeous prewar building in midtown Manhattan just off Broadway. The building had an ornate jewel case of a lobby that had been immaculately preserved and cared for over the years. Tourists would occasionally come in to take pictures of it. The upper floors were less ornate and more functional. Security was tight because major motion pictures that had not yet been released to the public were being worked on there. The lobby may have been retro, but everything upstairs was cutting edge.

The hip, young producer in charge of the production for Miramax was Z (this was not actually his real name). Z was given to multitasking. At the recording sessions and then in the final mix he would rarely speak.

All recording studios and mix studios seem to be laid out on exactly the same plan. The mixers, the librarian, the director, and sometimes a producer sat in chairs in front of a large console with thousands of blinking lights and dials that resembled the bridge of the Starship *Enterprise*. A large looming screen displayed the film being worked on. Just behind the console and between it and the screen in a slightly sunken space was a very large, beat-up, and well-worn sofa. Z would always occupy this sofa by himself, usually in a horizontal position. He generally limited his comments to one short sentence per hour, and the comments were often surprisingly insightful, especially coming from a guy seeming not to be paying attention and lying prone on a sofa.

Z's second in command was Y (also not her actual name). She was the day-to-day line producer who handled just about everything. A film school graduate, she tended to give detailed notes on every aspect of the film and wrote elaborate multipage memos. Her notes on the dialogue were voluminous and extremely picky. An actor would have given an Academy Award–level performance on a line and she would reject it because of a barely detectable sound of aspiration (spit) attached to the final "t" in "but." Because of this, nobody liked Y, and she often felt frustrated because Jack Fletcher wouldn't allow her to give her notes directly to the actors so as to avoid pissing them off.

During the mix one or another of the technicians would from time to time turn from their workstations to say how much they admired and appreciated the work of Hayao Miyazaki and that they knew most of his films. I heard this often and believed it was true, but it always gave me pause because at that time (legal) copies of his films weren't available outside Japan.

Normally a final mix would take about a five-day workweek. But because of all the discussion involved in deciding which of the alternate lines would ultimately be used, the *Princess Mononoke* mix was scheduled to take nine to ten days.

I was surprised to discover that during the mix the mix technicians don't mind if you talk to them and ask questions. They themselves would keep up a running banter while working (while the tapes are rewinding, which took a lot of time). After a week of all-day sessions and listening to them talk, I got to know them a little bit. I'm an early riser and, taking advantage of being in New York, I would get into the studio by 8 am, arriving each morning with a toasted bagel with lox schmear and a regular coffee (which in NYC means with milk but not sugar) and hoping to read the *New York Times* before anyone else arrived. But all the technicians would always already be in and at work when I got there, having commuted in from Queens or the Bronx or Long Island where they lived.

When Dom, the lead mixer, added in the English-language walla (background crowd noises) and then mixed it down so it became no more than an indistinct background murmur, I asked him why they bother to bring in all those actors (called the "Loop Group") and record the crowd noises again in English when they could have just used the original indistinct Japanese murmur. He explained that having the individual sounds and placing them exactly where they belong in the audio space makes the audience feel like they're in the scene if it's done right. Although it may sound like a single "murmur" to an untrained ear, each line is placed in a slightly different place. And since the English version is slightly different from the Japanese, it's important to get each line right. Miramax wanted to get it right.

Although you could chat during the mix you couldn't take phone calls. When you got a phone call someone came in to fetch you, and you had to go out to the reception area to take it. Y got a lot of phone calls, and when she was out of the mixing room Z would sit up on his sofa to run things. When this happened the mixing sessions went along more quickly. When Y was in charge things went very slowly. She wanted to review each completed line very carefully. Usually she wanted to confirm that all of the hard Ts were pronounced properly and that the lip synch matched up absolutely perfectly, something Hayao Miyazaki and other Japanese animation directors don't consider important. Whenever Y found a line which she felt came in a half frame too early, Dan, the second mixer, would groan. By day two he had stopped trying to hide his displeasure at her comments.

On day five Jack Fletcher joined the mix and was furious.

He had been told that the first four days would be music and effects only. He was sure that Y did this intentionally so he wouldn't veto her comments.

Jack insisted on hearing everything that had already been done and noticed sound effects that were not in the original. These added effects had escaped my untrained ears. Miramax had added unapproved sound effects that had previously been rejected, and Jack meticulously went through and identified them and then had them all removed. He was also not happy with some of the takes that had been chosen and insisted that we go back and change most of them. Jack said that if his name was going to be on the film he wanted to make sure that the lines in it were the ones that had been discussed and agreed on.

I had been told by Z and Y that the last several days of the mix were purely technical and that there was no reason for me to stay. Jack had me change my flight back to Tokyo and extend my hotel stay for another five days to be sure I was there to the end. Ghibli had final say over the mix, and Jack didn't trust Miramax.

All's Well That Ends ... (Well?)

I was just under an hour late getting back to the mix and found Jack Fletcher looking very pleased with himself. The producer Y was looking very unhappy. As Jack had known all along, many of the lines of dialogue that Miramax wanted to add in order to explain or clarify things had to be discarded. The Miramax writers had tried to take advantage of places in the film where the characters' mouths were not seen or where there were gaps in the action to add expository lines of dialogue. But they had not taken into account the music and effects. In almost every case the lines clashed with music or with effects and had to be left out. Even Y had to admit that they wouldn't work.

Once when Y left the room to take a phone call, the mixers and effects specialists spontaneously apologized for trying to add things to the film. They said they had never agreed that it was necessary or would make the film better, but were doing what they were told to do. Just then a scene came up on the screen where the men of the Tataraba Fortress were having a party. Sounds of dairy cows and chickens had been added to the soundtrack, and everyone in the room burst into laughter.

As we continued to go through the film we continued to discover layers of added sound effects. When Ashitaka jumps off a roof we hear a whooshing (Superman-like) sound effect that had been added. Y tried to argue we should leave it in and see how it sounds when the full sequence had been mixed. No one agreed with her. Everyone looked down at Z reclining on the front sofa, and he slid his forefinger across his throat. Lose it and move on. The tide had turned, and all the added things were finally being routinely deleted with little or no discussion. It frightens me to think how much it cost to have all these extra lines and sound effects added to the film and then cut.

Up until that point the mood in the mixing studio had been bleak. Jack was unhappy because we were spending too much time arguing about effects and alternate lines and not enough time refining the flow of the dialogue. Y was unhappy because everyone had been ignoring her notes. The effects guys were unhappy because they had done all that (good) work and still wished some of it could be used. The mixers were unhappy because Y asked to look at everything too many times and seemed obsessed with over-aspirated final consonants.

Z lightened things up by arriving the next morning with two boxes of doughnuts from a (then) new doughnut shop called Krispy Kreme. He refused to allow anyone to eat one until they had been microwaved for exactly ten seconds. That, he explained, was the perfect amount of time needed to recapture the way they would have tasted when consumed warm from the fryer at the Krispy Kreme store. The honey glaze doughnuts were gone in a flash. The chocolate ones were untouched.

When we returned to the task of mixing the film, midway through the day's session, Z, still reclining on his couch, suddenly launched into an exposition of the film's themes.

"Isn't the ideology of this movie like a big cycle," he said. "The iron taken from the Deer God's earth, once removed from the earth becomes evil, and shot into the boar-god Nago turns into a curse that kills him. The curse goes on to Ashitaka and makes a scar on his arm that has the same shape as the markings on the Deer God's body when he's in the form of Didarabotchi. When the scar on Ashitaka's arm encounters the Deer God, it reacts, like it wants to rejoin the rest of its body, the dark side of the god. He's a god of life and death and the scar is part of the death side. That side is held in check by the Deer God's head, which severed from the body can give eternal life, but also when severed from the body no longer keeps the dark side in check, which then escapes and wreaks havoc and destruction until the balance is again restored and the head is put back, by Ashitaka, who was summoned there because he picked up the curse from Nago, from the iron in the soil in the Deer God's forest that was removed from its body the sand."

Mouths opened and didn't close. A period of silence followed. Minds were absorbing the ideas. What Z had said was very, very interesting, very insightful, and very true. Jack lit up a cigarette and commented on the effects of coffee and sugar on an empty stomach. And then we got back to work.

Towards the end of the day Y asked to listen only to the music in a part of the film that was being reviewed.

Y: Do you hear that? The trumpet isn't hitting that high note properly. Play it again. Put up the volume.

DOM: You might be right. In a theater with a good sound system playing the film loud someone might hear that.

ME: If it's in the music it's the original Japanese music from the Japanese version of the film. That means that the director heard it in the mix and in a theater when they did the final check and he was OK with it. I don't think we should worry about it.

Y: There's a fucking wrong note. We shouldn't release the film with a fucking wrong note in the music. Let's get the original music stem and listen to it and see if it was wrong in the Japanese version. If it is we can correct it.

ME: Look, I can promise you they're not going to send you the stem. If you like I can give them the time code and ask them to check it in Japan.

Y: Don't give me any more of that FUCKING STUDIO GHIBLI BULLSHIT. YOU GET ON THE PHONE WITH JAPAN RIGHT THIS INSTANT AND TELL THEM TO SEND US THE FUCKING MUSIC STEM!! RIGHT FUCKING NOW!! DO YOU HEAR ME? NOW!!

Z: Why don't we take a short break?

The next day Y arrived to announce that she had been transferred to the LA office of Miramax and would be leaving for California. She wished us all well and from then on Jack Fletcher was running the mix.

Without Y in the room, the process of mixing began to run more smoothly, or at least faster, and the mixers thought we might even finish early.

At one point we came to a line in the film that mentions the guns used by the Tataraba people. Dom thought the line sounded odd. He said the word "rifle" would fit better and wondered why we didn't just call the guns rifles. Dom said he checked and there was an alternate take with the word "rifle" that fit much better.

I explained that Hayao Miyazaki had specifically cautioned me that these weapons should not be mistaken for or translated as rifles. Technically they are not rifles. Everyone looked back at me the way I had seen them looking at Y earlier.

DOM: Yeah but Steve they sure look like rifles. I think they look like rifles. Pretty much anybody watching the film would think they're rifles. Isn't it worse to make the audience stumble here?

JACK: I have to agree with Dom. They look like rifles to me. The line doesn't fit.

DAN: We should use the line with rifles. It's a better fit.

ME: But Hayao Miyazaki specifically said ...

DAN: Come on Steve, be reasonable.

JACK: It's a better line. Look Steve, Miyazaki will never know. Even if he watches it, which he won't, he'll never notice. He'll never find out.

ME: But ... they're really not rifles.

JACK: Look, do you think Hayao Miyazaki would want the audience at this point in the film to be not following it and to be worrying about the exact definitions of the weapons?

ME: He might.

JACK: Steve ... it's the American version.

ME: Fine. Rifles. Put in the other line.

The very last days of the mix were only about technical issues. The controversies over changes had finally ended. As we reviewed the earlier reels again, Jack noticed something in one of San's lines. Dom confirmed that up on screen and in the script San was supposed to say "Ugh, I smell a human," but in our mixed version there was no "Ugh" in the line. The lines in the alternate file were checked and none of them had the "Ugh".

Dom asked if Claire Danes actually said "Ugh" during the recording sessions. Jack checked his notes and confirmed that she did. Jack wanted to know what happened to his "Ugh." Jack called Ernie, the dialogue recordist in LA. Ernie checked his files for the tracks he recorded. Yes, he did have the "Ugh." Somehow it was left off the track that was sent to Miramax. Ernie then recorded the "Ugh" from his "archives" and promised to overnight it by FedEx to New York.

The next day, a Saturday, the tape from LA had not arrived. Dom called Dan at home to tell him the tape hadn't arrived. Dan called Jack at home in San Francisco (Jack would fly home every weekend to be with his family). Dan told Jack the tape didn't arrive. Jack called Ernie at home in LA to find out if the "Ugh" had been sent. Ernie called the recording studio and discovered that the FedEx guy missed the package and it was never picked up. Ernie then arranged for the "Ugh" to be sent via an ISDN line from the sound studio in LA to the sound studio in New York. In order to do that Miramax had to agree to rent time in both studios and pay the technicians double time because it was a weekend. Dan called Z at home for authorization and Z told him to go ahead. The "Ugh" then duly arrived and was added to the soundtrack.

When I heard the story on Monday I wondered how much it cost to do all that. Then I realized that I didn't want to know, but in another few months I was going to have to.

As it turned out, this entire process was nothing like the way all of the subsequent English-language versions of Ghibli's films were made. After *Princess Mononoke*, Ghibli's films were dubbed by Disney and supervised by Pixar's John Lasseter. There were disagreements about translation and what should or should not be in the scripts, but all the differences were relatively minor and all were resolved long before the superb casts that Disney/Pixar had lined up came in to record the voices. The experience of dubbing *Princess Mononoke* was an absolutely invaluable learning experience, because most of what we did on it was wrong. In theory you can sometimes learn more from making mistakes than from not making any.

And yet, the highly talented cast and technical crew that made the English-language version of *Princess Mononoke* still turned out a work that we were all proud of and deserved to be proud of. Minnie Driver in the role of Lady Eboshi absolutely nailed her character and gave a superb performance. Claire Danes and Billy Crudup recording in New York were fantastic. Billy Bob Thornton in recording sessions in LA that began at 11 pm did a fine Jigo Bo. Neil Gaiman came back and made the final fixes to the script. When it was all mixed and put together the result was good. We just did it a little more painfully and more expensively than was necessary. Though experience is the best of all possible teachers, not everyone can afford the tuition.

11

~~~~~~~~~~~~~~~~

The Circle of Life

To the Clouds

志雲より高く
Let that to which you aspire be higher than the clouds.

Tokuma Shoten founder Yasuyoshi Tokuma died on September 20, 2000, and the management inclined rapidly. The company was one of the largest entertainment publishers until the 1990s. Some of their products included music, computer and game software, movies, magazines, manga and books. One of their most famous subsidiaries was Studio Ghibli. The company sold off Daiei Motion Pictures, Tokuma Japan Communications and the headquarters in Shiodome. Studio Ghibli also left from the group and became an independent company. Tokuma Japan Communications was purchased by Daiichikosho and Daiei Motion Pictures was purchased by Kadokawa Shoten. Tokuma Shoten finished the arrangement of the debt by 2005, and is developing only the publication business now.

(from *Wikipedia*)

No one can deny that Yasuyoshi Tokuma had a flair for living. It extended to his death and to the funeral arrangements that followed. To both of his funerals.

I often heard Mr. Tokuma in speeches and in private conversation say that he would remain at the helm of all of his companies, vigorously running things, up until age seventy-five, after which he would retire. When he hit seventy-five he revised this to say that he would remain at the helm of all of his companies, vigorously running things, up until age eighty. But he never quite made it that far.

Mr. Tokuma's health had been failing. His death in September 2000, just short of his seventy-ninth birthday, came at a time when entertainment-related companies were having to seriously reconsider their business models. There had been a growing concern among the managers of the Tokuma companies (other than Studio Ghibli) that they might not survive without their charismatic leader. Not that Mr. Tokuma was directly involved in the actual management of his companies. But he did hold them together and keep things going by the force of his personality. That and his extraordinary ability to obtain bank loans. The short Wikipedia entry on the Tokuma business, apparently written by a non-native English speaker, captures the tone of the events, though it has the direction of management's trajectory reversed.

Due to the pile of corporate debt that Mr. Tokuma had managed to accumulate, the bankers were already in the process of taking over the Tokuma companies even before Mr. Tokuma passed away. The former bank executive who had been brought in to clean things up, or at least to stop the hemorrhaging of cash and assets, was just getting settled in when he suddenly found himself actually in charge.

The business of entertainment companies in general depends on the reading of the current and future tastes of a fickle public with an ever-shrinking attention span. When Yasuyoshi Tokuma died in September 2000 the things that everyone knew would probably happen to the Tokuma Group's fortunes did begin to happen. All the Tokuma companies at one point or another in their histories had become successful. But as the publishing industry and the music industry began to be disrupted by advances in technology and the growth of the internet, and by the normal migration of Japanese consumer tastes, many of the Tokuma companies began to decline.

At the time of Mr. Tokuma's death, only Studio Ghibli and the magazine *Asahi Geino* were profitable. *Asahi Geino* followed the Japanese time-honored tradition of mixing racy stories about political scandals, photos of alluringly posed women wearing suggestive or very little clothing (or just naked), and just enough legitimate political commentary for a man to claim he only bought the magazine for its articles. It was a profitable formula as long as the editors knew which scandals and which women would sell magazines.

But even *Asahi Geino* hit a speed bump when it was singled out in the Japanese Diet (parliament) as one of the worst purveyors of socially irredeemable, morally offensive smut and gratuitous profit mongering. Japanese politicians publicly accused *Asahi Geino* of cynically preying on people's prurient weaknesses.

Mr. Tokuma immediately took up the defense of his magazine by forcefully arguing in public that his magazine served a legitimate public interest. It exposed corrupt politicians, he said (except possibly those he was friendly with). It was a magazine that adhered to the highest standards of civic journalism, and he was proud of it.

But even Mr. Tokuma was shocked when he discovered that *Asahi Geino* (which he had stopped reading years earlier) had published photos of the all-time ten best "upskirt" shots, including one of England's Queen Elizabeth as she sat on a podium waiting to address an audience. A brief attempt to get the magazine to tone down the "V" photos failed. Apparently, if a magazine failed to provide the level of female crotch-related coverage demanded by its readers it could not hope to retain its audience. *Asahi Geino* prided itself on being cutting edge when it came to publishing pictures of mostly naked women, and Mr. Tokuma had to concede that it might after all be time to think about selling off the magazine.

The discussions on what to do about the money-losing businesses were ongoing when Tokuma-*shacho* died. His death, though not unexpected, provided a respite from the turmoil of a collapsing company. All deliberations about how to right the failing company were put on hold. The outpouring of affection for the man seemed to make it imperative that his demise be properly commemorated in a big way and in public. The practical financial discussions were tabled in favor of talking about how to celebrate the life of the company's founder. Upon sober reflection a person might feel uneasy about some of the things Mr. Tokuma did or about the way he ran his companies. And yet there was something about the man that attracted respect and affection. It was what I thought of as Pirates of the Caribbean Syndrome.

Pirates of the Caribbean is a children's ride at Disneyland. You sit in a boat packed with families and float along watching life-sized animatronic costumed robots enacting scenes of pirates ravaging a town. As the pirates steal, loot, rape the town's women, and murder their husbands, they chug down mugs of (animatronic) ale and sing *Yo ho yo ho a pirate's life for me!* Their floating audience oohs and ahs in appreciation. Yet, if you were to stop and think about it, shouldn't you feel that there is something not exactly right about presenting and applauding rape and murder together with excessive consumption of alcohol and joyful song as an entertainment for children?

When I first experienced this ride (attraction, as Disney calls it), I found myself floating along in my boat and wondering why no one else seemed bothered or concerned. Everyone seemed to be having a good time. So why be a killjoy and cause trouble by making a moral quibble?

Tokuma management focused all its attention on the funeral arrangements of their patriarch. There would be both a funeral and a special commemorative ceremony called the O Wakare no Kai (Leave-Taking Ceremony). An ad hoc committee was formed to manage the commemorative ceremony for Mr. Tokuma. The head of the committee was Hayao Miyazaki.

Hayao Miyazaki is above all else an artist and filmmaker. Miyazaki had never had any contact with anyone from the Tokuma businesses except Mr. Tokuma himself and Toshio Suzuki, the producer who had reluctantly moonlighted as the number-two man in the Tokuma empire. The Tokuma businesspeople hoped that Miyazaki would see his role as honorary and refrain from making statements to the press. Back at the studio Miyazaki was overheard saying, "Fine, now that the president is dead I'm through working with these people. I respected the man, but not his company."

The operational heads of the funeral committee were Mr. Tokuma's wife; the new president of Tokuma Shoten from Sumitomo Bank, O-san; and a representative from Tokuma Shoten middle management who actually did all the work, Tadokoro-san. The O Wakare no Kai itself was technically not a funeral but a commemorative ceremony and would be huge. The thousands of invited guests (about 3,500) would include a complete who's-who of Japanese politics and entertainment. In numerous meetings and in many detailed memos, Tadokoro-san and his staff carefully outlined and documented every expected or anticipated action that would or could occur at the ceremony. All Tokuma employees had assigned tasks at the ceremony that were explained in minute detail. Every VIP attendee had a Tokuma employee escort assigned to him or her.

The O Wakare no Kai was not an actual funeral, but invited guests could be forgiven for believing that it was. Accordingly, instructions were given that if the traditional funeral envelopes with money inside were offered, they had to be refused, or if refusal was impossible, handed directly over to Mr. Tokuma's wife. Since it was the company holding the ceremony, the contributions might have complicated the company's tax position. Offers of flowers also were to be refused. The flower situation had been thoroughly handled by Tadokoro-san's staff, and excess flowers would only confuse things. Because every aspect of the ceremony had been carefully planned and timed out, special instructions were issued for what to do in the unlikely event that the VIP for whom you were responsible arrived early or late—a serious issue in Japan.

In one of the many meetings that took place before the event, Toshio Suzuki, then a managing director of Tokuma Shoten and the head of Studio Ghibli, filled in senior management on the events of the last few days before Mr. Tokuma's death. Tokuma-*shacho* had been, as expected, upbeat and positive until the end. He was talking about having the company's usual directors' meetings and senior managers' meetings in his hospital room. Women who weren't his wife visited and left in tears.

Suzuki also kept us up to date on the protocol-related issues we faced at the O Wakare no Kai. At least one Japanese prime minister and several Living National Treasures would be in attendance. Many chairmen and presidents of major Japanese corporate groups would be there. Other famous and important people were invited. This created issues that required detailed attention. Who would arrive first? Who would leave first? Who would sit closest to the stage? Who would sit on the left and who on the right? If the prime minister attended where would his bodyguards sit (stand)? If an unexpected dignitary just showed up where would he fit in? If an ordinary VIP insisted on being re-classed as a special extraordinary VIP how would that be dealt with? If these sorts of decisions had to be made on the spot, who would be designated to make them?

Anyone who has ever attended a formal Japanese dinner will understand the issues. But this event was hundreds of times larger. At one point during one of the meetings Suzuki, sitting next to me, turned to me and said, "This is exactly how Japan lost the Pacific War."

The period just after Tokuma-*shacho*'s death was especially hard on Suzuki. Mr. Tokuma had been a mentor to him and an occasional adversary when it came to looking out for the interests of Studio Ghibli. Suzuki had played a large role in keeping the Tokuma companies afloat. After Mr. Tokuma's death Suzuki was burdened with meetings for the funeral arrangements, taking on some of Mr. Tokuma's duties and spending more time than he wanted to in the presence of elected public officials. At one point one of his key staff members approached him with the good news that he was getting married soon. "Look," Suzuki told the guy, "not now. You've managed to get by until now without being married. Get by without it a little longer."

Mr. Tokuma's favorite singer, the *enka* artist Itsuki Hiroshi, was asked to perform Mr. Tokuma's favorite song at the ceremony, a piece called "Chigiri." When the choice was announced it was soon vetoed at a hastily called emergency meeting. The song had certain connections to extreme rightwing nationalists with whom public figures preferred not to be associated. A sigh of relief was breathed when a second song, "Sanga" (The Mountain Stream), was proposed and accepted, until someone pointed out it was far shorter than the amount of time it needed to fill. Measures were then suggested to have it extended (artfully) to seven minutes, and the meeting was adjourned.

To the observer unfamiliar with issues of Japanese protocol the elaborateness of the preparations might have seemed like overkill. Perhaps, but in Japan it usually can't be avoided. When the Showa Emperor died and his son, the current emperor, stood at the head of the reception line welcoming the foreign heads of state who had come to his father's funeral, it was my own Tokyo landlord, then the head of protocol for the Imperial Household Agency, to whom the duty fell to let the new emperor know exactly who it was he was about to shake hands with. My landlord could be seen, there in the live TV coverage of the event, standing next to the emperor and whispering in his ear just before each guest stepped forward. Of course no one expects the emperor of Japan to recognize the president of Lichtenstein by sight or to know the name of his wife. But my landlord also found himself whispering into the emperor's ear, "This is Prince Charles from England and the tall lady with him is Princess Diana." In such situations, you take nothing for granted.

The O Wakare no Kai took place in a special building in the

Takanawa Prince Hotel complex near Shinagawa. At exactly 1 pm the doors to the hall were opened and the guests began to arrive. My job at the ceremony was to mind Michael O. Johnson, the president of Walt Disney's International Division, who had flown in just for the ceremony from Los Angeles. Mikiko Takeda from our office and I met him at the door, and we walked him over to the reception table where he was signed in and issued the oversized white corsage that marked him as a level-2 VIP.

A phalanx of stunningly beautiful professional event women in their late thirties and dressed in black prom gowns were hired to add a kind somber but graceful elegance to the event. One of them pinned the corsage to MOJ's lapel, and we headed upstairs to the VIP waiting room. In Japan VIPs don't wait at events with non-VIPs—they get their own private rooms. Across the hall, former Japanese Prime Minister Yasuhiro Nakasone and Tokyo Governor Ishihara Shintaro were just checking in. When we got upstairs and found MOJ's designated seat at the designated table, we sat down to briefly explain to him his duties at the ceremony and approximately what would occur.

At a certain time everyone would be summoned into the huge assembly room. The VIPs would be shown to their designated seats at the front of the auditorium. After a moment of silence Hayao Miyazaki would say a few words. Then on a big screen a video showing the highlights of Mr. Tokuma's life would be played. Next, three gentlemen would stand up to speak: Seiichiro Ujiie, the head of the Japan Broadcasters Television Association and chairman of the NTV Broadcasting Network; Yusuke Okada, the head of the Motion Picture Association of Japan and the chairman of Toei Films; and Toshiyuki Hattori, the head of the Association of Japanese Publishers and the chairman of the publishing house Kodansha.

Itsuki Hiroshi would then sing "Sanga" and the seated VIPs would stand and each be issued a single white flower. The VIPs would proceed single-file in precisely the predetermined order toward a giant picture of Mr. Tokuma, execute a formal bow, lay their flower beneath the picture, bow again, and leave. As far as what to do in the procession itself, the only advice I could give MOJ was to just do whatever the person in front of him does. I'd lived in Japan for almost thirty years and at formal ceremonies it's all I ever did.

MOJ noticed Hayao Miyazaki sitting by himself puffing on a cigarette and asked to go over to express his condolences. He began by telling Miyazaki a few personal anecdotes from his dealings with Mr. Tokuma and then asked after Mr. Miyazaki's family. MOJ seemed puzzled that Miyazaki's family were not present, and Miyazaki seemed puzzled that MOJ expected them to be there.

Whenever MOJ had met with Mr. Tokuma, usually the first thing he asked him was about his family. "How are your wife and daughter?" MOJ would ask. This always puzzled Mr. Tokuma, and he would usually take me aside to ask, "This Johnson fellow, what is he getting at? Why is he asking about my family? What does he mean? Is he after something?" Sometimes Tokuma-*shacho* was upset by the question. He had an unpredictable temper. I always tried to explain that Americans like to be friendly and it's usually a positive thing to care about, or to seem to care about, another person's family. But Mr. Tokuma never really grasped the concept.

Suzuki came over and introduced MOJ to O-san, the man from Sumitomo who was now running Tokuma Shoten. Mr. O insisted on holding the conversation entirely in English, and MOJ had a hard time following him. Mr. O had acquired his English while serving at his bank's New York branch. Apparently no one had ever mentioned to him that his English was less than fluent. MOJ kept looking over at me for a translation, but since he was already getting English I thought it might be rude to translate. O-san shook hands with MOJ, Suzuki said, "Mr. O, your English is very rich," and I returned MOJ to his table.

A young woman from Daiei Films came over to ask if we would mind if she brought the Japanese TV and movie actress Yoshiko Mita to sit with us. Apparently Mita-san was unhappy at her assigned table. Very few of the VIPs in the room were under seventy and I assumed it was an age thing. Yoshiko Mita is gorgeous in person. On TV she looked about forty-five, but in person she looked ten years younger. She was then actually over fifty. She also had a kind of permanently pissed-off expression on her face. Many Asian men find this appealing.

Ms. Mita did not smile when being introduced around at our table. She seemed reluctant to speak directly with *gaijin* and spoke only to Mikiko, MOJ's co-minder. This was probably just as well, because all I could think of to say was "Hey! *Hayame no Pabilon!* That's you right?" That was the slogan for the cold medicine she advertised on TV. MOJ for his part was looking for heads of major corporations to be introduced to and not movie actresses.

Suzuki came over to take MOJ to be introduced to Mrs. Tokuma. Mikiko and I didn't go with him. This sounds odd, since we were his designated minders and his translators, but we had heard stories about Mrs. Tokuma and I think we were afraid to come into contact with her. Either Suzuki handled the translation or she and her daughter could speak (some) English. When MOJ emerged from her private room five minutes later he took me aside.

"That was very strange," MOJ said. "Mrs. Tokuma seemed more interested in promoting her own business interests than talking about her husband. She asked me if I could help her in the US with her business. Then she started telling me that her husband treated her badly and left her with no money. Is that a normal thing to tell someone you just met at a funeral?"

I told him I thought it was probably not normal.

Back at the table Mikiko was trying to get a conversation going by explaining to MOJ what movies Yoshiko Mita had been in. But when Mita-san finally realized that we were from Studio Ghibli and not Tokuma Shoten, she said she wanted us to know that she had never been asked by Hayao Miyazaki to do a voice for one of his films. She said she felt strongly that she should have been asked, and that if asked she would do an excellent job, and should she be asked in the future, she would certainly consider it. I would have mentioned that Hayao Miyazaki was in the room somewhere if she wanted to ask him herself, but she was still not talking to *gaijin*.

When the signal came for the VIPs to enter the main hall we all stood and proceeded toward the door. Mita-san held back a little in order to allow MOJ to go in with her elegantly draped on his arm, but he missed the look and she gave up and went on alone. Once through the door and into the public space, though, we did discover that she had a very beautiful smile.

The first station on the route into the main hall was a battalion of the professionally ornamental event women dressed in their identical black evening gowns. When a person wearing a white corsage appeared before them they would brighten and bow him forward. When a designated VIP appeared without a white corsage there was a minor flurry of activity as they took him aside, located his corsage, pinned it to him, and then released him back into the flow of entering VIPs. Past the line of ornamental women was a line of middle-aged men dressed in black formal suits. These were a combination of Tokuma company executives, professional security men, and Japanese Secret Service agents who were examining the entering guests and nodding gravely as each passed inspection.

There was a last-minute bustle when Ujiie-san from NTV arrived late. The reception area staff had received instructions for his corsage to be sent up to the VIP waiting room. One of the assistants with a walkie-talkie called up to the VIP room to have the corsage brought down but the person in the VIP room refused. He/she had instructions to give it to him upstairs, and he/she wasn't deviating from his/her instructions.

Even though Ujiie-san was one of the four speakers at the ceremony, one of Japan's most powerful business executives, and an actual close friend and confidant of the late Mr. Tokuma, the reception staff weren't letting him in without his corsage. Just as it appeared there might actually be combat between the guarders of the gates and the minders of the VIPs, in a burst of creative improvisation, Haruyo Moriyoshi, who was Ujiie-san's designated minder, stole the corsage intended for Japanese Prime Minister Mori, who was delayed and wouldn't arrive for another half hour or more, pinned it to her charge—and Ujiie-san was allowed to enter.

Only invited guests were allowed into the hall, and the VIPs and the minders were separated. Minders joined the group of Tokuma employees and security men who would watch the ceremony on closed-circuit TV monitors in an operations room at the back of the building.

At the front of the cavernous main ceremony hall was an entire wall of white flowers topped with a giant picture of Mr. Tokuma and flanked on either side with giant video screens. Mr. Tokuma's smiling, benevolent, grandfatherly countenance graced both screens and several other smaller screens placed at intervals throughout the hall. Crystalline chandeliers glittered and threw off colorful sparkles of dancing light. The mellow tones of classical chamber music seeped into the hall from a screened-off area over to one side where a dozen unseen musicians played.

A professional MC standing at a podium at the front of the hall welcomed the attendees and guided things along. There were the speeches and a video montage of Mr. Tokuma's life. There was the tearful rendition of "Sanga" by Itsuki Hiroshi with his eyes fixed on an image of Mr. Tokuma projected on one of the big screens. As the camera panned the front row of VIPs, Mikiko and I were relieved to see that MOJ was still awake.

And then Mrs. Tokuma rose to speak. Her voice was firm and confident. She wore a simple black suit. No jewelry. Very plain. There was a certain tone of melodrama to what she said, and she was clearly not at all intimidated by the size and composition of the audience. She said that Mr. Tokuma had been diagnosed with cancer over ten years before and had been fighting it ever since. Usually in Japan people don't say the word "cancer" in public or recognize it as the cause of death, so the audience kind of snapped to attention and let out a collective gasp.

Mrs. Tokuma went on to say that only two weeks ago the doctors had given him less than two weeks to live, but that to the very end he had been planning this and that as if he never thought that soon he might be gone. She said that, as she had just been explaining to the nice gentleman from the Walt Disney Company who had flown here all the way from Los Angeles, her husband had wanted her to be independent and tough, like an American wife, and to take an interest in business. Suddenly the audience was wondering if she was saying she intended to run her husband's businesses.

And then Mrs. Tokuma said that there was one man in particular whom she wanted to thank for supporting her and her family in this very trying time. It was the man who had been sent from Sumitomo Bank to temporarily help run her husband's companies. The man who had protected her interests and her daughter's interests and who she hoped would continue to run her husband's businesses and look after her interests, Mr. O. "Mr. O would you please stand up and join me on the stage. Please step up here and let me introduce you."

This was an unscripted moment. Mr. O seemed reluctant to go up. He didn't want to give the impression that he was Mrs. Tokuma's man at the company but he could hardly refuse to go up having been publicly summoned in that way in that place. He had no choice. He shouldn't go but he had to go. He seemed to be wondering how this had happened as he stood on the stage in front of some of the most important people in Japan with Mrs. Tokuma's arm draped around his shoulder and her slender fingers smoothing the wrinkles in his suit collar.

Mrs. Tokuma continued to freely handle Mr. O as she continued to explain his virtues to the audience. By the time she was finished delivering what probably should have been the acting president's lines and allowed him to return to his seat, there was nothing he could do but weakly thank her for her support. Was she actually planning to take over from her husband and defy the bank's instructions? No one knew.

The speeches having concluded, forty-nine designated

VVIPs rose to lay flowers on the dais in front of Mr. Tokuma's picture. The name of each was called out and he or she came forward to receive a single white flower from a white-gloved female attendant. Each of them then went and offered the flower to the image of Tokuma-*shacho*. They paused to offer a silent prayer or to review a private memory, bowed, and then turned to leave the auditorium. After that, the non-VVIPs were allowed to proceed in predetermined order to offer their flowers, each taking one from trays held by black-suited male bearers. First the regular VIPs, then the company directors, then the company employees, and finally anyone else who was there.

Mikiko and I escorted MOJ back to his waiting limousine, and on the way back to the hall we encountered the current Japanese prime minister Mori and his security guard as they were mounting the escalator to leave. Just then, an expensively dressed older woman began waving and trying to get the prime minister's attention. The guards looked to their boss, and he shot them back a look that said, "absolutely not." Then the woman, exasperated, charged up the escalator toward them. The guards set themselves to repel her, but she just ducked underneath their arms and then wrapped one of her arms around the prime minister's shoulder and began talking into his ear. The PM looked helplessly at his bodyguards as she continued to talk. The bodyguards continued to alertly scan the area and even extended their protective cordon to include the woman. Prime Minister Mori exited the building with her still attached to his shoulder and talking into his ear.

I finally took my turn to pause underneath the large portrait of a benevolently smiling Tokuma-*shacho* and offer a single, fragrant white lily. Even though the flower was a bit beaten up from being at the bottom of the pile, standing there and offering it felt special. There is something about that moment when you stand alone with your thoughts while offering up a pinch of incense or a flower. You cannot help but reflect on the deceased, on death itself, and on life's larger moments.

Heads of state or great artists, scientists, or philosophers had passed away and their passing had been marked by less pomp and ceremony than what I had just witnessed. In the larger scale of things, what did this man, extraordinary to those who knew him and the sincere object of our admiration and affection, do to deserve this impressively grand memorial and send-off to the hereafter? All I could think was that someone simply had the money to do it and the will to do it and it happened. As Clint Eastwood's character William Munny observes in the film *Unforgiven*, "Deserve ain't got nothin' to do with it."

But standing there in that moment, before a wall of flowers and a mountain of floral offerings under the benevolently smiling portrait, I felt something else. There on a small table were Mr. Tokuma's two imperial medals, framed for display, with their big red and blue jewels glittering like the glass rhinestones in a child's cowboy or cowgirl outfit. This had been a ceremony that more than anyone else Mr. Tokuma himself would have loved. I felt with certainty and with no embarrassment a sincere affection for the specialness of the man. I thought of the things I had learned from him, either directly or secondhand through Suzuki. Don't let anyone write the screenplay of your life. Make your ambitions high. Real men don't apologize. And always remember, if you need money, the banks have plenty of it.

Who among us can actually live like that?

Back to Earth

The real funeral for Mr. Tokuma, a relatively private ceremony, took place at the Zen temple Chokokuji. A little over a month later there was an interring of the bones ceremony at the same temple for the purpose of placing Mr. Tokuma's ashes into his grave.

Chokokuji sits on a hillside off a small side street in the upscale Tokyo district of Aoyama. The main street in the area is Kotto-dori (Antiques Dealers' Street). It is where some of Tokyo's more famous dealers in Japanese and Asian art and antiquities had shops until soaring real estate prices drove them elsewhere. A few stayed and built deluxe condominium apartment buildings on top of their shops.

Once you pass through Chokokuji's large front gate you are in another, less modern world. Its wooden main buildings are among the few to have survived the bombings of WWII that devastated most of Tokyo (along with the subsequent sixty years of rebuilding). To the right as you enter is a smaller, newer building that houses a magnificent thirty-foot-tall wooden statue of Kannon (the Goddess of Mercy) carved from a single block of wood (mostly) in the 1970s. It's done in an unusual Art Deco style. The temple's in-training Zen Buddhist acolytes live, work, and meditate in the older buildings to the left of the entrance. To the right and behind the building that houses Kannon, there is a more modern building meant to host the activities that accompany a funeral. Funerals are the way Zen Buddhist priests earn their living in modern times.

The assembled guests at the ceremony, mostly Tokuma company executives and senior staff, arrived according to a fairly precise schedule and proceeded to the newer building. A series of memos at work had preceded the event so that everyone knew exactly when and where to arrive, how much of a contribution he/she was expected to make (Japanese funerals involve presenting a cash donation in a specially purposed envelope at the reception area), and which of the normal things that happen at funerals would not happen at this one (cash was delivered to the company in advance instead of in the special envelope at the reception). Those of us who arrived on time spent the next half hour milling about and chatting. Extra time had been built in for late arrivals, but this being Japan and involving a group of Tokuma-trained employees, no one arrived late. Dress at this kind of ceremony is formal, but slightly less formal than at the larger O Wakare No Kai: dark business suits; ties with subdued patterns and not black; no Mickeys or Totoros.

When the appointed time arrived, everyone was ushered into a large *tatami* room where we sat on the floor at low tables and were served tea and large butter cookies in the shape of doves. These cookies are always served to people sitting and waiting to go into a funeral ceremony, and I have never discovered why butter cookies or why doves.

Seated to my right was the Ghibli film director Isao Takahata and to my left Yukari Tai, the head of Ghibli's publishing division. Both were sitting in the formal *seiza* position and looking at me with mild disapproval. *Seiza* is that position you assume when seated on a cushion on a *tatami* mat at a formal occasion (tea ceremony or funeral). You sit bolt upright with your knees bent under you and your ankles somehow tucked underneath so the balls of your feet support your rear end. Most Japanese can do this but usually *gaijin* cannot. Japanese manage to look moderately comfortable sitting in this position and can even sip tea, eat a cookie, or chat with each other while doing it. When I do it, all I know is that I am in pain, a lot of pain, and in danger of tipping over.

Since everyone else was sitting in *seiza*, I forced my body to conform as best I could. At first you feel kind of elated since you have a nice, comfortable, spatially efficient, elevated perch from which to survey your surroundings and freely use your arms to reach for a teacup or unwrap a cookie. Then you notice a tingling sensation in your legs that soon becomes a tingling painful sensation. Tiny metallic ants are gnawing at your ankles. Angry bees are stinging your claves. An unknown assailant is slicing off your toes. The pain reaches a crescendo and you nearly scream out, but suddenly it recedes to a dull throbbing and then seems to stop altogether. At this point you discover that you can no longer feel anything from the waist down.

This is where the worst of it begins, because should you have to move at all or change positions, the bolts of electric pain in your legs as they begin to wake up are excruciating. And since your legs have gone to sleep, walking on them is a risky business, if you can even manage it. No information about the ground is coming back to you from your feet or legs, except for the pain as the lower half of your body begins to revive.

At my father-in-law's funeral I sat in *seiza* for what seemed like hours. When it was my turn to go up and offer incense, I thought that my legs underneath me had unbent and were ready to go, but when I moved to stand up I just toppled over onto my face. Japanese people are generally kind in this situation; my brother-in-law and his teenage son simply picked me up and dragged me forward until I could get my legs going again, and everyone else pretended it hadn't happened.

At one point I asked Tai-san sitting next to me and looking relatively serene, how Japanese people managed to do this.

"Doesn't it hurt?" I asked her.

"Of course it hurts," she said, "but the trick is not to mind that it hurts."

I had to wonder if this was really true or if she was just recalling Peter O'Toole's famous line from the film *Lawrence of Arabia*. I turned to Takahata and asked him if his legs hurt, and he grudgingly admitted that they did.

After about a half hour we were instructed to proceed to the temple's main hall where the service would take place. When we entered the main hall and I saw that we would be sitting on folding chairs and not on the floor I was enormously relieved. The Zen monks who do the service filed in, and they took the proper seating posture thing to a whole new level. They plopped down onto straw mats on the *tatami* and assumed the *seiza* position. Then they extended their arms into a rigid L shape, elbows bent, forearms up, palms facing in, making their arms into living (but not moving) bookstands for the sutra books they were holding that contain the chants they would be performing (offering) during the service. For forty-five minutes their bodies were absolutely motionless as they chanted the sutras.

The chanting was wonderful and very soothing. A senior monk led them and from time to time tapped on a giant metal bowl with a little metal mallet. Gongs bonged sonorously. Bells tinkled. A wooden block was struck with a wooden stick, making rapid staccato sounds. Chanting voices and the aroma of incense filled the hall.

Amunamudabiamunamudabiamunamudabiamunamudabi

... gonggggggggggggg ... ding-ding ... bonggggggggggg ... Amu-namudabiamunamudabiamunamudabiamunamudabi ... ding.

This went on for something like a half hour, and then there were some speeches and the offering of incense. Some people could be heard snoring during the sutras, others during the speeches. The offering of incense involved forming two lines and going up individually to sift a few pinches of incense onto a small burning coal and offer up a brief prayer to the deceased and then a quick formal bow to the deceased's family. By then everyone was awake.

After the ceremony in the temple the group moved outside to the gravesite. Chokokuji's cemetery overlooks the spacious and unspoiled gardens of the Nezu Museum. It extends across a large hillside in a maze of walkways, none of which forms a straight line. Here and there are ancient, gnarly cherry trees and a few massive ginkgo trees presiding over an undulating sea of gravestones. Some of the graves are hundreds of years old.

Mr. Tokuma had chosen himself a very lovely plot just in front of a bamboo grove at the edge of the cemetery. It was a picture-perfect autumn day. Wedge-shaped yellow ginkgo leaves sizzled on their branches. Birds warbled. Wispy clouds drifted across a pale blue sky. A small army of funeralgoers clad in black had snaked its way among the gravestones and crowded into a space not designed for crowds. At the center of the group the head priest of the temple and the immediate family and the Tokuma Shoten board of directors clustered around a newly carved gravestone that said "Tokuma." This was where Mr. Tokuma's ashes would be buried.

In the graveside ceremony the priest opens the urn with the deceased's ashes. The next of kin formally identifies the ashes, which are then interred beneath the granite tombstone. Mrs. Tokuma, however, declined to identify her husband's ashes saying, "I lived with the man for twenty-five years. That's enough. I don't need to look at his ashes."

The acting president of Tokuma Shoten, O-san, then

stepped forward and identified the ashes. They were placed under the tombstone.

Then we all snaked our way back out of the cemetery in single file and returned to the large gathering room in the new building, where an elaborate *kaiseki* box lunch was served. Again everyone assumed the *seiza* position, but this time I just couldn't. Appearances are one thing, but if you're going to eat a $200 boxed lunch you ought to be able to enjoy it.

12

DirecTV

Toshio Suzuki, my boss and mentor at Tokuma Shoten, Studio Ghibli's former parent company, used to impart his accumulated wisdom to me either in one-on-one lunches at his favorite restaurants or when sitting next to him in his car as we made the one- or two-hour drive, depending on traffic, between Shinbashi and Higashi Koganei. The restaurants Suzuki chose for lunch were all small and had been in business for decades. They were all in the older part of Shinbashi, a maze-like warren of small alleys south of the JR train station, or underground in the basements of the shabby office buildings on the station side of Dai-ichi Keihin-dori.

Suzuki's restaurants were drinking establishments at night, but during the lunch hour, in order to help pay the rent and stay in business, they offered *teishoku* (fixed menu) specials. The ingredients were the freshest, the finest, and mostly fish from the nearby Tsukiji market. The price of a lunch special was very low. These were places that only certain people knew about, but enough people did, and if you didn't get there before noon they'd have run out of food. 99.9% of all salaried people in Japan eat their lunch between noon and 1:30 pm. This says something about who ate in these restaurants before noon.

The year was 1997, early in my tenure at Tokuma Shoten. On one of Suzuki's regular visits to Shinbashi to attend a monthly department heads' meeting, he stopped by my office to invite me to join him for lunch. Mr. Tokuma was about to announce that the company would be joining a consortium that would operate a satellite TV broadcast service in Japan. Meetings at Tokuma Shoten began precisely at 10 am. The monthly meetings always ended before 11:30. Mr. Tokuma was a man of very precise habits, and Suzuki knew we could reliably be out of the Tokuma building by 11:31.

Suzuki and I left the Tokuma Shoten Building, crossed the wide Dai-ichi Keihin-dori, entered an older, grimy, featureless office building on the opposite side of the street, and descended to the second basement of the building. We found our way to a small restaurant with a seating capacity of nine around a burnished wooden U-shaped counter. The restaurant had just opened for business, and there were already six other in-the-know but seedy-looking patrons seated at the counter. Suzuki and I both ordered the restaurant's specialty, a ¥900 *uni-negitoro-ikura donburi*, a generous bowl of white rice topped with the very freshest and highest quality *uni* (caramel-colored sea urchin), *negitoro* (minced bits of rich fatty tuna mixed with chopped scallions), and *ikura* (plump orange salmon roe).

That was all there was on the lunch menu. You could get the rice with only one or only two of the three main ingredients for the same price. Serious eaters went for all three. By noon the restaurant would be sold out and closed until dinnertime, when the lone chef behind the counter was joined by an assistant. For dinner the little restaurant offered a full sushi menu along with some hard-to-find regional *sake*. The prices at night were much higher.

The lunch was an excuse for Suzuki to eat at one of his favorite restaurants. But he also wanted me to know the underlying details of how and why Tokuma Shoten was about to become a player in the satellite broadcast business.

Tokuma, along with the entertainment and communications conglomerate Softbank and the video rental store giant CCC, the parent company of Tsutaya, Japan's premium video supermarket and video rental company, were forming a partnership with Hughes Electronics to create DirecTV Japan, the Japanese version of DirecTV in the US at that time. The Japanese government had recently announced that by December 2003 all television broadcasting in Japan would be digital. There were only six national broadcasting networks in Japan, the main ones being NTV, TV Asahi, Fuji TV, and NHK. For a huge city like Tokyo there were surprisingly few TV channels. But once everything went digital that would change. Digital broadcasting would take up far less bandwidth than analog broadcasting, allowing for the creation of many more channels. It would also mean big sales in high-definition consumer electronics equipment for Japan's consumer electronics giants.

The question on the minds of potential broadcasters was, who would get the new channels and how would they acquire them? Usually the Japanese government assigned the rights to those who already had them. In other words, if you were broadcasting television now, you would be offered one or more of the new digital TV channels. This offer would extend not just to the six networks broadcasting terrestrial TV but also to those broadcasting via satellite or cable. Theoretically, as a member of a satellite broadcast consortium, Tokuma Shoten would be in line to acquire one of the newly available TV broadcasting frequencies.

Cable TV in Japan at the time was very limited. The few cable networks that existed covered only certain parts of central Tokyo. Satellite broadcast was even more limited. NHK, Japan's semipublic broadcasting network, already aired some programs via satellite. There was a satellite TV platform called WOWOW that broadcast movies and sports events and struggled to attract subscribers. With the prospect of digital TV channels becoming newly available, there was suddenly more interest in satellite broadcast in Japan. Hughes had come to Japan looking for DirecTV partners who could provide "contents." Rupert Murdoch's Sky TV sought an opportunity to expand its Asian broadcasting empire. And SONY, newly into the contents business itself, decided to enter the broadcast business with its own new company, PerfecTV.

CASTLE IN THE SKY

Dola's gang, including Charles and Henri, whom a Disney translator incorrectly gave Chinese names.

Suzuki had invited me to lunch both to share this information about the new venture and to tell me to stay out of it or anything at all connected with the new satellite TV business. He said that under no circumstances should I volunteer to help them, nor should I respond to requests for assistance.

Although DirecTV Japan was a partnership with Hughes, an American company, and my main job at Tokuma was to interface with foreign business partners, I wasn't being asked to help out. As the only native English speaker in the whole group of Tokuma companies, and the only person with non-Japanese contacts in the entertainment industry, I found it strange that no one would want my help.

Tokuma Shoten would be one of the smallest members of the DirecTV Japan group. Of the nearly one hundred broadcast channels in the new network, Tokuma Shoten would be responsible for only four of them. Tokuma's main job was to arrange for the bank loans to finance the venture, and to handle the government side of things. Television broadcasting in Japan was a highly regulated industry and required sensitive interface with the technocratic and the political sides of the Japanese government. Tokuma's expertise was entirely on the political side. And in acquiring bank loans.

Tokuma-*shacho* had called Suzuki in to tell him that Tokuma's four channels on DirecTV Japan would be a Ghibli Channel, a Daiei Channel, an Enka (music) Channel, and some kind of a Sports Channel, either golf or horse racing. Suzuki expressed surprise at this information. He reminded his boss, and his mentor, that Ghibli had at that time made exactly eight movies. He wondered how long a Ghibli Channel could survive playing only eight movies. What would the Ghibli Channel broadcast when it had exhausted its eight movies? Tokuma-*shacho* had seemed surprised but unconcerned.

Suzuki checked with the head of Daiei Film and learned that all of their movies were already licensed out for at least the next ten years. There would be no Daiei films available for broadcast on DirecTV Japan. Every known sport in Japan already had exclusive broadcast contracts. Very few *enka* artists ever made music videos. The Tokuma part of DirecTV Japan did not seem headed for success.

Mr. Tokuma made the DirecTV Japan announcement at the next monthly meeting of Tokuma Group division heads. He informed us that OH-san, currently a manager without portfolio, would be the president of the newly formed Tokuma subsidiary managing the DirecTV Japan business. OH-san, who I believed to be one of the least competent salarymen I had ever known, beamed as the announcement was made. He seemed completely unaware of what awaited him in his new position.

One of the managing editors in the publishing division, a very literate woman who happened to be sitting next to me at the meeting, slipped me a note on a folded sheet of paper. On it was written a well-known haiku by Matsuo Basho.

takotsubo ya
hakanaki yume wo
natsu no tsuki
An octopus makes its home in an octopus trap
Evanescent dreams
Under a hazy summer moon

A few weeks later, unable to control my curiosity, I took advantage of a Japanese tradition, paying an unnecessary in-person call on a newly appointed executive or newly opened company, and visited the brand-new offices of DirecTV Japan all the way across town in Meguro. I found OH-san in a modest office in the building that housed DirecTV Japan. OH-san had only two people working for him. Though he now seemed far less elated by his new position, he showed no signs of panic or worry as he described to me the main requirements of his job— to find programming for four television channels that would run 24 hours a day, 7 days a week, and 365 days a year (366 on leap year).

I was introduced to the head of DirecTV Japan. He seemed

very young for the position. He happened to be the son of a director of the bank that had lent Tokuma Shoten the start-up money it needed to join DirecTV Japan. He had no previous experience in the TV or entertainment business.

All the other partners in the DirecTV Japan venture had larger offices and bigger staffs than the Tokuma contingent, but they also had more channels to find programming for. Sitting in his small office, OH-san gave me an update on how things were going.

The Japanese partners in DirecTV Japan had assumed that Hughes would be supplying the same programming they broadcast in the US. Hughes had assumed that their role was only to provide the satellite, build the satellite uplink station, give instructions on how to operate the system, and offer technical support as needed. Hughes had originally begun their US DirecTV business thinking only of the American market. When they acquired the necessary broadcast rights for their network, they only acquired rights for North America. They had never tried and did not now own the foreign rights to any of their US programming. In most cases those rights were no longer available. So their expansion abroad was about finding partners with access to content.

I asked OH-san how he and his staff were going about finding programming. His answer was vague. I offered to help him in any way that I could and he thanked me and said he probably would not need any help.

A few days later I had breakfast at the Westin Hotel with someone I knew who worked for SONY and had been assigned to the PerfecTV satellite broadcast network. He told me that SONY had prepared for the launch of their satellite service years in advance, searching for and acquiring broadcast rights. He told me how difficult it had been to get access to enough quality programs to attract the number of subscribers it would take to make the venture profitable.

The announced launch of DirecTV Japan was only months away, and the DirecTV Japan partners had only just begun acquiring broadcast rights. My acquaintance pointed out that the only commercial satellite broadcaster in Japan, WOWOW, had been a spectacular failure and barely maintained the necessary subscriber base to stay in business. He wondered how the DirecTV Japan partners planned to get enough programming to operate. I said that I wondered the same thing myself.

As the date for the launch approached, none of the DirecTV Japan consortium partners seemed to be having much luck acquiring programming. Sky TV and PerfecTV had both announced they would begin broadcasting on about the same date. Japanese consumers were being bombarded with ads for all three new satellite services. At the monthly Tokuma management meetings, OH-san's updates on his business were upbeat, and he said that everything was going smoothly and according to plan. I couldn't imagine how this could possibly be true.

I asked Suzuki how DirecTV Japan was not a giant passenger liner about to collide with an enormous iceberg. He told me to please just mind my own business and stay out of it. I told him that the company, of which we were both members of the board of directors, had borrowed an enormous amount of money to run its satellite broadcast business, and from what I could tell there was no possible way the venture would succeed. He told me not to worry about it, that the bank wouldn't have lent the money if they didn't think it would be paid back, and that everything would work out in the end. I assumed that what he meant was that the DirecTV Japan partners would all receive digital broadcast TV channels from the Japanese government and somehow make up their losses using terrestrial digital broadcast rights.

On a fine early autumn day just before DirecTV Japan was scheduled to go live, all of the Tokuma Shoten Group department heads boarded a chartered bus to Mito in Ibaraki Prefecture, just north of Narita Airport. We had been invited for a tour of the newly completed DirecTV Japan state-of-the-art satellite uplink facility. Mr. Tokuma himself joined the tour, though he followed the bus in the comfort of his own chauffeur-driven town car.

There is something in the Japanese DNA that is triggered when riding a long-distance train or chartered bus. With the first jerk of motion, that subtle indication that the trip has begun and the vehicle is on its way, bags of dried squid and nuts are ripped open. All up and down the aisles is the popping off of tabs on cans of Asahi Super Dry and the soft snap of the twisting off of lids of Ozeki One-Cup *sake*. Shoes are removed and ties are loosened. Seat backs are reclined. Our bus to Mito had barely left the Tokuma parking area when the drinking and snacking began.

Both Tokuma Shoten and Studio Ghibli were among the last bastions of unreformed smokers. While the rest of the world was creating smoke-free environments in public places and relegating smokers to ever-smaller designated smoking areas, nonsmoking Tokuma and Ghibli employees had to leave their buildings and go outside for smoke-free breaks. By the time the bus to Mito hit the Shuto Expressway it had already filled with a cloud of smoke as thick and dense as a London fog in the days of Jack the Ripper.

Just before reaching its destination in Mito, the bus pulled into the parking lot of a very large, very traditional Japanese restaurant just off the highway in Ibaraki and everyone piled out of the bus to join Tokuma-*shacho* for a company lunch. It was a very elaborate, multicourse meal in a private dining room. Two long rows of low tables were arranged on the *tatami* mats to accommodate the thirty-odd executives in attendance. I was seated next to Mr. Tokuma, partly because he felt that a *gaijin* executive seated next to him made him look more important, international as opposed to just local, and partly because most of the Tokuma executives were afraid to sit next to him. A good deal of beer and *sake* was consumed during the excellent meal. Mr. Tokuma, as usual, held court, telling stories about the advice he had given to Japan's leading business leaders and politicians. Some of the stories were true.

When the bus finally arrived at the Hughes satellite uplink facility, we piled out and got a tour of the building and an explanation of its equipment from its all-American technical staff. A professional translator had been hired for the occasion. Her skills were mostly wasted since most of the audience, already possessed of a short attention span when it came to technical matters, was drunk and sleepy after the bus ride, the beer and *sake* and snacks, and the large formal lunch.

The facility had the look of a perfect setting for a space alien invasion movie or a world-ending disaster movie where the last men on Earth hole up in a protected military bunker and hunker down to try and save the planet. Only the Daiei Film executives who produced such movies perked up as we entered. Outside were enormous white weapons-grade microwave satellite dishes pointing up at the sky. Inside, an array of complicated-looking technical equipment sat quietly humming while LED lights on impressive control panels in low-lit, highly air-conditioned rooms flashed and blinked red, green, blue, and amber. Computers sat quietly in their own even more lowly lit, more highly air-conditioned glass-windowed bunker. The incomprehensible technical information imparted to us by the Hughes technician flowed over our heads, first in English and then in Japanese, as we stood and gaped at the technology.

The explanation of the process of uploading the data for broadcast seemed comically pedestrian compared to the lecture on the facility's equipment. Someone from the contents providers would arrive at the uplink facility in a van with a high-quality digital videotape. A technician then inserted it into a VCR. The satellite dishes would be pointed at the sky and the data beamed up daily to the satellite when it was in position. Either I missed something due to having eaten and drunk too much at lunch or that was all there was to it.

After more detailed technical explanations, which the translator skillfully translated, and which no one absorbed, there was time for questions. Mine was the only one. One of the technicians had mentioned that the location of the facility was carefully chosen to avoid having the microwave transmissions pass through any airspace used by commercial airliners. The intensity of the transmission beam was apparently potentially dangerous to airplanes flying overhead. I wanted to know, if a bird happened to be flying by low over the sending dish when it was transmitting, what would happen?

"The bird would be roasted. Cooked completely. Incinerated, depending on how close it was to the sending dish," was the answer.

Everyone went outside to pose for a group picture in front of the giant microwave uplink dishes. Then we all boarded the bus and headed back to Tokyo, our work for the day complete. The beer drinking and snack eating started up again as soon as the bus began to move and continued unabated all the way back to Shinbashi.

The launch of DirecTV Japan was bizarre in the extreme. All Tokuma Group executives had been given free DirecTV Japan subscriptions, ostensibly for the purpose of monitoring the broadcasts to provide feedback. Technicians appeared one day at my apartment in Azabu Juban and installed the equipment.

DirecTV Japan was launched with very few channels playing visual programming. The Tokuma channels played audio-only tapes of horse races, golf tournaments, and sumo matches that had taken place months and even years earlier, and music, mostly *enka* and Japanese teen-age-girl pop. The other DirecTV Channels were not much better. When my wife turned on the system and surfed through the channels, she called me at work to ask if it was broken.

"There's nothing playing," she said. "Most of the channels are dark and have audio only. Besides the regular TV channels we already get, it's nothing but hardcore Japanese anime, a few older TV shows, and audio tapes of old sports events. They're playing horse races and boxing, or music. Isn't there anything else on DirecTV? Why would anyone pay for this?"

I wondered that too. The service had managed to acquire nearly 400,000 subscribers, but I assumed that a large number of those were *kankeisha* and their families, that is, people related to the partner companies. Additionally there would be people without access to cable who had succumbed to the slick advertising campaign provided by Dentsu and/or Hakuhodo ad agencies. The bare-bones breakeven number of subscribers was judged to be around 1.2 million. DirecTV Japan's number never increased after the initial launch. Possibly because they were broadcasting 150 channels with nothing on them.

One day soon after the launch I was driving with Suzuki from Shinbashi out to Studio Ghibli in Higashi Koganei. I had launched into one of my tirades about DirecTV Japan and about how could we, as directors of the company, have allowed this fiasco to happen. I wanted to know how anyone could have been so stupid so as to let things get to this point. Finally fed up with listening to me go on and on about something I had been told to stay out of, Suzuki pulled the car off the road and shut off the engine.

"Look," he said, "there's more to this than you know about. I'll tell you if you promise to stop talking about it. The Japanese military has always wanted their own communications satellite. The US government has never been willing to allow them to buy one. When DirecTV Japan fails, the Japanese government is going to quietly buy the satellite and the uplink facility from them."

Because they were broadcasting actual programming on their services, both PerfecTV and Sky TV Japan did much better than DirecTV Japan, each with close to a million subscribers. But neither had enough of a subscription base to stay in business and they eventually merged to become SkyPerfecTV. Soon thereafter DirecTV Japan failed. What was left of it, its nearly thirty exclusive channels and its subscription base, was acquired by SkyPerfecTV. The uplink station is now a Japanese Jieitai (Japan Self-Defense Force) base, and commercial air traffic is carefully routed around its airspace.

It was a great relief to me to discover that the people in the company I worked for were not as stupid as they appeared to be. Not, at least, the ones who could see the invisible hand moving in the background. I suppose you just never really know, unless someone takes the trouble to tell you. Which is rare.

And that sums up what it is to be a *gaijin* in Japan. Lonely sometimes. Dependent on the kindness of others. And always fascinated by the unique and special history, culture, and people of Japan.

To paraphrase the great haiku poet Matsuo Basho:

初仕事
外人も
仲間をほしげ也。

Starting something new
Gaijin too
Need all the help they can get.

ACKNOWLEDGMENTS

The author wishes to thank everyone at Studio Ghibli for their patience, kindness, guidance, and willingness to suffer a clueless *gaijin*, but especially

Hayao Miyazaki

Toshio Suzuki

Koji Hoshino

Mikiko Takeda

Haruyo Moriyoshi

Shinsuke Nonaka

Yukari Tai

Evan Ma

Nao Amisaki

Seiji Okuda

Isao Takahata and Yasuyoshi Tokuma, who are no longer with us but whose works will live on forever

And my wife Yoko who has put up with me for more than thirty years.